HONESTLY

My life and Stryper revealed.

By
Michael Sweet

Founding member, singer, songwriter, and guitarist of the pioneering Christian rock band Stryper tells his life story – Honestly.

with
Dave Rose
and Doug Van Pelt

Michael Sweet, in this—his first autobiography—chronicles his life as the founding member, songwriter, singer, and guitarist of the pioneering rock band Stryper. As the first Christian band to see chart-topping MTV ™ airplay, Sweet gives an honest and moving account of the unexpected highs and lows throughout his often tumultuous path to success. The victories, as well as the failures, are all documented here as he takes the reader on an incredibly insightful journey through his life. Having sold almost 12 million albums worldwide and landed on countless Billboard ™ charts, Michael Sweet continues to enjoy a successful career in music. This revealing memoir shares the sometimes seemingly insurmountable challenges he has faced to reach this place in life. Michael is a husband and a father of two and he currently resides in Cape Cod, Massachusetts.

A note from Michael:
I wrote this book based primarily on my personal experiences and observations throughout my life. I drew from my archives and memorabilia, as evidenced by the old photographs within the book. In some cases, I may not have recalled a specific conversation exactly as it occurred, word-for-word, but I have provided the substance of the conversations and events as accurately as possible, based on my personal first-hand observations and recollections. The purpose behind what's written in this book is to tell the story of my life, from my perspective, as I best recall it. My intentions are not to offend or demean anyone, but to give you, the reader, a journey through my mind and heart to better understand what I've gone through and how I've gotten through it. I'm a man who speaks openly and often with that comes the risk of upsetting a few people along the way. I care deeply for my friends and fans around the world and please know that this is an opportunity for me to take you all into my soul and in the process, share a little bit of it with you. I ask you humbly to read with an open mind and an open heart. I also want to personally thank each and every person mentioned throughout this book, as they are the ones who have helped to shape me into the man and the artist that I am today. Each one of them has been instrumental to my development and to the life lessons that I've tried to impart upon myself. Saying "thank you" will never fully express the depths of my gratitude. So, grab a cup of coffee, find a comfortable chair and let's start this journey.....

I would like to thank everyone who helped make this book a reality: My wife Lisa, my daughter Ellena and my son Mikey, Bill Edwards and Marc Offenbach along with everyone at Big3, Dave Rose and Doug Van Pelt, Curtis Booker, John Booker, David McCreary, Richard Hughes, Nigel Skeet (family photo credit), Tina Enos, Paul Stevenson at Bookmasters, Brian Mayes and Kevin Chiaramonte, Jeff Wollschlager, and of course Robert, Oz, and Tim and the amazing fans and friends we have around the world. Without you there would be no story to tell. Thank you all ~ M

DEDICATION

I want to dedicate this book to my wife Lisa, my son Michael and my daughter Ellena. Playing in a band often separates you from the ones you love. The time away recording, touring, rehearsing, writing, and doing everything else associated with a band often takes precedence over what matters most. It's been a difficult task for me to balance being a husband and father with leading a successful band.

I look back on the years that have passed, and I think to myself, "Was I a good dad or did I fail as a father? Am I a good husband or am I a failure?" Fortunately, I took the opportunity to spend more time with my kids during my down time, yet I missed out on so many moments during their childhood that I wish I could build a time machine and set it for 1987 and have another go at being a dad, a better dad.

Often enough I neglect my wife Lisa and put many things above her and our relationship. I'm not proud of this. In fact, I'm ashamed. I continually ask God for focus and wisdom and maybe someday the light will go on and I'll figure it all out.

We can't travel back in time, but we can change who we are and how we relate to others. Despite our choices in life and how they have shaped us, we all have the opportunity to change how we make use of our time, how we prioritize, and how we treat those that God has blessed us with.

Our wives, our children, our family, our friends—they are our legacy. After we're gone, they continue to wave the flag and fight our fight. I couldn't be more proud than to have Lisa, Michael and Ellena waving mine.

I love all of you, more than I can ever show.......

FOREWORD

By Manager, Dave Rose

"That Jesus Dude"

The year was 1986. I was a freshman in college and laying the ground work to attend my very first concert. I was flat broke so like any good college freshman I asked my dad for the ticket money. And like any good dad, he didn't give it to me. But he did say that if I would clean out the garage, he would give me an old stereo that was in there.

So I did and got $25 for it at the local pawn shop. That was enough money for a ticket and gas for me and three other friends to pile into a car and drive five hours to hear Stryper in concert. I didn't catch one of the Bibles tossed into the audience, but I believe I slightly injured the church lady who scrambled for one at the same time I did.

I remember the long drive back from that concert—we certainly didn't have enough money for a hotel—and I recall saying to one of my friends, "That is what I want to do for a living." I didn't necessarily want to work *with* Stryper. That idea was, of course, way too far-fetched. No way could I ever work with a band of that caliber, but I just knew I wanted to be in music—somehow, some way. The feeling Stryper gave me at that concert was one I never wanted to let go of. And I didn't.

Fast-forward to 2001. Since my days of selling stereos at seedy pawn shops to get concert money, I had built a successful artist management company, Deep South Entertainment. Over the years we handled the careers of greats like Bruce Hornsby, Little Feat, Marcy Playground, Allison Moorer, Parmalee, and Vienna Teng. But Stryper remained my passion. So one day that year I decided to research what my old heroes had been up to since their unceremonious break-up in 1991. I knew Michael had put out some solo records, and I just assumed that, out of the four guys in the band, he would be the most approachable. On the Internet, he had a website but listed no email address. He did however list a PO Box for correspondence. I wrote him a letter and mailed it to him. In that letter I basically explained who I was, that I was a fan, and that I would like to help him with anything he needed.

A few days later I experienced the most surreal moment when our receptionist rang my desk and said, "You have Michael Sweet on line 3."

"You have got to be kidding," I thought to myself. *"He actually received the letter? And read it? And is now calling me?"*

We proceeded to talk about music and life for what felt like hours, but in reality was only about 20 minutes. A few weeks later I went to see him perform a solo show in Charlotte, North Carolina. We continued to stay in touch after that. I knew he was a little gun-shy of music business folks based on his past. So we took it slowly, but we began to develop a good rapport. We had about a two year "courtship" before we decided to enter into any sort of formal agreement.

It was now fall of 2002 and we had continued to talk seriously over the past couple of years about working together. I had even flown to Cape Cod to meet with him to discuss music and his career. We met for a simple lunch at Applebee's and that day could be considered the beginning of our working relationship.

As we were laying out the ground rules, as managers and artists often do in the early stages, I distinctly recall him saying one thing that resonated deeply. On several occasions he said, "Dave, I'd like for us to work together, but I should tell you, I will never play in Stryper again." Yet, later that year Stryper, with Michael included, embarked on a 7-week nationwide tour. It was their first tour together with all original members since their break-up in 1991.

I couldn't believe I was involved in reuniting the band that had meant so much to me over the years — that for all practical purposes was the reason I wanted to be in the music business.

What made Michael change his mind and decide to do a Stryper tour? To this day, I'm not really sure. I wouldn't say that I pressured him. I don't believe I did, although I'm sure I was nudging in that direction. But no amount of nudging can make Michael change his mind. It had to be something else that persuaded him. Perhaps he just felt it was the right time. Whatever it was, I wasn't going to question it.

When we started working together, it was with the intent of releasing some solo material. That material coalesced into *Reborn*, the first Stryper studio album since *Against the Law*. However, Michael had it in his heart that he wanted to be a solo artist, not because he didn't like Stryper, although there was definitely some deep-rooted pain associated with the band, but because he just wanted to be his own person and make a name for himself outside of *Stryper*. His longing for a solo career had less to do with his feelings about *Stryper* and more about his basic human instinct to prove to himself that he could stand on his own two feet.

As an experienced professional in the "new" music business of 2003, I knew solo work could be a very difficult path. Although I remained supportive of his solo endeavors, as I still do, I explained that the quickest path to gaining the attention of the world would be to tour with Stryper. It would be the most direct way to let Stryper fans know that he was alive and well, and sounding better than ever.

That 2003 tour was a success. And it gave birth to the live album *7 Weeks, Live in America* that would find its way onto three Billboard charts (Internet, Independent, and Christian), debuting at #4 on the Billboard Internet Chart.

That tour, which started as a one-time only engagement with no promises of a future, turned into a record deal with Big3 Records, which led to subsequent tours and albums. Stryper was back together.

Reuniting a band, who for all practical purposes had not been a proper business since 1991, required a lot of work. We had to completely re-build. We formed new corporations and hired lawyers, booking agents, accountants, and crew-members. The band didn't have a single Stryper T-shirt available for sale when we started the process. But day-by-day we laid the ground work to rebuild the business of Stryper.

I would spend the next several years getting to know the band that at one point were my childhood musical icons. I've come to know and love them all, but of the four I am the closest with Michael.

Michael is the hardest working of the bunch. He never stops pushing himself, and the band, to improve. When tour time approaches he hits the treadmill, he rehearses, and he practices his voice and instrument. He is truly working 365 days a year. That is probably why I gravitated toward him early on in my working relationship with the band. I understood his way of thinking and the lifestyle that accompanies it.

That said, his quest for perfection has often been the catalyst for my rising blood pressure and a few new grey hairs. He has postponed video shoots because he felt the band was not at their best. He has cancelled interviews because it would strain his voice and thus sacrifice the show. And in his mind, the show was, and is, THE most important thing. He will ask me to make demands on promoters that I may view as unreasonable, but that he views as necessary in order to put on the best show possible for the fans.

He's a perfectionist in every sense of the word. And sometimes that doesn't jive with the business world or, more specifically, me. I have to deal with the potential repercussions of a cancelled interview or an angry promoter, but in Michael's mind, that's what it takes to give the fans the show they deserve.

I don't always agree with Michael, but I *always* understand him, and I certainly always respect him.

I've been working with Michael since 2003 and consider him to be a true friend. I had the honor of delivering a toast at Michael and Lisa's wedding. We've been through a lot of ups and downs together, personally and professionally.

In the music world, after 10 years of working together, many are ready to put on the boxing gloves and duke it out. I'm happy to say this isn't the case with Michael and me, and I feel equally as comfortable with Michael in a church, in a movie theater, or in a bar.

I've always known Michael's hard work would pay off. I believed there was a world outside of Stryper where he would be recognized solely for the incredible talent that he is and not so much as a member of a groundbreaking Christian rock band. This is not to diminish the place of Stryper in his career. I just always had this gut feeling that his future held something exciting for him outside of the Christian rock scene.

That future arrived in 2007 when I received an email from Kim Scholz (wife of Boston's Tom Scholz) asking if Michael would be interested in performing at a tribute concert to Brad Delp, the former Boston singer who had died in March of that year. Members of Boston along with a smorgasbord of "Who's Who" in rock music were invited to perform.

Michael happily agreed to sing a few the band's songs with the other members of Boston.

The show took place August 19, 2007, at The Bank of America Pavilion in Boston. The most faithful of Boston fans were out in full force to pay respects to their hero, Brad Delp, one of the greatest rock singers of all time.

For the first time since I've known Michael, I was nervous for him. I wanted so badly for a world outside of Stryper to see him shine as the amazing musician and vocalist that I have always known that he is.

He was about to go on stage *in* Boston and perform with the remaining members *of* Boston to what could potentially be the most difficult crowd he'd ever performed for. He was about to sing Boston songs to Boston fans, all of whom were very emotionally charged coming off the death of Brad. This was a recipe for disaster.

I was truly a nervous wreck. Before the show I headed to a bar located inside the Pavilion. I needed a beer or two to calm my nerves and I knew if I hung around with Michael backstage he would sense my nervousness, and I certainly didn't want that. So I found a barstool and proceeded to calm my pre-show jitters.

As I sat there contemplating all the things that could potentially go wrong, but still convinced that Michael would handle the night with professionalism, five guys walked in the bar and sat down next to me. They were locals, no doubt about it. One was wearing a Red Sox baseball cap. Another had on a classic Boston Spaceship T-shirt. And they all had thick New England accents.

As I eavesdropped on their conversation, one of them spoke up with a tone of reservation, "I heard that Jesus Dude from the band Stryper is singing a bunch of songs tonight."

9

"Yeah. Whatever. No way he'll pull it off like Brad did, but it'll be cool. This may be the last time we get to hear these songs live," said Spaceship.

"That's true. This may be the last time we hear these songs live—So Jesus Dude better not f**k it up for us!" exclaimed Red Sox as they all laughed and high-fived each other.

No words I could have said would change their opinion of "Jesus Dude." They were going to have to hear it for themselves and make up their own minds. But this pre-show moment in the bar confirmed that tonight would be an amphitheater filled with skeptical naysayers. The only thing I could think to do was order another beer. Until now I had never simultaneously prayed *and* chugged an Amstel Light at the same time.

I finished my beer and headed into the concert area. I set up shop near the back row. I suppose I felt less nervous being furthest from the stage, but I also wanted to watch the crowd's reaction from the rear of the venue.

Michael came on stage with the confidence and grace I've come to expect from him, yet with all the humbleness and sincerity of someone paying genuine respects to Brad. Still, I was a wreck.

His moment arrived when the band started playing the Boston classic "Peace of Mind." My heart sank. I knew Michael had the chops to hold his own, but one screw-up and he was potentially facing a brutally unforgiving audience of Delp fans. It was an amphitheater filled with 5,000 or so fans like those I had just encountered at the bar, all with the sense that this may be the last time they hear these classic songs performed in concert.

Michael Sweet had performed to tough audiences before—most notably at heavy-metal festivals where the attendees are some of the most cynical music fans in the world. And he did a fine job at winning them over, but that was always within the confines of Stryper — his comfort-zone, so to speak. To date, Michael had never performed *in* another band of Boston's caliber, and here he was performing the vocal parts of a recently deceased singer. I had no doubt he was one of the best at winning over tough audiences, but this was different. Could he pull this one off?

The signature guitar sounds of Tom Scholz blared over the PA system and the crowd cheered loudly as they began to recognize the song. Within seconds, before he even started to sing, Michael had the audience on their feet with hands in the air clapping along. Then it came time for the opening line and he belted it out as strongly as I've ever heard that angelic voice of his. The crowd stayed right there with him, singing along, hands in the air, and going wild. This pattern continued throughout the night. He had done it. He was one with a Boston crowd, in Boston. He had the approval of the fans of one of the greatest rock bands of all time.

In my mind, that was *the* night. It was the night 5,000 people found out what I and other long-time loyal Stryper fans already knew — that Michael Sweet is one of the most talented rock vocalists in the world. On that night he held his own with a crowd that for the most part had no idea who he was, or at best knew him as "That Jesus Dude." In the end, they knew him as the guy who did great justice to the spirit of Brad Delp.

Michael went on to become a touring member of Boston during 2008.

I'd love to lean back in my chair, light a cigar, prop my feet on the desk and tell you I orchestrated the whole thing. But I didn't. His union with Boston and recognition the world over as a talented musician came about because of his hard work and devotion to his craft. It happened naturally — the way great music usually does —

11

without the intrusion of managerial finesse. It happened because Michael is truly an amazing talent.

When Stryper fans ask me, "What's Michael like?" I respond with "He's pretty normal." He's not, actually. He's insanely motivated and driven, and sometimes he has a fairly strange sense of humor. But as a human being, he's actually pretty normal.

I recall going to Boston during the recording of *Reborn* as the area got hit with a really bad snowstorm. I was in the studio with engineer Kenny Lewis. At some point we looked around and couldn't find Michael. We walked out the studio door and there was Michael with a big smile on his face shoveling snow off the sidewalk. He just disappeared, grabbed a shovel, and started shoveling snow without telling anyone. That's Michael Sweet, equally as happy recording a Billboard-charting record as he is shoveling snow.

I tell people all the time that I haven't worked a day in my life. It's because I do what I love—music. And I have Stryper to thank for putting me on that path. I feel as though I have truly lived The American Dream. I went from selling my stereo for Stryper tickets to managing the band, all in one lifetime.

This is the effect Stryper has on people every day. They give people hope and inspiration. They help you believe in yourself and that you have the ability to do anything you set your mind to. I am living proof of that. I walked out of my very first concert, a Stryper concert, saying "This is what I want to do with my life." And I did.

Thank you Tim, Oz, Rob, and Michael for giving me hope at such a young age, and for believing in me for so many years as your manager. You all are truly amazing people and I am forever grateful for being a part of your organization.

-Dave Rose, Raleigh, NC December 2013

ONE

I drink. Occasionally I smoke. If you ask my wife, my kids, my tech, my agent or my manager they'll all tell you that I curse more than I should. I've fooled around with women on tour buses. I've been arrested for indecent exposure. I've been reckless with money to the point of bankruptcy. My favorite bands are The Beatles, Van Halen and Judas Priest. I was pissed at God when my wife died of cancer and I despise religion.

I am a Christian.

I'm Michael Sweet. I'm a singer, guitarist, songwriter, producer and a founding member of the pioneering Christian rock band Stryper. We've sold almost 10 million records to date and were the first Christian band to air on MTV, and to have four #1 videos. We even had two top-10 videos at the same time, back when MTV actually played music videos. We've played soccer stadiums and biker bars, sometimes in the same week.

Despite having done all of that, I'm still often known as the Bible-Tossing-Yellow & Black-Bumble-Bee guy. The Jesus guy. The '80s hair/glam Christian metal guy. An irrelevant joke. Or, even worse—sometimes I'm not known at all.

So who am I? I'm a guy that grew up in Southern California—sort of a surf punk kind of guy who absolutely loved music. My brother, Robert, and I are the founding members of Stryper. Our band hit at the right time in the right place, and I thank God for every experience that I've had.

If you've picked up this book in hopes of reading stories about me hiding in a closet shooting up heroin, buying prostitutes with all my earnings or beating the crap out of a club owner because he looked at me funny, you should probably read the Motley Crue book instead, because you won't find that here. I'm not better than they are, but my story is different. I'm not an angel, either, and I think you'll find some pretty eye-opening stories, and I hope — whether you know my music or not — you'll find them enlightening or at least entertaining.

When I casually become a little introspective, I conclude that I'm a fairly normal guy — but that might just be wishful thinking. You read through the stories of my life and then you decide — am I a regular guy or am I just a big mess?

In one lifetime that seems like an instant I've gone from being a struggling musician on The Sunset Strip to being the songwriter in a multi-platinum selling band (Stryper), to going bankrupt (Stryper), to leaving Stryper, to topping the charts on Christian radio (solo years), to working at a campground and harvesting cranberries, to reuniting with Stryper, and then being a co-lead singer and guitarist in another multi-multi-platinum selling band (Boston), to losing my wife to cancer, to remarrying, to leaving Boston, to recording more Stryper records and producing more solo albums. God only knows what's next.

I live near Cape Cod and I'm blessed with two incredible kids, Mikey and Ellena, and an amazing wife, Lisa. I have a handful of people I would call friends and a whole lot of people who I know by face, but couldn't tell you their names if my life depended on it. My life is good. Still to this day I can't believe that I get paid for what I do, and not a day goes by that I take that for granted.

I have the most unique legion of fans. The vast majority of my fans are, like me, middle-aged family people. Good, normal people, many with some sort of Christian upbringing, but yet out of nowhere I find out that people like Larry The Cable Guy and Chris Jericho are fans. That Mike Wengren (Disturbed) and Richard Christy (Iced Earth) are fans. I read an article once where Wyclef Jean said he grew up listening to Stryper. Twiggy from Marilyn

Manson saw us back in the day and even dressed up as a member of Stryper for career day when he was in high school. John 5 (Rob Zombie) saw us multiple times when he was growing up and even caught a bible that he still has to this day! Drew Barrymore recently used a Stryper T-shirt in her film *Whip It*.

To the mainstream public or maybe even to the hobbyist musician, I'm the guy that may be slightly cooler than Kip Winger, but isn't nearly as cool as Bono. But if you get a couple of beers in people, you'd be shocked at who is willing to say, "Stryper? Hell yeah. They're one of my all-time favorite bands. *To Hell With The Devil*, baby."

How it got to this point, I have no idea. Some would call it luck. Some may call it a curse. I call it humbling divine intervention.

TWO

Whether you are a plumber, doctor, lawyer, or banker, there is someone, perhaps even several people, whom you can attribute to directly influencing your chosen career path.

For me, those people are Janice Sweet, Philip Sweet, Robert Sweet, and Jimmy Swaggart. We'll get to Jimmy later, but let me start at the beginning.

On July 4, 1963, my mother Janice Sweet gave birth to me, Michael Harrison Sweet, at Whittier Presbyterian Hospital on Washington Boulevard, about 20 miles east of downtown Los Angeles.

Robert is actually my half-brother. I also have a half-sister Lisa, who is also a half-sister to Robert. Robert, Lisa, and I each have different biological fathers. My mother, with all the promise of love-ever-after, married two times before she met Phillip, my biological father, who eventually became a brakeman for The Southern Pacific Railroad by day and was a very gifted musician by night.

My father later legally adopted Robert and Lisa.

My mom and dad loved us all unconditionally and equally. It is because of their love and support and lack of pressure that my chosen profession has been music. I wouldn't be writing this book today if it were not for the encouragement and support of my parents over the years.

I was born into a family of working musicians. Don Imus' brother, Fred Imus, was my dad's songwriting partner and together they penned the number one country song in 1976 called "I Don't Want to Have to Marry You", performed by Jim Ed Brown and Helen Cornelius. Jim Ed Brown, founding member of The Browns, had a number one hit in 1959 with the song "The Three Bells." My dad's song helped re-ignite Jim Ed Brown's career.

My mother, also a very talented singer, was in a trio with my aunt Reba and my grandmother Maxine. They sang in a live version of the show *Gunsmoke*. In 1958, my mom was in a beauty contest with Amanda Blake, "Miss Kitty" on *Gunsmoke*, as a judge. Not long after, she became friends with James Arness who played Matt Dillon on the show and she went to a few tapings that year.

The business of entertainment was in my life from the start. I didn't have to go searching for music. It came searching for me. It was a familiar part of my daily childhood. A normal weekend for me would be filled with babysitters while my parents were out performing at clubs.

My mom recalls that I used to rock back and forth, or as she calls it- "bop," in whatever chair I was sitting in, keeping time to whatever music was being played around me at the time. I never did really shake the habit. Still to this day, when I hear music I have to move some part of my body. My feet. My hands. My head. I probably drive people crazy with my inability to sit still when music is playing, and perhaps that's why I gravitated towards guitar as a way to channel and release my nervous energy.

My first memory of learning to play guitar was at the age of five when my dad began teaching me some basic chords on a Gibson 12-string acoustic. What kid learns to play guitar on a Jumbo 12-string acoustic? I did! Looking back on that, I'm amazed that my little fingers could manage such a task, but it's quite possibly the very thing that helped me to progress at such a fast pace.

By the time I was 10, I was a session player on my dad's country demos, where Robert, 13 at the time, played drums. Truthfully, my dad could have gotten the best players in the business to perform on those sessions, but he lovingly and patiently gave my brother and me a shot. That's my dad—very family minded and always willing to encourage us in all our interests. He believed in us and I'm forever thankful that he gave Robert and me an opportunity to record at such an early age.

The studio was always filled with seasoned pros and being around those guys was a real inspiration. Of course, at the time I didn't realize the magnitude of the influence they were having on me, but I learned so much from being a part of those sessions—watching the other musician's play and picking up everything I could from anyone who would take the time to teach me something new.

One player in particular that I remember was an incredibly well known country/blues player by the name of Lou Martin. Lou would give me tips and pointers when we were between takes or waiting for set-up. I tried to absorb everything I could from Lou. He was probably one of my earliest influences as a guitar player aside from Chuck Berry and John Fogerty. Looking back, I've often wondered if this was a strategic plan on the part of my dad to surround me with amazing musicians at such a young age. Planned or not, it certainly inspired my love for music and for playing guitar.

My parents were as encouraging and supportive as anyone could be throughout my childhood and my years as a growing musician. Whereas a garage for most Dads is typically sacred space for working on cars, collecting tools, or storing cold beer, my dad always gave up his "man cave" and let us turn every garage of every home into a rehearsal space.

When I was in the third grade, Robert and I entered a talent show at our elementary school. We played two instrumental songs, "Honky Tonk" by Bill Doggett and "Walk, Don't Run", a song first recorded by jazz great Johnny Smith, but made famous in 1960 by The Ventures.

We won 1st place! I played bass and Rob of course played drums. Despite the fact that the bass guitar was three times my size, and we looked like The Partridge Family in some fairly ridiculous outfits, it was our first taste of feeling the energy of a crowd from a stage. I liked it. It was just a third grade talent show, but to me, we may as well have been in a stadium playing for thousands of screaming fans.

From that moment on, there was never any doubt that this is what I wanted to do with my life. And what's amazing to me is that I still love doing what I do as much as I did that day in elementary school with my oversized bass and Keith Partridge shirt.

Prior to winning the talent show, I was a short, skinny kid with a bowl cut. Almost overnight I became a cool kid. Music has always had a way of lending a helping hand to my personal life along the way.

We moved a lot when I was young. I went to three different elementary schools, one junior high school, and four high schools. So naturally it was tough to fit in everywhere and I found myself constantly trying to make new friends. But the one thing that saved me was music.

Still though, I didn't quite dive into music with the same passion as my brother. Robert was married to music, I was just flirting with it.

THREE

It's ironic that the preacher who would eventually speak out boldly against Stryper was the same one who first led me to Christ — Jimmy Swaggart.

I was twelve years old when I first said the sinner's prayer. The sinner's prayer is basically the admission to God that you are a sinner, and a petition asking for forgiveness along with an eagerness to accept Christ into your heart with the acknowledgement that He is the only way to heaven.

In 1975, most families would gather around the TV set to watch Lawrence Welk, Hee Haw, or maybe an episode of Lassie, but not us. We were regularly watching Jimmy Swaggart flailing his arms about and sweating profusely. Jimmy Swaggart was the epitome of the TV evangelist. Threats of hell and damnation coupled with tearful outbursts of redemption blended with a lot of singing.

Swaggart's charisma drew our family in, particularly me as an impressionable young kid. I was too young to be skeptical of televangelists. Getting older and playing in Stryper would eventually change all of that — but for now, as a kid, I just thought it was cool to see all the energy and theatrics, not to mention the music and the message.

Our TV was an old RCA cabinet model — one of the hybrids that was a TV and a cheap piece of furniture all in one. It held precious space in our living room as though it were a member of the family — and those times when Jimmy Swaggart was on, it *was* a member of the family.

Like most televangelists, Jimmy would give an altar call at the end of his sermon. He usually cried during this part of the show. If he didn't, the audience most certainly did. One day, our entire family held hands right there in our living room, and we all unanimously accepted Christ into our lives. We gave God the rightful and prominent place in our hearts.

Not long after that, we went out and found a local First Southern Baptist Church and we started attending regularly. We even got involved with the worship team. But it didn't stick, not with Rob and me anyway.

We had dreams of rock stardom to pursue and our mission to "make it" involved a lifestyle that didn't seem to mesh too well with early morning church services. As Jesus teaches us in Luke, "He who is forgiven much, loves much." I can testify that I threw myself into the business of having much to be forgiven. It's ironic given my ultimate career as a Christian musician that I initially saw church as an obstacle to my goals instead of a counterpart.

Rob's passion for becoming a successful musician was more deeply rooted than mine. Although my days as a third grade talent show superstar planted the musical seed, I wasn't quite ready to be in a serious relationship with music. Rob and I began to slowly spend less and less time together. As he became more and more serious about music, I became more and more serious about being a punk brother.

When Robert and his band mates practiced in the garage, they would often light candles. Once when they weren't around, my best friend and partner in crime, Greg Rahmeyer, and I went into the garage, lit the candles and melted wax all over their equipment. The wax hardened and sealed the knobs.

I'm surprised Rob and his band mates didn't give us a beat down. I was a real punk. Although I was running around getting into lots of neighborhood trouble, I still knew I wanted to play music. I just wasn't quite ready to make it a career.

Robert however was nose-to-the-grindstone serious about music. But there was only one problem. He couldn't find and/or keep, a good singer.

FOUR

Years earlier, when I was around 6 or 7, Rob, Lisa and I would stay with our grandparents one, two and sometimes three nights a week while my parents performed at local bars or clubs. My grandparent's names were Maxine and Melvin, but we called them Nana and Popo. Nana is one who should be equally credited for giving me the foundation to eventually become a professional musician.

She came from a family of 12 kids, the Lamb family of Oklahoma. When we would visit, there was always music in the air. She was a singer and a songwriter and she even played a little guitar. Music was the centerpiece of our visits. Nana would sit around the living room playing guitar and singing. Her voice relaxed me as she would teach us country, classic rock and even traditional hymns. Every visit turned into a jam session.

"Michael, I'll give you a quarter if you'll sing." she'd say, knowing I would be reluctant and shy—and I always was.

Rob was never hesitant to join in. He'd bring out pots and pans and bang on them with wooden spoons. It took a little more coaxing to convince me. Sometimes when I wouldn't sing, Nana would raise the stakes, saying in her thick southern accent "Okay, 50 cents? Sing for us, Michael. Come on now!" Sometimes if the money wouldn't work, she'd bribe me with food by telling me she'd make a cake or Popo would make some ice cream. Nana was a great cook and Popo made the absolute best homemade banana ice cream. That always worked, even if the pay didn't.

I was, and still am, a very shy person. Singing in public, or doing anything in public, never came naturally for me. It was something I learned, largely from my Nana. When I would begrudgingly join in singing, she would go on and on about it. "Oh Michael. My

23

God, You're so good." Even at a young age I knew that was something grandmothers were just supposed to say to their grandkids, whether they were actually good or not. But as other people would hear me sing around the house, I would receive similar comments and compliments and as a result I began to gain a little more confidence.

I wouldn't say that I ever overcame being shy, but I did start to become more comfortable singing to an audience. So eventually, over time, I'd join in with no coaxing at all.

Nana gave me my first electric guitar and gave Rob his first drum kit. She and Popo took Robert down to the local K-Mart and bought him a set. I remember seeing it for the first time and watching him pound away on that kit and I thought to myself, now this is cool.

Nana really helped to bring me out of my shell and always went the distance to encourage Rob and me in our love of music.

Later in life, as Rob was going through different singers for his band, my dad would always say to him *"You should audition Mike. He's a good singer."* Rob would brush it off and proceed to audition another round of local guys for whatever band he had going at the time. This was fine by me. I was 12 and really had no interest in being in a band. There was trouble to be made and gotten into, and I had mischief to find with neighborhood friends. A band felt like work to me and I wasn't ready for that.

After going through several singers that didn't work out, Rob finally caved and agreed to give me an audition. It was not a big deal to me. After all, it was my brother's band, and I had heard them practicing and rehearsing dozens and dozens of times. My neighborhood friends were likely unavailable on the day I auditioned, so I was probably just thinking "What the heck. There's nothing else to do today. I guess I could give this band thing a try."

But to my Dad, it was a much bigger deal. He had been suggesting to Robert for months, if not years, that he give me a try as the singer. So when Rob finally did agree to give me a shot, my Dad was obviously happy about it. He must have known something good would come out of this. To celebrate the occasion, Dad bought a Shure Vocal Master PA System, one of the most iconic PA systems in music history. It was one of the first portable sound systems, complete with a half-ton mixer/power amp and two speaker columns that were six feet tall. As long as I had a roadie, this hundred pound stick kid was set. Although I couldn't even lift the thing, it was the coolest system I could have at that time.

The audition took place in the garage of our house in Whittier, on Chatfield Street. We set up the PA and were just as excited about hearing it as we were about playing. Larry Richardson was the guitarist, Rob was the drummer, Dean Cerny was the bassist, and I played guitar and sang. We played mostly cover tunes by Hendrix, Bowie, Aerosmith and whatever else we knew. Occasionally we would break into a free-for-all jam—a slightly awkward attempt at creating our own music, I suppose. But mostly we covered rock classics that day. We played for about an hour or so.

When it was over there was no ceremonious joining of the band. There were no papers to be signed stating my new title as lead singer. Basically Rob looked at me when it was over and said, "Well, that sounded pretty good, I guess."

From that day on, Rob would be in my life musically and professionally and I would be in his to the same degree.

Following the audition, we lined up a grandiose tour of backyard parties and VFW halls. We would play for anyone with a yard big enough. We'd bang out a couple sets of covers and a few originals thrown in as well. We'd play anywhere and everywhere.

Once, someone wanted us to play a backyard party under the condition that we'd mow the lawn. The yard was big and it looked like it hadn't been mowed in months, but we mowed it. Just to get a backyard gig we brought out a couple of mowers and took turns cutting the grass — all in the name of rock.

Gigs were fun then. They were small-time stuff, but they meant the world to us. Weeks of planning would go into each one of our shows. We'd carefully construct a set-list, print flyers to help advertise, and we'd spend days picking out the perfect stage wear. We'd set up in the corner of a backyard somewhere with the Shure PA system in front of our instruments. If the backyard had a concrete patio we'd use that, but more often than not, we set up right in the middle of the lawn.

We did our best to make sure each show was a success. There were no aspirations of stardom or recording contracts. Our biggest concern then was how we would sound and how many people would show up. If we made $100 and could buy pizza, guitar strings and drum sticks, we were happy.

It's a lot more complicated today of course. Logistics, business decisions, branding, profitability, budgets, and contracts are more the topics of discussion when it comes time for a gig today, but I can't help fondly reminiscing of a day when the most difficult part of a gig was to find a working lawnmower.

Members came and went throughout those early years. I have distinct memories of them all, but one guy in particular stood out as I approached my high-school years.

FIVE

"F**k school! F**k the Principal! Don't go back to class!" our stand-in guitar player shouted over the microphone during a lunchtime show at Whittier High School in 1978. Our band, Firestorm, had the opportunity to play during lunch break and we almost caused a riot that day.

Rob and I swore that we'd never talk to that guitar player again. And we almost never did.

Whittier High in 1978 was your standard mix of Southern California teens. There were geeks, jocks, rockers, cheerleaders, preps, poor kids and rich kids. It was a melting pot of personalities and ethnic diversities. Richard Nixon went to Whittier High, so it wasn't exactly the bad part of town, but it wasn't necessarily the best part of town either.

We were doing our best to make a name for ourselves and we were just starting to get the hang of booking our own shows.

After much persuading on our part, Whittier High School agreed to let us perform during lunch. Mind you, a rock band during lunch break was not an everyday occurrence at school, especially at that time. To my knowledge, we were one of the first. And after that day, we may have been the last.

From our family station wagon, we lugged all of our gear onto the site and were a bit drained from setting up all morning. I remember it being an unusually hot day for Southern California, but we pressed on, ready for the big gig.

Like when the lights dim over a sold out arena, or when the national anthem crescendos at a ball game, there's that anticipatory moment just before the crowd rips into a roaring cheer. Our

27

moment came when the starting lunch bell rang and the students emerged through the front doors of the school. It was on that day, at Whittier High School in 1978 that we became rock stars to our adoring fans toting homemade PB&J sandwiches.

We did a few Van Halen covers along with some of our own songs. We weren't exactly inimitable, but we were an acceptable rock band — at least for the lunch crowd. Toward the end of the set, after giving it our all, we were covered in sweat from performing in the mid day heat. In our minds, and particularly in the mind of our guitarist, we were good enough to have deserved an encore, maybe two. There was only one problem — the ending lunch bell had just rung and it was time for our crazed audience, along with their lunch boxes, notebooks and backpacks, to go back to class.

Well, the guitarist wasn't having it. He wanted and deserved an encore, or so he thought. Having been fairly quiet throughout the entire show, other than his rehearsed backing vocals, he decided to speak and when he did, that's what came out of his mouth:

"F**k school! F**k the Principal! Don't go back to class!"

Our jaws dropped. Some students were actually taking his advice and not going back to class. Teachers and faculty were obviously upset with us as they tried to calm the crowd and get them to go back into school. We were counting the seconds for the cops to show up. Miraculously, they never came.

Rob and I were so embarrassed and we could have gotten in a lot of trouble because of that incident. We had put our reputations on the line with the school administrators in order to book this gig, and our guitarist sealed our fate with a few uncontrolled expletives.

We decided that day we would never, ever perform with this guy again. Ever!

If you're wondering who he was, his name is Richard Martinez, also known as Oz Fox. Yes, that stand-in guitarist who lost his cool would one day become our lifelong partner in Stryper.

Rewind about a year earlier to the spring of 1977. There was a rock band in our area called Jekyll And Hyde, led by Richard Oderbagan (Odie), a black-eyeliner wearing, long-haired, double stack and SG slingin' rock star (at least in our minds). Robert knew Odie and took me, his twelve-year-old brother, along to hear the band at their rehearsal space.

Back then it was the "thing" to go hang around other band's rehearsal rooms. Other musicians would come to these band practices, and it was usually in someone's garage or an old warehouse. Everyone, including the band, would sit around and drink, talk, smoke pot and jam. Almost always there were grandiose tales of rock-stardom that usually started with "I can't wait 'til we make it!"

Oh yeah, and sometimes the band would actually practice, too.

In later years, when Roxx Regime was in full force, I wasn't into the "hang out at other bands rehearsals" scene. I was too busy writing songs and trying to figure out how to make *our* band successful.

But in the spring of 1977, I was only 12 years old and Robert took me along to Jekyll And Hyde's rehearsal. There were a few people hanging around and Robert introduced me to one of them he knew from Whittier.

"Hey, I'm Richard but people call me Oz" he said to me reaching out his hand from his non-descript t-shirt and tattered blue jeans.

"Hey, I'm Michael," I said with as much coolness as a 12 year old kid at a Jekyll And Hyde rehearsal could muster.

That was the first time I met the guy who, for the better part of my professional career, would be my band-mate in Stryper, Oz Fox.

So in 1977 I met this nice guy named Richard Martinez. In 1978 that same guy, bereft of any social graces common at a high school concert, almost got us banned from Whittier High permanently. And in 1981 he joined Roxx Regime.

How we got from that moment in 1978 to him becoming a member of Roxx Regime in 1981 had a little bit to do with a brown Datsun Pick-up, a little bit to do with an unknown guitarist at the time from New York named C.C. Deville, and a whole lot to do with a ton of convincing on my part to persuade Rob to give Oz another shot at redemption.

SIX

Whether or not I've been willing to admit it, or even know it, God has always had his hand in my life and in this band. It's been incredibly humbling to see the ways He has worked through us, and with us. From finding the right band members in the early years to capacity-crowd touring in the later years, He has always done amazing things within our lives.

Fast-forward several years to the Soldiers Under Command era, for instance. We were billed to play a death metal festival in Holland. "Death Metal" by the way was the promoter's description and billing of the show. Testament and Raven along with a dozen other similar acts were on the bill. The audience at this show was made up primarily of males, a sea of testosterone. I don't recall seeing many females in the crowd at all. Most of the crowd was dressed in black leather jackets and studded wristbands, and all of them couldn't seem to get enough of trashing something, including themselves.

We approached the festival in a white 15-passenger van, and as we pulled up to the backstage area I saw guys being carried away on stretchers. There was blood on their clothes and I remember thinking and saying, "Why did John book this festival?" Until that point, we weren't fully aware this was a thrash/death metal festival. We thought we were just performing at another rock festival in the middle of nowhere.

As we observed the festival from backstage, we started having second thoughts about being there. This was NOT a Stryper crowd. As our time-slot approached and we began tuning our guitars backstage, we could hear the entire crowd beginning to chant something. It seemed to get louder and louder as each person in the audience joined in. *"F**k Stryper! F**k Stryper!"* the masses shouted as if it were the start of a sporting event, and we were the opposing team.

At one point we stood side stage and saw someone holding up a 6-foot, upside down cross that had Robert's face overtop a cardboard cutout of a girl in a bikini. Odd. Why Robert and why a girl in a bikini, I have no idea. I can only assume it was some sort of reference to us looking like girls. Then they started burning the cross and tearing it apart. It was crazy.

This crowd obviously did not like us. Actually, they hated us. We briefly discussed the idea of cancelling, out of fear for our lives. It felt as though the audience was planning to rip us to shreds.

But we chose not to cancel. Instead, we decided to alter the set eliminating the ballads of course and anything with a "pop" sense. We did every "heavy" song we could. The first three songs were mostly spent dodging bottles, food, and chains that were getting thrown at us. Yes, chains. There was a moment during the first song where I looked up and saw a chain with a padlock attached to the end hurling in my direction. I ducked. It missed me, but it could have easily taken my head off.

After the third song, I felt God's anointing. I hadn't felt God's direct presence like this, of this magnitude, ever before in my life. It was as if He was standing right there with us on stage. It was powerful.

In an instance the crowd turned. Their anger and our fear subsided. I'm convinced it was God's spirit moving over the crowd. It wasn't the songs. It wasn't anything we did. God brought peace to that festival and everyone there. What once was intense mayhem, was now immense calm. Within another couple of songs, things went to a whole different level—the crowd was now head banging and seemingly loving the band! They had their fists in the air and were cheering after every song. I've never witnessed anything so powerful in all my life. It was mind-blowing to experience and something that I will never forget.

After the show, new fans approached us saying things like "We had no idea. We didn't know you were this good. You changed our opinion of the band forever." When I left after the show to head back to the hotel, I remember clearly thinking, "God is really doing something special with this band." I knew then He had huge plans for us.

To me, this is one of the many miracles God has shown us. But that festival in Holland stands out as one of the most powerful and life changing.

Years prior however, the miracles came in less obvious ways.

During the audition process to find an additional guitar player, we auditioned a new guy in town from New York by the name of Bruce Johannesson, otherwise known as CC Deville. I had met CC previously and we hit it off. He seemed like a great guy and we got along well. Our band had been playing out as a trio for a quite a while, with me handling all the guitars, but we were actively seeking a fourth member. CC came in to our rehearsal studio and we went through a typical audition process playing some covers and some of our tunes, just to get a feel on how we'd gel together. Musically it felt great but at the end of the night, he inquired about the yellow and black. Rob was adamant about keeping the yellow and black, so when CC suggested he wasn't really into the color scheme, I could sense Rob's defense mechanism kick in. The yellow and black was Rob's baby and he was convinced we should stick with it. So no matter how good CC was, if he couldn't wear the colors, he wasn't going to be in the band. CC politely declined the opportunity, stating he really wasn't digging the yellow and black thing and that he was more of a pink and purple kind of guy. And our auditions with others continued. But to think, had our color scheme been pink and purple, CC Deville just might have become a member of our band.

Just another one of God's miracles, both for him and for us, I'm sure. I can't imagine Poison without CC, and I'm certain he is thankful as well for the path he took.

We also auditioned Doug Aldrich. Doug had just arrived from Philly and was pursuing a gig in town. Doug and I met on the strip and became the best of friends. We hung out and were inseparable for a while. That audition didn't work out either. It wasn't really a decision on either of our parts — I think we both just kind of knew it wasn't the right fit musically, and Doug went on to join the band Lion soon after. I think the world of Doug and I consider him to be one of the best guitarists of our generation.

During my high school years, as we continued to audition guitarists, I would regularly run into Oz at school and around town. He owned a dark brown Datsun pick-up truck with a shell and would often give Greg and me lifts home from school. During the short drives he would play cassettes of whatever rock band we were into at the moment and we would talk music the whole way home. We'd listen to UFO, Scorpions, Black Sabbath, Yesterday And Today and anything else that was guitar driven. I began to establish a friendship with Oz and I got the sense that he was a good guy and that he and I had the same direction in music, and we did.

After the infamous Whittier High gig, I continued to press Rob, asking if he would consider having Oz back in the band. Rob was so against it. He didn't want to have anything to do with Oz. As I've said before, it seems that once Rob is done with something, he's done with it. And the Whittier High incident made Rob done with Oz.

But I was persistent, as I often can be, and Robert eventually opened up to the idea. We eventually asked Oz to join the band, and he agreed. Now, if we could just solve our revolving door of bass players, maybe we'd have a real band.

SEVEN

Remember when you were in high school and there was that hot girl, usually a cheerleader, who was untouchable? And although you'd love the chance to date her, you knew that you couldn't because she was dating the quarterback. Even if she wasn't dating the quarterback, you probably still wouldn't have a shot with her. Remember that girl?

Timothy Gaines was the musical equivalent of that girl. In terms of bass players, he was unattainable, at least so we thought.

But God had a plan.

Tim, legally known as Timothy Hagelganz, was the bass player for Stormer, one of the more popular bands on the LA scene at the time. They drew fairly large crowds and Tim was very much a centerpiece for that band with his youthfulness and vibe, not to mention the fact that he had the chops to back it up. He was, and is, a great player who was envied by many-a-band seeking a bassist, including us.

We used to talk about Tim a lot saying, "Man, he'd be perfect for our band, but that'll never happen." I just couldn't imagine Stormer without Tim. He was such an integral part of that band.

Stormer was always featured and interviewed in BAM Magazine, the free entertainment rag in the late '70s and '80s. The magazine launched in San Francisco, but soon had a Northern California and Southern California edition. It was distributed prominently at liquor stores, clubs, restaurants and music shops. That magazine was as iconic to the time as anything about The Sunset Strip.

All bands wanted to be featured in BAM. The publication brought recognition to many rising acts. If you were part of the Hollywood club scene, BAM was your road map. It was a huge deal to be featured and interviewed in this magazine and Stormer was.

BAM was also known for their musician classified ad section. We were constantly scouring each issue in search of the perfect bass player.

Up to this point, our lives had been changing subtly but significantly and the idea of making music for God was continuing to bounce around in our heads, and in conversations. We continued to toy with the idea of going Christian with our lyrics, but we weren't really taking the necessary steps. Our hearts were certainly changing and we grew weary of the routine on The Strip.

I had just spent the last 7 years of my life on Sunset Strip living the sex/drugs/rock & roll lifestyle, but there was always this feeling in my heart that told me I needed to change. I attribute this largely to when I first accepted Christ and got into church. The seed was planted then and that seed obviously took root.

Even though I was getting hammered on a regular basis and waking up with women I didn't know, not even knowing where I was, I kept feeling that something was wrong—that I needed to change. I kept thinking, "This isn't what I want to do. This just isn't right."
My long-term and solid commitment to a life with Christ wouldn't take place for another six months, but I could feel the seed growing and I knew I needed to do something.

It was almost as if our meeting Tim was set up before we even knew what was going on. It was as if God had a plan and knew exactly when the right time would be to bring Tim into our lives. Robert and I had accepted Christ at an early age. Oz's mother, who was a Christian and went to a Pentecostal church, was always talking to him about God and pleading with him to go to church. God was in Oz's life from an early age. And then there was Tim—

37

the awesome bass player in Stormer—your standard Hollywood rock band.

So here we were—Oz, Robert and myself—three guys who were Christians and really wanted to make a go at this, but didn't really know how. Or it's equally possible that we just didn't have the courage to take the stance we needed to take, and therefore we were suppressing those feelings of needing to change our lifestyle and lyrics.

One night Oz and I decided to hit Gazzarri's when Stormer would be playing. After the show Oz and Tim talked for a while and managed to exchange numbers. Nothing came of it, but we continued to go see Stormer play over the next few months. And if we didn't see them play, we could always pick up a copy of BAM and read about the latest with them.

Then one day I happened to be down on The Strip and I picked up the latest copy of the magazine. To no surprise, there was Stormer featured once again, only this time Tim wasn't in the picture with the band. They had another bass player.

I immediately brought this to Robert's attention and told him, "Hey man, I don't think Tim is in Stormer any longer. We should give him a call."

The next day after rehearsal, we all gathered around the phone while Robert called Tim. His mom answered the phone and told Robert that Tim wasn't home. Robert, thankfully, pressed on and went ahead and told her that we were a band and we were looking for a bass player.

Tim's mom, a bit thrown off, explained that Tim didn't do that anymore. She said that he became a Christian and decided to leave Stormer for that very reason. He had rededicated his life to God and was getting out of that scene.

Tim's father was a Presbyterian preacher, so just like Rob, Oz, and me, he had the seed planted at an early age and it, too, had apparently taken root.

Robert spoke up quickly and said "Wow. Well, we're Christians, too, and that's what we want to do, play Christian music."

I think Tim's mother was surely skeptical, but regardless, we convinced Tim to come down the next day and meet with us. No audition necessary. We agreed on the spot that we wanted him in the band, and he agreed as well.

It was all coming together. God was laying the ground work for us to all come together at the right time and place and it seemed miraculous.

That week we started rehearsing together. We were still known as Roxx Regime, but the birth of Stryper was just around the corner.

EIGHT

We were contemplating the whole "Christian thing." I wouldn't say we were 100% committed at this point, but we were paying good lip-service to the idea. It wasn't as if we were lying to Tim's mom when we said we were Christians. We were. But by no means were we men of conviction — however that was about to change.

In 1979, we were performing as Aftermath at The La Mirada Civic Center. There were four bands on the bill that night and one of the bands had a local keyboard player/singer named Kenny Metcalf. Ken wasn't a Christian at the time and I'd even go as far as to say that he was quite the opposite.

Fast-forward to when Tim joined the band and Kenny heard about us. I saw Kenny around town from time to time and someone told me that he had become a Christian and devoted his life to Christ. Having known of Kenny's reputation for quite some time and then being told that he was now a believer was amazing to me. I ran into Kenny on another occasion and he mentioned to me that he would like to stop by a rehearsal.

Sensing my apprehension, he said that he too was now a Christian and he wanted to check the band out and see what we were up to. I agreed to let him stop by, unsure of his motives.

So that night we started rehearsals as usual, running through song after song. Mind you, the lyrics weren't from a Christian perspective at this point. They were the same songs we had been playing and recording. Kenny came in and listened through part of our set, and after we were done we got into a long conversation with him and he shared in depth about how he had given his life to Christ.

He said that we needed to do the same and if we did, God would do incredible things with the band. It was odd that although he was telling us what to do, it wasn't in a forceful "turn or burn" way at all. He wasn't pointing fingers at us telling us we were sinners. It was non-judgmental and as a result, we were receptive. He was very enthusiastic and encouraging at the same time.

"Look guys. God wants to do some incredible things with you," he said as he looked around the room making eye contact with each of us. "You all know God. You've been there. And at one point in your life you've all made a commitment to God. If you devote this band to God 100%, He's going to take you places you've never dreamed of and He'll open doors and it's going to be incredible."

It was as if he saw our future. Or perhaps God saw our future and had put it upon Kenny's heart to tell us that if we didn't take our commitment seriously, doors to our future in music would remain closed.

Kenny continued to talk and we all took it in. Toward the end of the conversation he asked if we could all pray together, and we did.

I wasn't sure what tomorrow would hold, but what he said laid heavy on my heart—and, come to find out, it was laying quite heavily on the hearts of the other guys as well.

The next day, we continued to discuss this experience as a band. Rob, Oz, and Tim were obviously open to it, but again, nobody really knew what we should do and I think we were all a little nervous.

Picture this. The year is 1983 and we look around and see all these bands getting big record deals. Bands that had at one time opened for us were now of national and international acclaim. They all lived the Hollywood lifestyle. So it was a little—scratch that—it was a LOT intimidating to think about being a band that stood for the complete opposite of everything that was successful and popular at the time.

We finally had the bass player of our dreams. Were we going to waste away playing on Sundays in Church for the rest of our lives while everyone else got signed and found a career in music? Were we about to make the biggest mistake of our lives and throw all of our hopes and dreams out the window? Wouldn't it be enough to just be Christians, and not really sing about Jesus? Perhaps for some, that's the right path, but for us it wasn't the path we were supposed to take.

We decided to meet with another guy by the name of Michael Guido, whom Tim used to be in a band with. Tim invited him to come meet with us and he really brought encouragement into our lives and began to ease our fears. Guido, as we call him, had done a complete U-Turn with his life since his days in the band with Tim. Guido was heavily into alcohol and the lifestyle that typically goes along with most bands, even getting in a few bad accidents as a result of his drinking. He was fortunate and blessed to be alive.

I believe seeing this transformation of Guido first hand really had an effect on Tim, although all of us were affected by the encouragement he offered.

Very shortly after meeting with Guido, the four of us- Rob, Tim, Oz, and I- got together and unanimously agreed that this was something we wanted to do. We wanted to dedicate this band to God. We were done talking about it and it was time to actually do it.

That night we sat and we prayed. We individually and collectively recommitted our lives to Christ. It was an emotional night as we prayed and encouraged each other. No matter what happened, we were going to devote ourselves 100%. We agreed that night to hold one another accountable for our actions, and agreed to support one another along what we were sure would be a difficult and unknown path.

After that night, I took the first step and said to the band, "Guys, if we're going to do this, one of the first things we need to do is change the lyrics to our songs." They agreed, but I think with a little uncertainty.

I worked relentlessly over the next week or so rewriting the lyrics to all of the songs. Some of them didn't need much rewriting. I was already writing songs about love and relationships, so some just needed small changes, yet others were a little more drastic.

Thinking back on this time in our lives excites me. Our faith was fresh, sincere and uncluttered. Our fears of what others would think, or whether or not we might succeed, no longer mattered. We were committed and that's all that counted. The bond within the band was indescribable. We were both happy *and* sober, something that up until that point we didn't believe was possible.

Each night at rehearsal we would read the Bible and pray. When I think back on those times, I miss them. We don't do enough of that these days. Sure, we still pray, but sometimes it feels stale and rushed. It's almost as if we're saying, "Okay guys, hurry up, let's pray. We're on in 10 minutes." And that's not what prayer should be about. Prayer should be from the heart with an interest in sharing with God, without limitations. Instead, sometimes it feels more like "We've got a show to do in 2 minutes — let's pray because we forgot to."

Prayer in the early days of the band was a lot less rushed. We would take time to not only talk to God, but to each other. Our faith was alive and real, not just a set of doctrines that we all agreed on intellectually. We had a very personal relationship with God.

43

Before shows we would meet and without thinking about it, we would take the time to sit, talk and pray. Sometimes we'd have crew and friends in the room and there would be a dozen or more people gathered. We'd dim the lights and just talk and pray. We'd pour everything out to one another, and many times it led to tears. Other times it was just short and simple, but always real.

I think just the fact that we never prayed the same way twice shows me that it was not ritualistic at all. We just completely opened our hearts and laid everything out. Sometimes we'd spend an hour or more praying and talking and it would get pretty deep, yet other times it was short and light-hearted. We did it because we wanted to. All of us genuinely looked forward to prayer. It bonded us together more than we ever could have imagined.

This is what the "behind-the-scenes" was like when we were just getting started. And we weren't shy about it either. If you were around when we prayed, I don't care if you were the house sound guy, the janitor, the bouncer or whatever... if you were standing nearby, we'd invite you to join us. It was casual yet amazingly powerful.

NINE

"Whose birthday is it?" I asked one of the people at Enigma Records on the first day we met with the label.

The candles and cake were a dead give-away. But it wasn't your typical one or two candles on a cake type setting. There were candles everywhere in the office, almost like some ambient mood lighting for the occasion. Either way, I just assumed it was somebody's birthday. Or maybe I was just making small talk because I was a nervous wreck about the meeting with Bill and Wes Hein (label founders and owners).

Come to find out, I was right. It was somebody's birthday.

On the day we took our first meeting with Enigma Records, the entire office was celebrating the birthday of Aleister Crowley, one of the most influential occultists of all time who is recognized by many as a key predecessor to Satanism.

"Wow. This is no way to start." I thought. "Probably not the right label for us. Oh well. We're here. We may as well take the meeting."

Had we not already been escorted half way down the carpeted hallway lined with gold records and album marketing posters when I found out whose birthday it was, I probably would have turned around and left.

Glad I didn't.

Since the addition of Tim Gaines, we had really been working hard trying to get the coveted record deal. Hair bands were starting to get signed and we just couldn't seem to cross that bridge from the land of "Semi-Popular Sunset Strip Band" over to "Major Label Band Ready To Conquer The World."

It was frustrating. We'd hear all these stories of this band or that band taking meetings with labels. We'd here about so-and-so showcasing for this label or for that label. We were dancing with local success, but no labels were interested, until we met with Enigma.

A week prior, Robert and I carefully pieced together a faux record jacket/sleeve and the infamous early "demo" cassette to send to Enigma. We creatively labeled it with a thin-tipped black Sharpie and a yellow highlighter with the words "ROXX REGIME DEMO." We taped the package closed and placed it in a padded envelope scheduled for overnight delivery just a few cities away in Torrance.

By 10:30 the next morning we received confirmation that the package had arrived, and we exercised what little self-control we had and didn't follow up with a phone call. We had decided that if they didn't call us by the end of the week, we'd call them.

They received the demo on a Tuesday and called us that Thursday. The following week, we took a meeting with the Hein brothers and their team at Enigma Records.

Enigma was diverse in their signings. They had everyone from Motley Crue (early on) to Poison, but they had never signed a Christian band.

We later found out that the logo for Enigma records is an illustration of a woman's breast and "junk," for lack of a better term, and we became even more hesitant about the road we were traveling down.

What's strange about that time in our career, now looking back on it, was that we weren't really into Christian rock music, nor did we even consider the thought of soliciting Christian labels. It wasn't as if we were against the idea, we just didn't *have* the idea. We were surrounded by bands getting signed to LA labels, and well, that's just what you're supposed to do when you're a rock band from Hollywood— get signed to a rock label like everyone else. We knew two kinds of music at the time. It was either Rock or Metal (read: Judas Priest, Iron Maiden, Van Halen, and Black Sabbath).

In 1983 the only semi-notable Christian rock acts were Petra, The Rez Band, Phil Keaggy, Mylon LeFevre, and Larry Norman, and we certainly weren't listening to any of them. Nothing against those acts personally. I know most of those guys and I respect and admire them immensely. It just wasn't our kind of music, so signing with a label who signed those bands never even crossed our minds. We sounded nothing like them, so it wasn't even in our consciousness to consider looking at labels that had signed Christian bands.

So, we met with Enigma and they were all incredibly nice. They liked what we were doing, but they didn't like it enough. They asked for a private showcase as the next step.

Our friend (and brief former guitarist), Odie, had a warehouse in Whittier where his new band was rehearsing and he agreed to let us use the space for an evening.

We set up a showcase for Enigma Records to take place a few weeks later at the warehouse.

Showcases, particularly private ones, are odd affairs. You're essentially playing a live show, but your audience is made up of only a few people from the record label with the sole purpose of deciding your fate as an artist within their record label world. They are there to judge you, plain and simple. "Are you a big enough rock star with big enough rock hooks to make our label millions and millions of dollars?" And this all takes place on a Tuesday at 7:00 in the evening.

So we decided to make it a little less awkward, and unbeknownst to Enigma, we invited a bunch of friends so we could have people (fans) who knew the music and who would stand up near the stage, giving us the energy that only a live audience can give.

So half-a-dozen people from the label show up to this warehouse and we've got 30 or so friends there just hanging around. One of the label staff asks, "When are you planning to clear the room and get the showcase started?"

"We're a rock band," I said. "And a rock band has fans. Fans are part of our show and we feel they should stay."

They seemed to agree.

We were blaringly loud that day in our tin-roof showcase warehouse. You could hardly distinguish the vocals over the din of the instruments. It sounded horrible to me, but apparently not to Enigma, because they got really excited and shortly thereafter offered us a recording contract.

Not long after that showcase, we went to Enigma's offices in Torrance and filed into their boardroom to sign the deal. Enigma was THE hot independent label at the time. They were a driving force in the market and although they weren't Capital or Warner Brothers, we felt good about our decision. Turns out, Enigma was one of the best career decisions we ever made as a band. To this day, I have incredible respect for what Bill and Wes Hein did for this band.

We had such magical camaraderie with Enigma, a rare experience even at that time. We worked together on launching the band, setting forth goals and specific actions to achieve those goals. Bill and Wes were brilliant and undeniably instrumental in the success of Stryper.

Ironically, it wasn't until *after* we signed the deal that they realized we were a Christian band, and a very outspoken one at that. I still find that hard to believe, but that's what they said. Not that it really mattered to them. It wasn't as if they were saying, "Oh man, what have we done? We just signed a Jesus band. How can we get out of this one?" Or maybe they were thinking that, but they hid it well.

Even with the distorted vocals in that acoustically flawed warehouse, how could they not hear the words "Jesus is the way!" in the song "From Wrong To Right", or any of the other blatantly bold lyrics at the time?

So there we were, the sole Christian band signed to a label that celebrated Aleister Crowley's birthday. What next?

Well, the first order of business from the label was direct orders, or more like a firm suggestion, to change the name. This was the moment I began to really like this label. I always hated the name Roxx Regime. But Rob wasn't as easily convinced. He liked the name a lot.

Over the coming weeks we threw around a few dozen options and eventually settled on Striper. We changed the "I" to a "Y" and we became Stryper. Rob said it rhymed with "hyper." And that's the story behind the name. The label didn't like Roxx Regime, thankfully, and we, again thankfully, came up with Stryper.

It wasn't until later that we would associate the name with the words of Isaiah 53:5 — "By His Stripes We Are Healed." And it was a few weeks after that when we would create the acronym "Salvation Through Redemption Yielding Peace Encouragement and Righteousness."

It didn't take long for word on the street to spread that we were now a heavy metal band devoted to Christ, and our crowds got even bigger. We were packing clubs throughout LA and Orange County. Soon after signing, we performed at The Troubadour and sold it out. The line stretched from Santa Monica to Sunset. We could have done 2-3 shows that night and filled the place. The buzz began......

Record-signing shows were common then. It was partially a way for labels to show off their new trophy bands, and partially a way for bands to say to other *un*signed bands, "Hey, look at us, we're signed!" They were always lavish and over-the-top extravaganzas, each label trying to out-do another and each band trying to have their 15 minutes of bragging rights. It's a little silly when you think about it, but that was how it was.

We found out later that they turned away over a thousand people for that show at The Troubadour. The next day there were pictures of the line in the paper. If anyone overlooked our bragging rights that night at The Troubadour, they surely saw it the next day in print.

Things started to happen fast at this point — really fast.

Soon after, we played a show at the Reseda Country Club with Poison and Bon Jovi. Bon Jovi had just come out with "Runaway" and they were really starting to take off, so it was another capacity crowd. To the masses they weren't yet rock stars, but within their own minds, they may as well have been The Rolling Stones. That's probably an unfair judgment of them having only been around them for such a short time, but that's the way I perceived them and the way they came across.

We had of course crossed paths with C.C. Deville previously, and the guys in Poison were sweethearts. All of them were really nice guys and took time to talk with us.

We used to try to take the time to talk to the bands we performed with, looking for any open door to share our faith. We never cornered bands and preached to them. We were just acutely aware of opportunities that could lead to the sharing of our faith, where we were in our lives, and why we believed what we did.

There was only one little speed bump during our honeymoon time with Enigma. They weren't ready to lay down the money to record a new album. They planned to release our demos as the first album. They basically just said "We like your demos. Let's release these."

Thank God we met someone who would become a life-long friend and an investor in the band and would give us the opportunity to record our low budget demos professionally. She had heard about us doing this "God thing" and decided to come to a show to see if it was for real or not. She saw the band and was blown away. Here we were, a band devoted to Christ but at the same time selling out clubs on The Sunset Strip. Her name was Daryn Hinton, and she would become instrumental in the next phase of Stryper.

TEN

Nowhere is the popular saying about the journey being more fun than the destination truer than in the music business. In hindsight I wish I had taken time to appreciate the early journey a little more. I should have taken just a few more moments to breathe in those early days and enjoy the sunrise that was taking place before my very eyes.

In 1983 we were kids with all the promise of a future, but still wanting to be kids and continue playing with toys.

Our most prized toy was a recording contract. The rest of the industry probably thought we were crazy, but we didn't care. The sense of hope and a bright future was palpable within the walls of the Stryper camp. We were hangin' with industry big-wigs. We were, finally, of interest to the press. Our peers were envious, or so we assumed. And we had an entire world to toss Bibles to.

Daryn Hinton strengthened our excitement about our future.

There's a popular saying in the music business about bands and record companies. When a record label doesn't really want to invest in a band, they instead throw a bunch of albums out just to "see what sticks." People would say about a record label that doesn't develop acts, "They just throw it against the wall and see if it sticks."

Well, thanks largely to Daryn, we stuck like glue.

Enigma, not ready to invest and wanting to see if we "stuck" first, was considering releasing the demos "as is." Those "as is" recordings were later released as '"The Roxx Regime Demos" through our own label Fifty Three Five Records.

As our bond with (and love for) Daryn began to grow, she agreed to invest in us. $100,000. This was an unheard of amount of money to us. We signed an agreement to pay her back with interest, and we did. Because of Daryn and her risky investment, we were able to go back in and re-record those demos, get some new equipment, and we even had a billboard on Sunset Strip that stayed in place for months and months.

Locals were thinking, "What the hell?" A Billboard on The Strip dedicated solely to one band was not common-place at the time. People took notice. How could they miss us? A bunch of guys that looked like girls dressed in yellow and black striped spandex? Yeah, not really a Billboard you could overlook on Sunset Strip.

We went into Mad Dog Studios in Venice to re-record the demos, having tracked the drums at a place called Music Grinder. Mad Dog relocated in 1996 to Burbank but still has a history of having recorded some great artists like Dwight Yoakum and Buck Owens.

The music was coming together just like I had imagined it would. If only I had the right equipment and studio to capture the sounds as I was hearing them the first time on the demos. I've always been a stickler about the sonic quality of Stryper, tending to over-obsess with every detail. It was so satisfying to finally be happy with a recording.

Enigma was obviously pleased. Why wouldn't they be? The record went from a mediocre sounding demo at best, to a polished, professional recording — on our dime, loaned to us with interest.

But still, we were a "Jesus Band", as they used to refer to us around the office, and Enigma had never marketed a Jesus Band. So the process began on artwork and packaging for the album. We turned in our 8-mile-long list of thank-you credits that we wanted on the album. First-time releases by young bands always have too many names on the thanks list. We were no exception. We thanked people on our first album that we haven't seen or spoken to since.

Enigma's uncertainty about how to market Stryper really sank in when we turned in the lyrics. Conversations went back and forth debating the merits of including the lyrics in the album. We of course wanted to, but the label wasn't so sure.

I guess maybe they thought that the rest of the world wouldn't notice the "Jesus thing." I remember talking to the label and hearing the uncertainty in their voices over the lyrical content and thinking for a moment that we may get dropped before we even release the record. Fortunately, we were not willing to compromise our music and message, and so the lyrics stayed, Jesus and all.

On July 21, 1984, *The Yellow and Black Attack* was released. Miraculously, it built its own momentum and sold an unexplained 150,000 copies in the first three weeks! It exploded. We were the talk of LA, if not the country. I imagine Enigma Records thought differently of us from that moment on.

Although I never heard these words, my gut was telling me that behind closed doors at the label they were thinking "Okay. This Christian thing isn't so bad after all. This might actually be pretty easy."

The label made us a priority and got behind us one hundred percent.

I believe it was God who had his hands on this and He was in complete control. I truly believe the Creator of the Universe was the fifth member of Stryper, keeping a watchful eye on us. He closed all the right doors at the right time, and opened the right ones at the right time as well.

Despite our naiveté about the steps leading to getting signed and putting out our first record, our hearts were truly humbled. We were praying and having Bible studies more than ever, and really looking to God to lead the way, and boy did He, right into the fast lane.

We didn't know what we were doing business-wise, but our hearts were pure. We just wanted to do whatever we felt God was leading us to do. And we believed. Our faith was strong. We didn't doubt the path we had chosen. It all seemed to come together at the right time almost as if God was saying, "Now you're ready. *That's* the kind of faith I'm looking for." It was the faith of a mustard seed.

It's mindboggling to me as I reflect on that period of my life and realize all that was accomplished with such little knowledge of exactly how to accomplish it. I can't explain it any other way other than God's hands were upon us. And this was just the beginning.

ELEVEN

A black 1984 T-Top Corvette. This was the first indication that I'm a spender. Some people are spenders and some are savers. My wife Lisa is a saver. My daughter Ellena is a saver. Saving money comes as naturally to them as one would expect. But spending, on the other hand, comes naturally to me. That's not to say I'm incapable of saving money. I can, and I do save. But it's like playing guitar both left handed and right handed. It doesn't come easy. It requires a lot of extra thought and effort.

We sold an astonishing amount of *The Yellow & Black Attack* in the third quarter, and it was time for Enigma to pay fourth quarter mechanical royalties. A mechanical royalty is a royalty paid to the songwriters, and since I was the primary songwriter, I got the biggest check — almost $40,000!

I cashed it. I didn't open a savings account. I didn't even put any in a checking account. I cashed the check and was walking around with a stack of hundred dollar bills rolled up with rubber bands wrapped around them.

That same day I walked into the local Chevy dealership and was treated like a complete loser by a pompous salesman. His attitude told me all I needed to know — that he was completely wasting his time showing a 21-year-old longhaired kid around the showroom. He was condescending and rude.

I, of course, wanted to test-drive the car before purchasing it, although that was just a formality. As long as it started and smelled new, I was buying it.

I glanced around the showroom filled with exactly zero customers and only two other salesmen. My guy made it pretty obvious that he thought I was "just looking" and certainly couldn't afford a new Corvette.

He didn't join me for the test drive, which I thought was a little odd. If he didn't think I could buy it, surely he must have considered the possibility of me stealing it.

Regardless, he didn't go with me on the test drive. When I returned I walked into his office and pulled out a ball of cash from my jacket and laid it on his desk. "I'll take it," I said. I plopped down the cash on his desk, rubber bands and all.

The look on his face was priceless. I think I enjoyed that part of the experience as much as the actual car — although in hindsight I wish I hadn't given him the satisfaction of making a commission.

Chalk that day up to a "coming of age" experience. I suppose there are worse ways I could have spent that money and worse people who could have received it. Drug dealers, tax collectors and televangelists come to mind (*I may get letters for that statement but wait until the end of the book before sending any out. You may want to add more to your letter*).

I came to know Christ through Jimmy Swaggart. But that was about the extent of my appreciation for Swaggart. Shortly after we became successful, he spoke boldly against Stryper and said some really hurtful things about us.

It was confusing and hard to understand since he was so instrumental in my conversion. He actually held up our records at quite a few of his telecasts and told his viewers that we were "wolves in sheep's clothing" and not to support us! Of course not long after his judgmental rants about our ministry, his ministry came crashing down. More about ministries crashing down later.....

Within a year of purchasing my dream car, I got in a minor fender-bender with my Corvette on the way to Robert's house. My wife Kyle, who was pregnant at the time, was in the car with me when it happened. Knowing that Corvettes are made of fiberglass, it was enough to scare me into selling the car. I sold it to Rob minutes later for $20,000. I said "Dude, it's yours right now for 20k if you'll just take it." He did.

I bought a brand new 'Vette and sold it less than a year later for $20k? Yep, I was shaping up to be quite the businessman with choices like that. Don't let Rob tell you I never did anything for him. I took that $20k and bought a sensible 4-door sedan complete with cup-holders, seat back pockets, and an AM/FM/cassette radio.

In 1984, having been on the air for almost 3 years now, MTV played music videos and featured VJs such as Nina Blackwood, Mark Goodman, Alan Hunter, J.J. Jackson and Martha Quinn, who would come on the airwaves with all the authority and integrity of Walter Cronkite and tell, or rather *show*, young music fans what they should be listening to. Although I believe there are a lot of variables that led to our success, one decisive element was MTV. They liked us, and we liked them.

Our first music video was for the song "You Know What to Do" from *The Yellow and Black Attack* that we shot at the Santa Monica Civic Auditorium during an actual live performance.

Matt Crouch, son of TBN's Paul and Jan Crouch, directed the video. To this day he's a dear friend of mine and has always been there for me through thick and thin. He's gone on to become a very talented director and film-maker with his company Gener8ion.

We were working on a very limited budget so Daryn Hinton called in as many favors as possible to help with the video. One of those favors was a makeup artist—a beautiful woman by the name of

Kyle Tucy. Kyle was one of the most sought after makeup artists in Hollywood working on films like *Terminator, Repo Man* and *Wisdom.*

Having makeup applied is a unique experience. I'm in a chair while the makeup artist leans in close, walking around from side to side getting up-close and personal, attempting to achieve the perfect look. It's a very intimate experience that can either be really comfortable or really awkward. In this case, it was a little of both. I didn't want to get out of the chair that day because something just happened from the moment I met Kyle. I could sense something special, and I literally felt my stomach turning. She was beautiful, but it wasn't about that. I got the strangest feeling around Kyle from day one. It was a feeling I had never felt before.

She wasn't a Christian and was thrust into this job with a bold Christian band. She didn't know what to think. I believe she was a little shocked by the whole thing, but I do recall her telling me how nice she thought we were. But here was this makeup artist getting thrown into the ring—the hair, the spandex, the Christian lyrics and message. She must have thought, "What in the world is this?" But back then everybody seemingly had that reaction to us.

She and I exchanged numbers and talked almost nightly on the phone the next week. I talked to her a lot about my faith and my beliefs, not so much hoping she would believe the same, but just wanting to gauge whether or not she would be okay dating someone who had dedicated his life to Christ.

I finally got the nerve to ask her out the following week. I drove to her house on Flores Street, just off Santa Monica Boulevard. We walked a block away to the famous Barney's Beanery, a casual Burgers and Billiards place, located less than a mile away from the Whisky A Go Go and the Key Club. It was an amazing night. Time stood still, yet moved so quickly. Before I knew it we had finished our food, but I didn't want the night to end. Neither did she.

We decided to walk another block up Santa Monica to an ice cream place where we sat and talked for another hour or so, until they finally had to tell us they were closing for the night. I walked her home, briefly kissed her goodnight at her front door, and then I drove home thinking about all the possibilities that might lie ahead.

I was a bit skeptical about jumping into a relationship with Kyle. She had moved to LA from Massachusetts with her fiancé, a musician named Dave Amato. The two of them had only broken up a short while before I started seeing Kyle, and it was a bit awkward at first. He was still coming around and occasionally I would be there when he'd stop by. I got the sense it felt to him as though I had taken Kyle away from him, which wasn't true. They had already broken up before we started dating. Nonetheless, it was a little uncomfortable to say the least.

Dave was and is quite the admired musician in LA. Not long after his breakup with Kyle, he would become the guitarist for Ted Nugent, and now he is a member of REO Speedwagon. Ironically, his first band back in Massachusetts was called Aftermath, formed around the same time Rob and I had a band in LA by the same name.

He's a great guy and a dear friend now and I can see why the two of them connected. Dave and I have actually remained in touch and I recently joined REO Speedwagon on stage when they were touring through Boston. Dave pulled me on stage, handed me a guitar, and I faked my way through the REO hit "Keep Pushin." It was classic.....

Kyle was 7 years my senior. What this 28 year old, well educated woman saw in a Jesus-loving 21-year-old musician, I'm not sure. But thankfully we clicked.

Getting to know and grow closer to Kyle was a bit of a roller coaster thanks to my childish erratic behavior. We got serious about each other fast, and as a result I began to back-pedal, wondering if I should play the field. Stryper was dancing with success and I was questioning the idea of settling down. And I was a jerk throughout the process.

I couldn't be a man about it and just tell Kyle how I was feeling. No, that would have been the smart thing to do. Instead, I just started being mean. Not calling. Treating her rudely. Or just ignoring her altogether.

We didn't really break up. I just stopped calling.

I did this not once, but twice. After the first time, I came to my senses and she took me back, miraculously. And then I did it again, and again a few months later. That was me at the time—a selfish kid who didn't know what he wanted or needed.

The second time she wasn't quite as understanding and just moved on, dating a stunt man she was working with on a movie.

So like the yo-yo I was, I went running back to her again. This time on bended knees asking for her forgiveness, apologizing profusely, realizing what a fool I was. I told her that I realized there was most likely no way she would take me back, but I would be forever committed if she would.

Thankfully, she took me back and I was committed. We were obviously very attracted to each other and passionately in love. One day after band practice I came to her apartment and the look on her face told me that my life was about to change forever. Kyle was pregnant.

A few days later we eloped, telling nobody—not my parents, not the band. Nobody.

We went to a friend's house in Palos Verdes, got a minister and a couple of necessary witnesses, and we got married. The next day I moved out of my room at my parents' house and into Kyle's apartment. My parents were obviously upset. But I was ecstatic. I was 22 years old and embarrassed by still living with my parents and sleeping in a bunk bed. Bunk beds should end pre-teen, right? Friends would come to the house and I wouldn't even take them to my room! Well, I was outta there as fast as I could pack and gather my belongings. But between my immaturity, the pregnancy, eloping, and upset family members, we weren't exactly standing on solid ground.

We had previously not lived together, so we were also learning all the quirks and idiosyncrasies a new couple endures. Toilet paper roll over or under? Squeeze the toothpaste from the bottom or the middle? Should the dishes get washed nightly or sit in the sink? We were now financially joined at the hip, a situation that never makes for an easy adjustment, particularly when one of us has spent his entire, and to that point, only paycheck on a depreciating sports car.

Yes, there was a definite learning curve, more so for me. She was a much more mature person than I, and she was capable of handling this lifestyle change. Kyle was a college graduate with a major in Child Psychology from Colby College and I had only a G.E.D. Throughout our life together, although I was envious of her at times, I appreciated being married to a woman who was smarter than I was.

We were in love and worked through things. I learned to squeeze the toothpaste from the bottom and she learned that toilet paper should always dispense under, never over.

Most importantly, in a day when it wasn't uncommon for a Sunset Strip rocker to get a girl pregnant prior to marriage, it *was,* however, uncommon for a Christian rocker to own up and take responsibility for it. Although I was young, I knew I needed to do the right thing. But it really didn't have as much to do with that as the fact that I loved Kyle with all my heart and soul. She was the one that I wanted to spend the rest of my life with. Getting Kyle pregnant prior to marriage was not part of my plan. Regardless, I had committed my life to her, and the fact that we had a baby on the way made life even greater.

Within a year we purchased our first home in Fullerton, California and our son, Michael, Jr. was born. We were living the fairytale life in our new home with great neighbors, a well-manicured lawn that I took pride in maintaining, and an interior of designer furniture and state-of-the-art appliances. No more bunk beds for me. We were a family now. And I was happy.

TWELVE

I have a love/hate relationship with our Yellow & Black motif. Actually, it's mostly a hate relationship. Just the thought of yellow and black and I begin to feel anxious and uneasy, wishing we had never gone down that road. It has been the single most persistent antagonist of my career.

That is not to say I wish we had eliminated the motif all together, I just wish we had toned it down a bit. By the time Stryper was in full force, Rob had everything painted in yellow and black stripes. If it wasn't yellow and black, it wasn't on stage. I even remember Rob suggesting we dye our hair yellow and black. Seriously.

Would Stryper have become successful without the yellow and black? I would argue we would have been even *more* successful. Although Rob was the first to introduce it, and push it to extremes that left me uncomfortable, I'm also to blame. It wasn't as if we suddenly, in one day, painted everything we owned yellow and black. No, it started with the drum kit, then the guitars, then the clothing, then the mic stands, then the guitar cables, then the cars! One element at a time, and before I knew it, we were living in a striped world and I was getting a headache.

Rob was always focused on the show whereas my focus was the music. Rob was the visual guy hence the name "The Visual Timekeeper", and I was always the music guy. It's always been that way as far back as I can recall.

Rob was consistently and acutely on the lookout for our next big gimmick—Always on the search for new ideas. I can't say for sure where he got the idea for yellow and black stripes, but I can say that he had an obsession with that combination of colors. As teenagers, long before the development of Stryper, we would go out and steal yellow and black road signs to line the walls of our studio. For me it was just fun to get rowdy and go out stealing road signs. For Rob it was a quest to acquire more yellow and black, or so it seemed.

Rob was really into Kiss, and I think that played a role in his desire and need for us to have a visual gimmick. I liked Kiss too, but not like Rob did. I was more drawn to bands like Bad Company, Van Halen and Journey who had great songs, talent and production. I couldn't care less what the band looked like. But Rob really enjoyed seeing a band and saying, "Look at those guys! Look at those outfits! Look at those lights, look at that stage!!!"

In that sense I suppose we are the perfect Yin and Yang. Yet I can't help but feel the attire, makeup, and glam of Stryper often detracts from the substance of the music and the message.

We certainly weren't the first band to introduce stripes into our overall theme. Honestly, a lot of things that fans may perceive as unique to Stryper aren't that unique at all. We weren't the first to do many of the things that became synonymous with Stryper. Matthias Jabs of The Scorpions, for example, used to wear stripes, as did David Lee Roth and Kevin DuBrow of Quiet Riot. Matthias even implied once in an interview that perhaps Stryper had stolen his yellow and black striped look. Perhaps we did subconsciously. I honestly don't know how it all got started. I just know that I went along with it but I wasn't necessarily a huge fan of it.

We also weren't the first to introduce a sideways drum kit either. I believe Kelly Keagy of Night Ranger was the first to do that.

I would like to think the name Stryper largely came about because we had already donned stripes. That may have been part of it, but I've heard stories that the idea for the name Stryper may have been inadvertently planted in Rob's head by a local band from Texas named Stryker, whom Rob supposedly had met in a local park several years earlier during our Roxx Regime days. Stryker, according to insider legend, had met Rob and told him about their band, even going so far as to telling him that they chose the name Stryker and spelled it with a "y" because it rhymed with "hyper." Hmmm, sounds a little all too familiar. Stryker's logo even looks a lot like the Stryper logo. It wasn't until after we hit it pretty big that Stryker released their first national album having changed their named to Stryken— so that made them look like the copycats although if the stories are true, it just may have been the other way around.

I did always wonder why they changed their name from Stryker to Stryken though. You would think if a band were going to undergo a name change, partially because your name sounds like another band, then you'd make a more drastic change than one letter. Who knows?

The name, the colors, the outfits, it's a bit of a tender spot with me.

For almost 30 years, whether in a hardware store, a grocery store, a book store or wherever, some form of the following conversation has haunted me.

"You look like you're in a band."

"I am."

"What band?"

"A band called Stryper."

"Hmmmm. I'm sorry. I'm not familiar with you guys," they say with apologetic overtones.

"No worries. I don't expect you to be."

"Would I know any of your songs?" they say, hopeful to redeem themselves, or at least to make the already uncomfortable conversation a little more comfortable.

"Maybe. We had a few songs you might know. 'Honestly'. 'Calling On You'. 'To Hell With The Devil'. 'Always There For You'." I don't expect them to recognize any of these. Continuing the list would only prolong our mutual embarrassment.

"Hmmmm. Doesn't ring a bell, but I'd probably know them if I heard them." Ha! Or then again, probably not.

I take one last stab at it, more for their sake than for mine, and say "We wore yellow and black outfits."

"Oh yeah," I *do* remember you guys. The yellow and black band. Yeah. Wow. That's cool! That's REALLY cool!"

"Not really," I think in my head. You have basically just told me that you don't know our band or our music, but you do know that we dressed like bumblebees.

Oh well. We could have done the yellow and black thing in a much cooler way. It was just so over the top that it opened the door for mockery at times. I feel as though it diluted the legitimacy of the band. Had I been more outspoken about it in my younger years, I think we could have found a way to have an image that wasn't so gimmicky. Elements of yellow and black stripes here and there could have still given us a visual edge without making us look like, well you know — bumblebees.

To me, bands that use visual gimmicks do so because they don't often have the music to back it up. I believe that we did and *do* have the music to back it up, and as a result, I always found myself fighting against our image.

I feel we have something incredibly unique without all the bumblebee crap. Oz, Tim, and I sing well together creating some unique and impressive harmonies. Our songs. Our message. Our harmony guitar solos. Rob's drumming. All of that sometimes takes a back seat, or isn't taken seriously, and to me that's very unfortunate.

It's depressing to pour the very core of my heart and soul into writing a song or an album, only to read discussions, often jokes, about our attire. So much time, thought, and effort go into the music and the production. It's not 3-chord rock. Some of it is pretty intricate stuff. And to work so hard on something, musically, vocally, and lyrically, only to be overshadowed by the look — well, it's frustrating to say the least. We didn't need a gimmick, but we got one any way.

I'd like to be remembered for our message and music. Had we just toned down the yellow and black, even just a little bit, our legacy might hold a little more legitimacy.

From the moment the yellow and black stripes extended beyond the drum set, I have always encouraged toning it down, but it wasn't until the *Against The Law* album that I put my foot down. Rob seemed to resist the color change. Our compromise was to keep elements of stripes in the band, but we did away with the yellow and black. To me, that was the best the band had ever looked. Visuals aside, that was a humbling and even embarrassing time in my life for other reasons.

THIRTEEN

If I were to describe John The Baptist, I might imagine him to be a lot like my friend Michael Guido. Strong facial features, a defined jaw line hidden behind a salt and pepper beard. Long, curly hair, callused hands and sun tanned skin from his time outdoors praying for and with people. Outspoken in his faith, but quick to listen intently. Deep set eyes that speak to your very soul when you gaze into them. Sometimes his eyes are saying, "Well done my child" and other times they are saying, "I'm disappointed in you." Nonetheless, they always say, "I care."

Guido accompanied us, along with 10 of our closest friends and crewmates on our very first tour following the release of *The Yellow and Black Attack.* 15 of us filled every available seat in a 15 passenger van on a ten day tour through Texas and Arizona. It was our only tour to support that album before we went on to record *Soldiers Under Command.* By the way "15 passenger van" is a terrible name for those vehicles. Yes, they *can* hold 15 people, but there's no accounting for all the gear that a band must carry along.

As we headed deep into the heart of Texas, most of us took turns driving. I, of course, was the best driver, meticulously obsessing over every road sign and turn signal (at least that's what I thought but I guarantee you everyone else would tell you a different story). I required a co-pilot at all times, glued to the Rand McNally, ensuring the most direct route to each venue. I remember driving late one night and being especially tired. As we approached the outskirts of the next town, we came to a fork in the road and I had already decided to go to the left, at 85 mph! Oz was to my right and shouted "No, No... Stay to the right! Stay to the right!"

A sudden jerk of the steering wheel and I lost control of the van. The screech of the tires was muffled only by the uncontrollable outbursts of fear within the van. The women were screaming. I was screaming. It was a miracle the van didn't roll. Our first "real" tour outside of LA and we almost met God that night. I could see the headlines: "Christian Rock band's fatal crash on I-20. 15 people dead." I gained control and sighs of relief filled the van. Then laughter. We're alive, and on tour!!

Later that month, I read a national automotive report declaring 15-passenger vans have a 400 percent greater chance of rolling over when they are filled to capacity. It was time for us to get on a tour bus or reduce our number of traveling companions. To this day I won't tour in a van. Not because I'm above it. I just don't feel safe.

We banged out 7 shows in 10 days on that first tour, including an amazing show at The Bronco Bowl in Dallas where we sold over 1000 tickets. The incredible turnouts at each show pleasantly surprised us, but at every stop on the tour I was confident nobody would show up. And then miraculously, each night, we had more than respectable crowds. I was absolutely amazed by the outpouring of fans. Hundreds, sometimes thousands in each city turned out, many of them already sporting yellow and black attire. This helped me realize we were about to embark on something big with Stryper and made me even more excited and anxious to get back into the studio to record the album that I knew we were capable of making.

Despite having seen a smorgasbord of diverse cultures back home in Los Angeles, we were relatively naïve to the world. We had not yet toured beyond a 60 mile radius of our home, so we were thrilled to be away for the first time. To this day, Texas remains one of our strongest markets and I attribute that to the early years of touring there regularly. Los Angeles is our home. Texas is our most beloved home away from home.

Three days into the tour, I'm already beginning to wonder why we have brought so many people. This van was just too small for 15 of us. But we loved it. We needed the 15 of us, especially Kenny

Metcalf and Michael Guido who helped embrace us with the love, encouragement, and support to be strong and self-reliant.

Guido prayed over everything. "Guys. This is the venue. Before we go in, let's pray over the venue." And we did. In the middle of the day, as people strolled by, we would put our hands on the walls of the building and Guido would lead us in prayer over the venue. Before sound check Guido would gather us to pray over the instruments. We would of course pray before taking the stage as well. One night in particular the local opening band was obviously nervous about their performance. Guido gathered us all around to pray for them, and with them, so they might experience God too. This shocked the band as they were not Christians — but they still smiled with appreciation, or perhaps confusion, as the prayer concluded.

This constant prayer could be both comforting and yet annoying at times to a young rock band out on their own for the first time, but Guido knew we needed a foundation and he was happy to help provide it. Sometimes we didn't want to pray. Sometimes we just wanted to get out of the van and head down the street looking for the local music store or coffee shop. Sometimes I just wanted to get away from everyone and be by myself, a tendency that would never abandon me as I grew older. But we prayed. Over the buildings. The van. The clothes. The equipment. The shows. I was thankful to be surrounded by this sort of commitment. And as inconvenient as it may have been, I didn't lose focus on the importance of prayer.

The fans at these shows were so supportive. Most were Christians who had heard about us through fanzines, word of mouth, and what little radio play we received. We were still flying safely under the radar from the skeptics and naysayers. They, for the most part, didn't rear their ugly heads until after *Soldiers Under Command* started to climb the charts.

As we headed back across Arizona into California, there was a quiet sense of accomplishment inside our van. We were of course pleased to have completed our first tour, but we basked in silence. All of the shows far exceeded our expectations and we felt strangely at peace with our place in the music business. Yet I was sad to return home, despite knowing the next item on my agenda was to make what was certain to become the groundbreaking album of my career. Still, as I saw the "Welcome to California" sign I missed the call of the road already. The uncertainty before each show. The near fatal van accident. I missed the smell of the venues and the nervous butterflies I got when the house lights dimmed and I could hear the roar of the crowd from behind the stage. It had been only 24 hours since our last show, and I missed it, terribly. I was already being pulled back to the ambivalent role I would play on the rock-n-roll touring circuit. And I realized, "This is what I live for. This is who I will be for the rest of my life. Forever I will be constantly torn between home and the nomad's life where every city looks the same. Forever I will constantly battle between the need to make music in the controlled environment of a studio and the anything-goes chaos of a tour." As I crossed the California State line I knew that for the rest of my life, wherever I was, I would want to be somewhere else.

FOURTEEN

In 2010 I was diagnosed with Attention Deficit Hyperactivity Disorder (ADHD). Today I make light of it, laughing at it from time to time. It's just my way of not letting it get to me, because it can be very frustrating at times. It's probably the most confusing thing I've dealt with throughout my life.

Not long ago I was working in my studio hanging pictures on the wall. With hammer and nails in hand, I hang my first picture. Stepping back to make sure that it's level, I realize I've lost my hammer. I haven't left the room so it's got to be here, yet I spend the next five minutes looking for it. I'm too focused on whether or not the picture frame is level to remember where I put it down. While searching, I find some old pictures of Lena and Mikey, and I get further distracted. Finally, I find the hammer and hang the second picture. Somehow, I lose it again. I spend another five minutes looking for the hammer, all the while continuing to try to take my focus off questioning whether or not my pictures are level. The phone rings (my most common distraction), and after the conversation I spend another few minutes looking. I find it again. A few hours later, I complete a job that would take a "normal person" 15 minutes, but I've found some pictures and now I need to figure out what to do with them. Maybe this is why I can scream so high and so loud—it's the frustration! That is what my life has been like for as long as I can remember.

In the mid seventies, as I was developing my signature guitar tone (and ultimately the signature Stryper guitar tone), ADHD was not widely accepted by the medical community as a disorder. Back then I was just hyper. Or I just didn't pay attention. Or worse, I paid attention to only one thing and nothing else, but that one thing had to be really interesting to me in order to keep my attention any longer than a few moments.

The one thing I did pay attention to at the time was my guitar tone.

I can sit in a room for hours trying to achieve the best tone from an amp, guitar or pedal. I'll change pickups, strings, readjust the amp, readjust the pedals, change the pickups again, and so on and so on. Before I know it an entire day has passed.

At the age of 13, after hearing the first Boston album, I became hyper-focused on achieving greatness with my own signature guitar sound. Later in life I discovered there were a gazillion tracks of guitars on those Boston albums, but at 13 all I knew was that I too wanted the perfect guitar tone. I spent many afternoons as a young teen working with different gear to achieve just that.

Tom Scholz, founder of Boston, capitalized on his sound by selling rack mount EQs, pre-amps, choruses, and delays—and every aspiring guitar player wanted that Boston sound. I would go so far as to say that the Boston guitar sound created one of the most influential tones ever recorded.

It's funny how something can be so profound when you're a kid and then when you're older (and perhaps a little wiser), you see it for what it truly is. I had the opportunity to join Boston and play alongside Tom Scholz. As a contributing member of Boston, I realized that the simplicity of a guitar tone is often the root of its greatness.

Ultimately, a Gibson Lab Series L-5 head combined with a Marshall head would be the combination to create what would become known as the Stryper tone. But to get there, it took hours and hours of obsessing over every small detail and countless combinations of knob-turning and "tweaking."

In the '80s the most guarded secret on The Sunset Strip was how a guitarist achieved his guitar tone. If aspiring, or even established musicians liked your tone, they became obsessively inquisitive about how you achieved it. And The Strip was a battle ground competition toward the ever coveted recording contract, so to just freely give away the secret of your guitar tone would be like handing the opposing team your playbook before the game. You just don't do that. Every band wanted to win the race to the front door of the record label, and part of that was hiding your playbook.

Back when we were a trio, I used to hide some of my equipment so the audience, or more specifically other musicians, couldn't see what I was using. One night playing with Ratt at the infamous Gazarri's, Robbin Crosby and Chris Hager began asking me questions about my guitar tone. "Hey man. What are you using to get that sound?"

I showed them what I was using, but I hid the main ingredient, the Gibson Lab Series, and it seemed to successfully confuse true guitar aficionados. No way was I sharing my trade secrets, at least not yet. Oddly enough, the unique configuration of guitar amps that I and my fellow Sunset Strip musicians were developing in the '80s is now commonplace among today's artists. I get a certain guitar-geek satisfaction from knowing I was at ground-zero of an era that set the pace for many of the sounds you hear on today's modern day rock records.

Now when people ask me how I achieve my guitar tones, I just tell them that I hang really straight pictures. If said with a smile, they smile back, more confused than before.

When you're ADHD, finding someone you trust to be your guitar tech is a major task. I put my trust in a guy by the name of Rick Pietila. I love and trust Rick. He's a martial artist, so not only is he great with guitars, he's also great at protection when it's needed. He's probably 160 pounds soaking wet in his work boots, but I'd never want to take a punch from him. Thankfully we get along great. I'm equally as thankful that he's never used his martial art skills for my protection (at least that I'm aware of), but it's nice to know he's there. Sometimes early in the morning I'd wake up and look out the window of the tour bus or hotel room and see him practicing his routines as if nobody else in the world was around. He'd find a small space of solitude behind the hotel or in a corner of the parking lot, and spend hours practicing and meditating. He's a really disciplined guy and it shows both through his lifestyle and his guitar tech skills.

When I joined Boston, I brought Rick over from our camp to the Boston camp. One night on the 2008 tour, Tom Scholz's limited edition Les Paul (one of 100) got kicked over on stage and the headstock broke off. This is a guitar that is easily worth in excess of $100,000. Rick fixed Tom's guitar and you would never know the headstock had broken off. Tom was incredibly impressed, and that's saying a lot.

For the better part of my life I've been a somewhat frustrated guitar player for a number of reasons. The most lingering frustration has been that I don't feel as though I'm looked at as a guitarist often. I'm viewed as a singer, which I am, of course. But the idea that you can't be both, and be good at both, has always frustrated me. The industry and often fans alike want to compartmentalize musicians. You're either a drummer or a bass player or a guitar player or you are a singer. The idea that someone can be equally skilled at more than one thing often seems like a foreign concept. This can be frustrating to me as it relates to my guitar playing.

Virtually everyone who has followed Stryper's career, whether fan or critic, has viewed Oz as our primary guitarist. Honestly, I'd venture to say that many people probably see him as the band's only guitarist. Even though I do my best not to care or think about it, it's a difficult pill to swallow when you work so hard at something and don't get recognition for it. Actually, I'll go one step further and confess that it really irks me from time to time. Yes, Oz is *a* guitar player in Stryper, but he's not the only guitarist in the band.

76

It's difficult to write this without coming across as petty, but the fact is that I'm the one who created the Stryper tone and sold Oz on it (and still do). I also take the time and energy to write many of our guitar solos and even most of the harmony solos. Often enough, I'll teach Oz a guitar part and we'll sit with a metronome and or a small recorder, and we'll go over it again and again until he works out the right harmony part.

By saying this, I don't mean to insinuate that Oz is not a good player. He is, and I appreciate our work together. Our work has inspired many players over the years. Steve Vai even made a positive comment once about our solos and harmonies and hearing that from guys like him makes me appreciate the hours I have spent working hard.

But despite my role in developing our tone and solos, Oz remains, at least in the public eye, the primary guitar player for Stryper, and I remain somewhat frustrated by that perception.

I try to remain reasonable and realistic about it all. I try to remind myself that it's really not that big of a deal. Who really cares if Oz is viewed as the guitar player? Well, as hard as I try to tell myself it shouldn't matter—it does. And I do care. I've obsessed over my guitar playing a thousand times more intensely than any crooked picture ever hanging on a wall. So yes, *I do* care. And even though in my heart of hearts I know that it shouldn't matter, it does. It matters a lot. I wish it didn't. But it does.

Fortunately, as I would soon find out, all of this—having ADHD, my obsession over guitar tones, my relentless rehearsing of guitar solos—would pay off in the making of the *Soldiers Under Command* album. ADHD, for the first time in my life, would prove to have a very positive side.

After our recent tour of Texas, we played a hometown show at Knotts Berry Farm in Buena Park California, and a rising and now legendary metal producer by the name of Michael Wagener came to see us perform. Michael had produced Motley Crue's *Too Fast For Love* as well as Dokken's *Breaking The Chains*. Up next on his agenda, from a hand-shake deal in the dressing room of The Good Time Theater, he would be producing the album that would soon become *Soldiers Under Command*.

FIFTEEN

The guys in Metallica seemed nice enough, although we didn't speak a lot other than exchanging a few words here and there. The obligatory "Hey, how are you?" was the extent of our conversation. They certainly weren't rude, but neither of us really made an effort in getting to know one another. They appeared light-hearted and care free.

Conversely, I'm focused and ready to work, sitting quietly on a '70s style burnt-orange loveseat in the lounge at Amigo Studios where we are recording *Soldiers Under Command*, the album that would one day become my favorite in the Stryper catalog. Michael Wagener is in the producer's seat, and we're thrilled about the possibilities that lie ahead.

Amigo Studio sits a few blocks off the Hollywood freeway in an undistinguished industrial section of North Hollywood surrounded by mid-rise apartments, pastel California-style bungalows, and mixed-use office buildings. Just down the street sits the slightly more modern Record Plant. All of this is about a 45 minute drive from my parent's house in La Mirada where I'm living at the time.

I prefer the vibe Amigo offers over the area's surrounding studios. It's creative, warm, and comfortable—like our garage, only with much better equipment. It's a vintage studio with light fixtures and décor suitable for an Austin Powers movie. Rustic shag carpet lines the walls only to be covered by a plethora of Ted Templeman gold and platinum album awards. Ted has used Amigo to track many legendary artists from Van Halen to Little Feat to Christopher Cross. Somehow I'm not intimidated. I'm as confident in the band as I am the songs and myself, and I'm ready to get to work.

But for the moment our work will have to wait.

Metallica is here today meeting with Michael about producing their *Master of Puppets* album. Their meeting takes precedence over our recording time and as we all sit in the narrow back-room lounge of Amigo, one of them shows his manners by burping and eventually, passing gas. Don't get me wrong, we burp and fart too but when you meet someone for the first time you usually restrain yourself. After all, there are ladies present. Aside from Darren, Kyle is also in the room.

I try to not be thrown off by what I view as a lack of respect. Instead I focus on my hand-written lyric collection on sheets of paper scattered across the empty half of the loveseat. I've been writing the songs for this album for almost a year and we've been performing them live almost equally as long. Only "Battle Hymn of the Republic" would be created while at Amigo. Everything else on this album has had time to develop, both in the garage and on stages throughout southern California. But despite these songs having been rehearsed time and time again, I continue to obsess over the lyrics. I analyze each line of every song just to ensure no last minute changes, all the while attempting to ignore the rudeness in the room. But it lingers and I think to myself *"Seriously? Come on guys. Have a little respect."* Then one of them burps, and then laughs. I refocus toward the lyrics and what I'm there to do.

Looking back on this it's pretty hilarious. Had this taken place twenty years later it would have been one of us that farted. I have definitely loosened up a bit in my old age but I've always tried to retain some level of respect.

Today we're recording guitars a few days ahead of schedule because Robert managed to hammer out his drum parts in one very long day. Michael Wagener was convinced we needed two to three days to record the drum tracks and he had scheduled as much. Robert, however, was convinced he could get them all done in one day. That session lasted a grueling 15 hours into the early morning dawn, but he delivered as promised.

The band is sounding tight and together. Although I feel like it's just the beginning for us, (and in many ways, it is) more years under my belt would teach me that this album would be our shining moment musically and spiritually. This album would be the one I believe best captures what Stryper is all about: the unity of the musicians, the boldness of the message, and the energy of the performances. Yes, in my opinion, the second album in my 30+ year career would be Stryper at its best, keeping in mind that your best moment doesn't always equate to your most successful one.

Oz and I burn through the guitar parts with relative ease. I am particularly pleased with our performances on the title track and "Reach Out."

During our two weeks in the studio we rarely break to go out to eat. We order take-out from down the street. A lot of Chinese, Mexican and Italian food is consumed during the making of *Soldiers*. To this day I can't eat Mexican food without fondly remembering Amigo Studios.

Days after wrapping guitars I find myself unnaturally at ease when recording my vocal parts. Our first album saw respectable success, and by all accounts I should be nervous. A band's sophomore album is typically the time when the group either turns the corner toward success, or they stall, like an old used car. By that measure I should be concerned, but I'm not. I'm confident not only in my personal abilities but in the band as well. We're playing and singing as a group. We're on a spiritual high and surrounded by love, support and encouragement. Even the last minute changes I make to the lyrics don't seem to affect me. With each scribble of my pen, each lyric marked through to be slightly revised, I remain confident that God has His hand on this band and a definitive plan for our future.

81

Throughout the making of *Soldiers*, I'm present for every aspect of tracking and although I'm a member of the band, I feel as much like a fledgling producer eager to soak up all I can about the recording process.

Despite having recorded many times before, this was my first project on a big label with a highly respected producer. I hang on Michael Wagener's every word, learning all I can about his reasons why he does what he does in the studio. Mic placement. His opinions on guitar and drum tones. Performance techniques to get the best out of each musician. I soak in all these details and don't dare to miss a second of it for fear that I'll miss something important. If I could have, I would have slept there every night. But instead, each morning, as I drive North on the 5 to the 101, the anticipation of learning more about the recording process excites me almost as much as the process of being a musician making the album.

12 or so days after we first walked into Amigo, we're wrapping the recording of *Soldiers* and it pains me to think about missing out on the mixing sessions soon to take place. We can't stay for the mixing as we're scheduled to go to Japan for the first time where we're about to discover a world we had no idea existed. A world where Stryper fans are in the thousands, screaming as if we were The Beatles. Despite being absent for mixing, I find solace in knowing it's not just me missing out but the entire band. I would have cancelled almost anything if it were a situation where the rest of the band could be at the mixing and I couldn't. These are the early signs of my deeply rooted desire to be involved in every aspect of Stryper. While Michael begins the mixing process, we prepare to leave for Japan.

And on this day, walking out into the warm evening air as the sun sets over our last day in the studio, I am completely happy with this band. I love Stryper and everything it is. What it stands for.

What it has achieved and what it is about to achieve. I love my brothers in the band and we are united, with God guiding us throughout the process. The sense of fellowship and brotherhood is almost tangible. I am one of the most fortunate guys alive. Thankfully, at this moment, I have no idea that time has a funny way of changing things — my perspective on the band, my feelings toward my brothers, and at times even my feelings about God. Thankfully, tonight, I'm all smiles with no knowledge of, or worry about, what the future may hold and what lies ahead.

SIXTEEN

I'm afraid to fly. There was a time in history when a person may be scoffed at for admitting this fear, but ever since 9/11, and subsequent plane crashes becoming more highly publicized, people have seemingly become less judgmental on the topic. Saying "I'm afraid to fly" post-9/11, you're likely to be met with more sympathetic eyes than you would have pre-9/11 and pre-internet. With information now traveling instantaneously, the catastrophe of a plane crash is reported on and commented about to the nth degree. Rather than hearing about a plane crash a few times on the evening news, like we would during the pre-internet era, you now hear about it hundreds and hundreds of times from multiple outlets. The crash is played and replayed through tweets, video clips, and more. The information age, and 9/11, has made a lot of people afraid to fly.

But long before people were sympathetic to the fear of flying, I was afraid to fly. Actually, I can give you the exact date when this phobia took root. January 9, 1975. I was 11. It was a Thursday. It was a clear sunny day and not particularly cold for January, around 60 degrees I suppose. If I were to trace back my fear of flying to the very moment, it all started at about 10 minutes after 4pm on that day. The late afternoon sun was starting its decent over southern California.

I had just arrived home from school to our Chatfield house in Whittier. Mom was home. I was actually in the bathroom doing my after-school business. If ever there were an appropriate, and literal, time to say "That scared the s**t out of me," it would be this time. I heard a loud boom. But it was more than just a boom. It rumbled. It was an explosion. The sound had a depth and energy larger than anything I had ever heard before in my 11 years on this planet. And I'm positive I even heard voices screaming. But at the sound of that boom, I immediately knew it was something big, and likely tragic.

I ran outside as quickly as I could. Looking around I saw an ominous cloud of dark black smoke just a few blocks away, hovering over the landscape of picturesque southern California neighborhood houses. I jumped on my red dirt-bike-style bicycle and pedaled as fast as my skinny legs would allow. I didn't know what, if anything, I would discover but my curiosity had the best of me. What I had heard in the distance, from within the walls of my bathroom, was unlike anything I had ever known, and I was determined to find out what it was.

The cloud of smoke seemed only steps away in a northwest direction from my house, but turns out it was a little over a mile away in the vicinity of Katherine Edwards Middle School.

As I got closer and closer to the cloud, emergency response vehicles had already started arriving—even whizzing past me on Mines Boulevard as I headed in the direction of the school. I was pedaling as quickly as I could, but I felt like it was all happening in slow motion. As I drew closer to Katherine Edwards Middle School I started seeing large pieces of metal in people's front yards, with smoke still emitting off the debris. In one area near the school I saw several medics and firemen frantically throwing blankets overtop of what I now know to be body parts, but at the time, I didn't know what they were covering. I saw blood stains on the blankets.

Nearing the school yard I saw what I felt sure to be an airplane wing lying on the ground, smoking. It was all coming together for me. That boom must have been an airplane crash. And these blankets, they were covering dead bodies, or body parts. I saw pieces of luggage scattered about. I later even saw a lone airplane seat resting on its side in someone's front yard.

I pulled my bicycle up as close as the authorities would allow. They had already blocked off many of the streets by the time I arrived, roughly one-mile from my house. I stopped at one of the road blocks and put my two feet on the ground straddling my bicycle and holding the handlebars. I gazed into the distance as I listened to the commotion coming from the crowds. People gathered around talking about what had just happened. I didn't hear their words distinctly—I just knew they were discussing a tragedy. The sirens, the crying, and the tone of despair in people's voices—I didn't need to hear the words they were saying to know this was bad. A man stood next to me paying no attention to my presence. But I recall his look of distress and bewilderment as he held both his hands over his mouth as he gazed into the distance.

I stayed and watched from behind police lines for another hour or so as the sun was setting and then I pedaled home, not nearly as swiftly but instead with a steady pace of slow reflection on what I had just witnessed.

When I came home, my mother had the news on and I saw the stories of what I had just seen. Apparently two small planes had a mid-air collision and rained luggage, bodies, and debris across the schoolyard and community of Whittier California. 14 people died instantly. There was an outdoor basketball game happening at the time of the collision and over 300 people at the game witnessed the wreckage first-hand. It took me days to really process the enormity of what I had experienced, and I certainly had no idea at the time how profoundly it would affect me for the rest of my life. That collision still remains on a number of worst plane crash lists and has been discussed in much detail among those who witnessed the tragedy that day.

From that day forward, I've always had a deep rooted anxiety about flying. I do it because I have to, but given the option I prefer to avoid air travel.

So when we got word that we'd be going to Japan to perform I was a mixed bag of emotions. Fear and anxiety were coupled with excitement and hope. I certainly didn't want to fly to Japan, but travel by boat wasn't going to be an option given our time constraints, so I did what I've done most of my adult life. I sucked it up, did my best to mask my fears, and hoped that I could sleep through the majority of the trip.

Boarding the airplane heading for Japan, I can't help but look around and notice the excitement on everyone's faces. I feel a little nervous inside as well. We're performing in Japan for the very first time, and a production company has been hired to film the show in Tokyo for release through Enigma.

Although I've begun to notice tension between Daryn and my mom, I ignore it. Although I'm curious how we can afford to fly massive Stryper stage equipment to Japan, I ignore it. I purposely disregard the idea of inquiring into topics that might disrupt the daily satisfaction and thrill I get from being a member of this band. Although hindsight tells me that this tour to Japan will be one of the early indications that we are a financially irresponsible band. Still, in the moment, I ignore these thoughts pushing them as far to the back of my mind as they will possibly go.

Both my mom and Daryn have strong personalities, a great quality to have in a manager, but because they co-manage us together I begin to feel the first signs of disagreements over how the band should be managed. It's nothing big, yet. At this point I'm just noticing small stuff like how to handle travel arrangements and publicity. I don't believe the tension has anything to do with them splitting management commissions. Money doesn't seem to be a big topic or concern at this point in our career, although in hindsight it probably should have been. There's something else brewing between Daryn and my mom and I can't quite put my finger on it.

Still, none of this matters to me though because I'm about to share my faith with a nation that is largely Buddhist. It's a new chapter in my life that's leading me into unknown territory. I'm experiencing things that most people can only dream of. It's amazing, and nothing will stand in the way of my enthusiasm.

I've also been ignoring Kyle. I'm not really sure why, but I'm noticeably keeping my distance from her. We're not even sitting together on the plane. I'm slightly aggravated that she's even going on this trip, although I do find comfort knowing that she is. I'm going through one of my phases where I'm doing all I can to let her know she's in the way.

The future is exciting and unknown. The possibilities are limitless as to what the next few months and years will hold. We've just made an incredible album that is in the process of being mixed.
It'll soon be released and I'm naively confident that this album, *Soldiers Under Command,* is a game changer.

So every moment, every thought where I feel tied to Kyle makes me even more agitated. It makes me want to ignore her even more. Not so much because I want someone else. That's not it at all. I'm days away from turning twenty-two. *Do I really want to be tied down to a woman several years my senior? Do I really want to be tied down at all?* As I ask myself these questions, the resounding answer is *"No, absolutely not. I don't want to be tied down."*

So, I'm a jerk, and I ignore her. She seems to weather it well though. She is happy, not because she's here with Stryper. Kyle is a happy person by nature. She exudes warmth and it's contagious. People like being around Kyle, so while I'm all the more eager to ignore her, I'm somewhat annoyed that everyone else seems to enjoy having her around. Doesn't everyone else see what I'm seeing? That she's cramping my style? And if she's cramping my style, why are the guys not supporting me by also making her feel like an intruder? Instead they sit next to her and laugh at her jokes. They appreciate her kindness and are eager to be in her presence.

The tour consists of a number of shows in three cities—Osaka, Nagoya, and Tokyo. We arrive into Tokyo by plane and spend the remainder of the tour traveling by planes, trains and automobiles.

Mark Joseph, a friend of Daryn's, has arranged the tour. He is the son of missionaries and has lived much of his life split between Japan and America, thus speaking both English and Japanese fluently. It becomes obvious early on during this tour how well-connected Mark is in the Japanese music business so before we even play our first show, I feel at ease knowing we're in good hands. As Japanese businessmen talk to him, it's as if they are seeking his approval. Although I can't understand a word they are saying, I can tell that in a room full of businessmen, all of them have a high respect for Mark.

Later in life Mark would become an incredibly successful author and film business icon, even playing a role in the production of the Mel Gibson movie, *The Passion of The Christ*. But this week he is my lifeline, offering me familiarity in unfamiliar surroundings.

As I exit the plane into the terminal, I look behind me to see if perhaps some other celebrity was on the plane with us, because the sea of screaming Japanese girls would indicate that either The Beatles or, because it's 1985, Michael J. Fox, are traveling alongside us. But this thought fades quickly as I notice the hand-painted Stryper signs. *"Wow,"* I think. *"All this is for us?"*

Today is my 22nd birthday, July 4, 1985, and it's the day of our first show in Tokyo. I wish we had a warm-up show here before the concert that will be filmed, but we don't. I'm excited but I'm nervous as well. We know that it's being filmed, but we're also aware that we have no creative control over the final product, something I would never allow to happen in my later years. The film company will tape, edit, and mix the audio for the video *Live in Japan* that would eventually become certified Multi Platinum and one of our biggest selling products of the Stryper catalog. Had I known how big this video would be, I would be more apprehensive than I am now.

But now, today, it's my birthday and I've just finished a long sound-check. All the gear and stage props are in their proper place. The "No Devil" and "No 666" signs are flashing on cue from the lighting director. The sound system is rumbling loud. My guitar sounds great and the 2000 seat Shibuya Public Hall will soon be filled with music fans that likely have no idea about the message behind our music. This makes me nervous. I carefully consider how I should relay our message between songs. *"Do we pray at the end of the set?"* We decide not to. *"How much should we share of our message between songs?"* I'm just not sure.

We do however get together to pray after sound-check and after we've had our make-up applied.

About the only words I speak to Kyle during this first part of the trip are to ask her about our make-up and wardrobe. Despite me keeping my distance, she does a great job at making us look our best. Regardless of our distance, she remains a professional, and a caring one at that.

Make-up and wardrobe are in check. The sound and stage setting is in place. We've prayed as a group asking for wisdom and strength. All we have left to do is make a few statements for the fans in Japan that will haunt us for the rest of our lives.

This feels like it's important, so I guess we need to do this. We follow the person in charge to the stage. The hall is still empty. He walks us over to stand in front of our yellow and black amps. He assertively directs us to *"Say something for people of Japan."*

90

"What do you want us to say? What's this for?" we ask.

"Just say something for the people of Japan. Not much time. We need quickly," he says in broken English.

And so we did. Turns out saying something to the people of Japan should have been a little more thought out on our part. They ended up using those interview segments to close out the video as a segment they called "A Message From Stryper." I wish I had known it would be forever etched in the video history of Stryper. All of us would have planned our speech a little better. I can't watch those interviews without cringing. They're embarrassing partially because they're incongruous with our typical interview style. It's not as if we were new to the world of being asked questions on camera. We had done dozens and dozens of on-camera interviews by this point, but because of the rushed manner in which we were thrust into these interviews, with no real understanding of who the intended audience was, it came across somewhat insincere and quite corny. But, we were young, and just doing the best we could to get our message out.

My uncertainty on how to relate to a non-English speaking audience is evident during the show, and upon later review of the video, it's clear I'm a young performer unsure of what to do and what not to do.

We open the show strong coming out of a building keyboard intro going into "Makes Me Wanna Sing" and then we rip into "Loud N Clear" and "From Wrong To Right." The show feels good at this point but I'm beginning to over-think what I will say between songs.

Our first break comes after "From Wrong To Right" and Robert approaches the front of the stage where we toss a stack of about 50 Bibles into the audience. I can see people scrambling to get their hands on a copy. I should say something. *"Keep it simple,"* I think to myself.

"Stryper rocks for Jesus Christ! You guys having a good time?"

"Maybe that was too simple," I second guess myself. *"Should I say something else?"*

I don't. Instead I start playing a riff on my guitar to buy some time until Robert returns to the kit. When he does, we start in on "You Know What To Do" and then go straight into a newer song, "Surrender." I had revised the lyrics to "Surrender" while in the studio recently. I'm still second guessing what to say and I lose focus on the lyrics. As a matter of fact, I forget them all together.

There's nothing more nerve racking to a singer than realizing you have no idea what the lyrics are to your song, four bars before the opening line. The more you focus on trying to remember them the harder it is to do so. 4 bars away. 3 bars away. 2 bars. 1 bar. Time to sing. Still, nothing. My mouth opens in hopes that my brain will catch up with it. No such luck. I make up lyrics on the spot having no idea what is coming out but hoping I can regain my composure. Heads in the audience are still bobbing and fists are still pumping, so whatever I'm doing must be working.

I made it through "Surrender" and another break is coming up but I decide to let the music speak for itself, so I go straight in to announcing "Together Forever." I forget the words again and resort to an older version of the lyrics. Thankfully, Tim moves quickly to the keyboards for "First Love" and it sounds great. I'm proud of the job he does on this tour. We considered bringing Kenny Metcalf to play keys, but it wasn't in the budget apparently. As with most financial decisions, I don't question it although I am curious how we can fly God knows how many pounds of signs, equipment and a drum kit the size of a tank, yet we can't afford a keyboard player.

As the set rolls on, I'm finally becoming more comfortable and really starting to enjoy the show. "Loving You" moves in to "Soldiers Under Command", where I only forget a few lyrics but it no longer bothers me. We're having fun and the crowd is responding in kind.

In the studio weeks earlier when cutting the vocals for "Soldiers Under Command", I attempted a ridiculously high note at the end of the song and nailed it. So as we roll through the same song on stage, I debate attempting to re-create this scream live, but given my lyric amnesia I play it safe thinking my vocal chords might too develop a case of forgetfulness. I can live with ad-lib lyrics being forever etched into history, but a sour note or botched scream I'm not so sure. So as the note approaches, I decide to take it down an octave.

As we come out for the encore, "C'mon Rock", I notice half-a-dozen yellow roses lying at the front of the stage so I pass them out one by one to the girls in the front row. I'm loosening up quite a bit at this point and wish we could continue on. At one point I even jump on Robert's drum riser, grab his gong mallet and just start beating away at one of his massive gongs. I may as well give it some use, we paid good money to fly it across the Pacific. We close the show with "Battle Hymn of the Republic" and head back stage all smiles from a rough, but successful night.

The other shows on this tour went much better, but unfortunately this is the one that is captured on video.

We then head to Osaka, back to Tokyo for two shows at Yubin Chokin Hall, and then wrap up our first tour of Japan in Nagoya. We pound out the last shows as a professional rock band would. I get more comfortable on stage in Japan as each show proves to be as successful as the last.

On the train ride back to Tokyo in preparation for our return to the states, we're all proud of the job we've done here. God granted us an opportunity to bring His message to the masses in a way never before done, at least never before done in yellow and black spandex.

The adulation we receive in Japan will later only be rivaled by that of Puerto Rico.

I'm curious as to why we are so popular here. There are very few Christians in this country, so each time we step on stage during this tour I'm slightly skeptical as to the reception we will get, yet as the shows progress, I'm pleasantly relieved to always feel more-than-welcomed. I can only assume our music is about to cross big boundaries.

I'm tired yet excited to get back to Amigo and listen to the final mixes for *Soldiers Under Command*. I sit next to Kyle on the plane ride back to Los Angeles.

SEVENTEEN

"The Church of Satan Welcomes You" was scribbled backwards in red lipstick on the mirror in my room at a low budget motel we were staying at one night during the *Soldiers Under Command* tour.

That tour was my first realization that being in Stryper could become difficult mentally at times. Fortunately I was still young in my faith and I was eager to take on whatever challenges might be thrown my way, without complaint.

Today, if I saw strange messages mysteriously written on my hotel room mirror, I'm not sure how I would handle it. My immediate reaction to this backwards lipstick message was laughter. I assumed that one of the guys in the band was playing a practical joke on me. How else would someone know this was my room? It had to be Rob, Oz or Tim.

But after inquiring further, I discovered it was not a joke. I was a bit thrown off by the whole thing and I suppose I became even more uncomfortable when I realized that this was real.

How could someone have known this would be one of the rooms we'd be staying in? Furthermore, how did they get in the room before I arrived? I never did find out. And surprisingly, it didn't scare me enough to do anything about it. I just grabbed a paper towel and cleaned it off without giving it much thought.

It was on this tour that I realized I would encounter some strange people in my life, for the rest of my life. Ironically, it became almost impossible to predict who would be "strange." Christians hated us. Christians loved us. Satanists hated us. Satanists loved us. Atheists hated us. Atheists loved us. It was impossible to predict who was going to support us and who was going to curse the very sight of us.   We couldn't spot our enemies visually — therefore, we couldn't spot our friends either.

Just because someone was wearing a Motley Crue shirt and a pentagram around his neck didn't necessarily mean he was our enemy. And someone wearing a "Jesus Saves" T-shirt was equally as likely to throw a rock at my head as someone wearing a "The Devil is my Friend" T-shirt. Although to be perfectly honest, the "Jesus Saves" T-shirts probably cast more stones, at least at the time.

No other band that I know of has had such an inability to distinguish their friends from their foes. Most bands can spot their antagonists from a mile away. Not us. We had an equal number of fans and enemies on both sides of the religious fence.

This was a strange and eye-opening reality that came to fruition during the *Soldiers Under Command* tour.

Very few people were indifferent about us. If you knew about Stryper at this point in our career, you most likely had a strong opinion one way or another. If you were a Christian you either loved us dearly or hated the very thought of our existence. If you were a non-believer, you were equally as likely to accept us for our music and appreciate our freedom of speech as you were to be upset that a "Jesus Band" could possibly infiltrate the world of rock and metal that you held so sacred.

Imagine not being able to spot people who may be opposed to you so passionately they are willing to go to extreme lengths to see you fall, even die. Yes, we received death threats. At one point we were receiving several death threats per week by mail. Most writers seemed harmless and immature, but occasionally they knew just a little too much about our personal lives. We would turn those letters over to the police, but to my knowledge nobody was ever arrested for these threats.

I suppose going into this band, I just assumed that most of the haters would be non-believers. I guess I was naïve. It shocked me the first time I saw Christian's protesting one of our shows, and this would become a regular routine throughout the *Soldiers Under Command*, *To Hell With The Devil* and *In God We Trust* tours.

I was young and innocent in my spirituality during this time in my life, and as a result, I was willing to do anything required to keep spreading the message that I felt called to share. There was a sense of true innocence in my faith, and all I cared about was serving God. I believe because of this, God started to bless me and this band on a level we never dreamed possible. We were starting to get a taste of success, and it tasted good.

I think back on how little I had then, yet how little I complained about it. If I got a PB&J sandwich for dinner at a show, I was happy and content.

I complain more now than I used to—I believe in part because I forget. I forget that sense of innocence I once had. As I get older, I get tired and exhausted a little easier and that opens the door to bitterness if I allow it. Back during the *Soldiers* era we just never allowed that door to open. Once it does, it's a difficult one to close as we would discover in years to come.

Had it been 2012 instead of 1986 when someone wrote a welcome message on the mirror in my hotel, I likely would have cancelled the show on the spot. But not then. In 1986 I was ready to conquer the world. Today, I'm a bit less tolerant than I once was.

The tour for *Soldiers Under Command* started in October 1985 and continued almost non-stop through the end of April 1986. It was the first time we had hit the East Coast and we were playing everything from clubs to small theaters and even a few high-school auditoriums. We loved it.

A notable stop on that tour was performing at the Dove Awards in Nashville in April. To say the audience looked like deer in headlights doesn't even come close to describing what I saw when I looked out from the stage when we began our performance. It looked more like a congregation of Southern Baptists expecting to see a film about The Ten Commandments but instead they were watching a Farrelly Brothers movie. They were shocked to say the least. And I even dressed conservatively that night, wrapping a scarf around my waist just before we went on stage so my spandex pants wouldn't offend anyone in the first few rows.

I can't say that I was surprised by the crowd's initial apprehension. After all, it was artists like Sandi Patti and Michael W. Smith who were the big winners that year. We didn't exactly fit in. It wasn't until 1988 with the *In God We Trust* album that we would win a Dove Award. We'd win two that year — "Hard Music Album of the Year" and "Hard Music Song of the Year" (for the title track).

Those awards shows are always scripted and often have somewhat embarrassing banter between the co-hosts before and after each performance, but I think our night takes the cake. After we played, the male host Pat Boone, said something along the lines that he would rather kids see Stryper than Motley Crue or The Rolling Stones. I was about 10% offended by that. Basically he was saying, "All rock music is garbage, but if you must listen to it, you might as well be listening to Stryper." I don't blame Pat for that statement. I've presented at the Dove Awards on multiple occasions and I know that the script is written for you. There's very little room for ad-libbing. Pat was just saying what was on the teleprompter. He probably thought it was a little offensive too. Pat actually supports us and rock music. He even put out a "metal" album once. So I'm sure he, like many who present at these awards, probably feels a bit awkward about some of the statements he has to read.

To make matters worse, we had to play to tracks at that show. They wouldn't let us perform live. They played the recording and we had to pretend like we were performing. They claimed they wouldn't be able to set us up quickly enough for TV. We weren't buying it, but we also didn't complain.

We went through the motions and put on the best performance we knew how, and afterwards we received a standing ovation. It was unique to play the Dove Awards and receive praise from the Christian community, yet regularly on this tour we ran into protestors from the church.

As we made our way through The Deep South, Louisiana most notably, I experienced my first moment of feeling deeply betrayed. Jimmy Swaggart had sent his church members out to protest. Remember, Robert and I came to know God through Jimmy. He was our mentor of sorts, although to this day I've never met the man. Yet when the tour came through his neck of the woods, it was as if the devil himself showed up in Jimmy's backyard. I couldn't believe it the first time I saw protestors from Jimmy Swaggart Ministries with signs saying things like "Stryper: Wolves in Sheep's Clothing" and "Rock Music is the Devil."

This went on for years, Jimmy Swaggart's contempt for Stryper, and really for all rock music. We were once featured on a CBS News program where Jimmy said that it was impossible for any rock music to be Christian, going so far as to say, "Christian Rock-n-Roll" was no different than "Christian Prostitutes" or "Christian Pimps." Really?

"How can it be that Jimmy Swaggart is so against us?" I would think to myself. Supposedly we were on the same team, spreading the same message, loving the same God — yet Swaggart followers seemed to hate us with a passion.

Each time this would happen, and it happened frequently over the next few years, I, along with Michael Guido, or Kenny Metcalf, or Robert, would go and talk to the protestors. We would not approach them with malice or anger or even resentment, but instead we would approach them in love. We would invite them to the show, and all of them admitted never to have even seen us live. Again, how could it be? Protestors would be standing in front of an auditorium protesting a band that they had never even seen live before. Rarely would the protestors take us up on our offer to attend the show, but on those occasions when they would, they almost always left with a new respect for us. They may not like us, but at least they understood us better.

To my knowledge, Swaggart himself never showed up at one of these protests. However, the ultimate slap in the face came when I saw a video tape of Jimmy Swaggart holding up a copy of our album *The Yellow and Black Attack* on national TV, condemning us, telling his followers that we were fakes. He made references to our tossing Bibles into the audience saying that we were casting pearls to swine.

That hurt. It didn't weaken my relationship with God, not in the least. But it did weaken my faith in supposed Christians who were so outspoken against us, with Swaggart leading the pack.

During this tour and subsequent tours it was normal for fans to show up seeing church protestors holding picket signs with bullhorns denouncing Stryper. You would have thought Slayer was in town. These protestors would spew Bible verses in an attempt to convince people that we were phonies yet few of them ever took the time to come witness the miracles that would often take place at a Stryper concert. There's no denying that people's lives were changed because of God's work through the band. I saw it first hand on a nightly basis. People who were living in very dark places with drugs, addictions, suicide, alcoholism and anything else you can think of were turning their lives around because they first discovered God's power at a Stryper show!

But the bullhorns kept blasting and the protestors kept protesting. And we kept inviting them to the shows. Some started to take us up on our offers and actually became Stryper fans once they saw we weren't biting the heads off of bats or making porno films on stage.

In 1987 Swaggart would dedicate an entire section to Stryper in his manifesto "Religious Rock 'N' Roll: A Wolf in Sheep's Clothing" — once again denouncing us, saying that we were just in this for the fast cash. How could a band look the way we looked, play the music we played, and still be Christians?

Sadly it was Jimmy who would take the hard fall in 1988 when he was caught with a prostitute.

We pressed on, like the young faithful soldiers we were, and continued the course tossing Bibles into the audience and sharing our faith knowing that God would protect us. But I have always felt somewhat betrayed by the man who first led me to God.

The *Soldiers Under Command* album definitely reeled in its share of controversy, most notably the album cover where we are pictured in front of a yellow and black van holding guns. We of course wanted to make a bold statement of being soldiers, and this certainly did it. That picture was taken in a church parking lot by photographer John Scarpati. The van came from the 1979 movie *Angel's Brigade* in which Daryn's brother Darby appeared in an acting role. Robert had it painted yellow and black and this would all add up to the infamous and highly controversial album cover. The guns, by the way, were plastic pellet guns we bought in Japan on our first visit there.

Soldiers Under Command, the album that took us only nine days to record, would ultimately spend thirty-six weeks in the Billboard Top 100 album chart and would reach number 5 on the Contemporary Christian Album charts. We shot one video during that album. It was once again a low-budget video for the title track shot during a concert in Fresno. We went back to Smoke Tree Studios to stage some footage of us singing around a microphone, and that was intertwined with B-roll backstage footage. Although the album, for the most part, was recorded at Amigo, we recorded the song "Together As One" at Smoke Tree. We were looking to get a full, grand piano sound for that song and they had the right equipment for what we wanted to accomplish. John Van Togren played piano and would subsequently play on the *To Hell with The Devil* recordings as well as the *In God We Trust* album. We met John through John St. James, the original owner of The Casbah studio in Fullerton, where we recorded the demos that led to our record deal.

I first saw that video for "Soldiers Under Command" on TBN (Trinity Broadcasting Network) and I recall the feeling of knowing we were one step closer to success. The video also had a few late-night airings on MTV as well but it wasn't until the *To Hell With The Devil* album that music videos would change our lives forever!

EIGHTEEN

Believe it or not, I don't really like most Christian rock, particularly that from the '80s. During the period when we were on the rise ('84-'86) there was definitely a Christian rock movement happening. Magazines like Heaven's Metal were formed. Entire churches were developed around the Christian metal movement, the most notable being Sanctuary lead by the amazing Pastor Bob Beeman. Pastor Bob is still serving today. This was a time when Christian rock and metal started becoming a main attraction at festivals around the nation.

Christian rock was, for the first time, becoming a legitimate, or at least noticed, genre of music. And I wasn't a fan of most of it. With very few exceptions, I didn't like the genre or the industry that surrounded it.

If I were to name the top 10 times I've been "screwed" in the music business, I would say 9 of those 10 were from people in the Christian industry. Most weren't intentionally screwing me — they just weren't responsible business people and instead relied too much on God to provide, without taking responsibility for their own actions.

Some of the worst situations I've been in have occurred because Christian promoters, record execs, or managers relied too heavily on the term "just pray about it," at the same time neglecting what God calls us to be — good stewards.

Stryper stood out from the rest of the Christian-rock-pack, I believe, for two reasons: We had a unique sound with great songs and we didn't preach to the choir.

Let me address the first. I'm not here to judge other Christian bands from the '80s. Sure, there were a few that stood out in their own way, but most did not. The few and far between Christian bands that really stood out were the ones who were good enough or had something unique enough to cross them over into mainstream.

It's sad. You would think someone called to play music by God would have talent and creativity far beyond that of the secular world and would excel far beyond the norm, but that just wasn't the case, or at least it didn't seem that way to me. I think a lot of it has to do with competition. Stryper grew up on The Sunset Strip where competition was fierce. We didn't just have to be better than other Christian bands but we had to strive to be better than the best of the best on The Strip. The Strip had the most critical fan base in the world. So for us to sing about Jesus *and* appeal to the fans on The Strip was quite unusual. We had to have great songs, a great look, and really shine above and beyond the rest. Our competition wasn't the church band from down the street. It was Motley Crue, Ratt, and Poison. So we did everything we could to try to be as good as, if not better, than the acts we were seeing on a nightly basis.

So as long as these Christian bands were moderately good, and inserted "Jesus" into a lot of their songs, they didn't really have to try as hard to be accepted by most Christian rock fans. As a result, mediocre songs became good enough for a good handful of these groups.

We've been booed. We've been spat on. We've been taunted relentlessly. There's nothing like brutal criticism from an unforgiving club or festival crowd to make you buckle down in your rehearsal space for the next month and do everything in your power to figure out how to keep that from happening again.

There's an interview on YouTube where Scott Ian of Anthrax, with his selective memory and all, recalls their first gig in Southern California and he describes Stryper opening for them. It's a good example of the less-than-welcoming atmosphere our band could often be subject to, but Scott blows it way out of proportion. He paints the picture that every Bible we threw in the audience that night got thrown back at us and implies it was a mistake having us on the bill.

In order to play the venue in question, The Country Club in Reseda, you actually had to draw people. We had a good following in the area already, so the promoter added us to the bill because Anthrax wasn't capable of filling the room on their own.

We had a big following there that night. And yes, Stryper fans mixed with Anthrax fans was an odd pairing, I'll admit. We may have had a few bibles tossed back at us when an unsuspecting Anthrax fan would catch one. We even received a few middle fingers from the crowd. But it was nothing like Scott describes in the video. Not even close.

As a matter of fact, most of the Stryper fans left after we played leaving the room less than full. And from what I recall, some of the Stryper fans that stayed, gave Anthrax an equally lukewarm reception.

These moments of receiving a less-than-stellar response from a tempered secular crowd didn't faze us. It only made us want to work harder. And we did. But many Christian bands — not all, but many — were never met with these challenges of trying to win over a non-religious crowd. Most Christian bands played within the comfort zone of the church-going rock fans. Why improve when the audience already loves you?

Stryper stood out from other Christian rock bands because we had to, for survival. We either had to stand out and rise above musically and professionally, or we were done. Clubs wouldn't book us if we couldn't hold our own with a skeptical and primarily non-Christian crowd.

Barren Cross, Whitecross, Bloodgood, Rez Band, and Guardian were a few that danced with crossover success. I'm not sure if it was because of Stryper. Maybe the world was looking for other great Christian rock bands and these guys just happened to be climbing the ladder, or maybe it was because these acts truly had the capability of appealing to an audience outside of the Church. Yet, all of them sadly fell just a bit short of making that complete crossover to mainstream.

In saying all of this, I should emphasize that not everyone's calling is the same. The choir sometimes needs preaching to. And if their calling was to preach to the choir, then they were doing just what they were supposed to do. That was not *our* calling, however. Our calling was to take the Word to the streets and share our faith with people who never in a million years would dream of stepping foot in a Church. And you don't do that through mediocre music or visual presentation.

I know—who am I to speak about fashion? Yes, we had some of the most ridiculous outfits ever. But it worked, for the time. The spandex, the hair, the make-up, and even the yellow and black—it all played a part in an image that was suitable for mainstream.

Although our songs were bold lyrically, we didn't preach. We stated two main points at our shows, points we still carry with us to this day. Those were we believe in God, and you can believe anything you want.

This, I feel, set us apart from other acts in the Christian rock genre. Most other acts, although I'm sure they wouldn't admit it, came across more along the lines of we believe in God, and you too had better believe in God, or else.

That doesn't work. People don't want to be pushed or pressured into anything. Fear rarely works in motivating people to accept

Christ. Love does. Acceptance does. Unconditional understanding and appreciation for someone's background — that will make people pay attention to what you have to say. "Turn or Burn" has never been my preferred method of leading people to Christ.

The Christian rock scene that was emerging in the mid-80s felt a bit like a bandwagon to me. This was likely more the part of the Christian music industry than it was the bands themselves, although I would imagine it to be a little of both.

If Iron Maiden was popular, the Christian music business needed a Christian version of Iron Maiden. Enter, Barren Cross. If Ratt was popular, the Christian music business needed a version of Ratt. Enter, Whitecross. If AC/DC was buzzin' — X-Sinner. It was as if the Christian music industry needed an answer for every mainstream band.

I even recall seeing flyers and stickers in Christian bookstores that would say things like "If you like Iron Maiden, listen to Barren Cross." Or, "Instead of Madonna, try Amy Grant." I always thought that was odd. Amy Grant sounds nothing like Madonna. In many ways, Amy Grant is better, but they're certainly not comparable.

But this was the way the Christian music industry was working — jumping on bandwagons and trying to capitalize on each artist's mainstream counterpart. I get it. I know what they were trying to do. Mom and Dad were shopping at the bookstore hoping to turn their child on to some music other than what they were listening to. These were suggestions to help Mom and Dad. But the kids saw right through it. They didn't want a clone of Iron Maiden. They didn't want a clone of Ratt. Kids wanted something raw, fresh and exciting, regardless of the message in the songs.

Stryper, with all of our faults and flaws, tried really hard not to sound like the bands we played with on the Strip. We didn't sound like Motley Crue, or Ratt, or any of those. Stryper had its own sound, or at least we tried really hard to do so, and I believe we succeeded and was part of the reason we stood out from the pack.

To me part of being a musician is to be an artist, and to be a great artist you have to be original and express your own artistic views. It was incredibly important for Stryper to be unique and original in all aspects of our art.

It was around the beginning of the *Soldiers Under Command* era that we made a conscious decision to try to do as few shows as possible with Christian bands. We had performed with bands like Bloodgood, Barren Cross, Rez Band and a few others, but we always felt that we needed to be taking our message to people and places that no other Christian band had gone. We needed to stay the course and continue playing clubs and theaters and tour with acts that were not Christian bands. This is a philosophy we still hold true to today. Just recently we performed in Indonesia and India, both countries rarely visited by Christian rock bands.

There were some great musicians rising in the Christian music scene at the time, though. Rex Carroll (Whitecross) and Tony Palacios (Guardian) were (and are) two of the most talented guitarists in any genre. Ted Kirkpatrick (Tourniquet) is an incredible drummer and one of the best out there. Kevin Max (DC Talk), Bob Carlisle (Allies) and Bryan Duncan (Sweet Comfort Band) are three of the most amazingly talented singers around. I was, and always will be impressed with these guys and their God given abilities and talents.

I personally like most of the Christian musicians that came of age around the same time as Stryper. They are, for the most part, great people. I just never really got into their music. I wish that were not the case. I wish there had been 20 Christian bands in the '80s that rose to the level of Stryper. I would have loved nothing more than to see the Billboard charts filled with bands representing God. It was saddening to me that this never happened. I was, and still am, rooting for any band that shares their faith openly and does what God calls them to do. Yet I can't help but feel most Christian bands from the '80s should have worked harder to set themselves apart from the rest.

NINETEEN

To Hell With The Devil. Little did I know as we were preparing to make this album, those five words would become synonymous with me and my band for the rest of my life. The title-track from that album was never even a major single, yet it's presently one of our highest viewed videos on YouTube—a live version no less, which wasn't filmed until years later in Puerto Rico during the reunion tour of 2003. Somehow, that song and title have stood the test of time and become as much a part of Stryper pop-culture as the yellow and black stripes and the Bible tossing.

We toured to promote the *Soldiers Under Command* album from September of '85 through May of '86. Even to this day, I've always enjoyed having the Christmas holidays off, and this year was no exception. So we took a brief break and that's when I did a lot of the writing for *To Hell With The Devil.* I was writing all the time back then, in hotel rooms, on the bus, in dressing rooms and any off time at home. I was still living with my parents on Fonseca Avenue in La Mirada.

I've always done a lot of writing over the holidays. For some reason I feel creatively inspired during the holiday season. I did a lot of writing Christmas of '85. I had a small keyboard in the rehearsal studio and early one morning inspiration hit and I began to experiment with some chord progressions on that keyboard.

Although Iron Maiden, Judas Priest and Van Halen have always been a huge influence on me musically in terms of all things hard rock and metal, there's another side of me that has enormous appreciation for the power ballad talents of artists like Styx and Journey. On this particular day I was feeling more Styx and Journey than I was Maiden or Priest, so I began to experiment with some tones and chord progressions on the keys instead of guitar. It took me just short of a day and I would emerge from the garage with a song that would become the most notable and biggest selling song of our career, "Honestly."

I've never written ballads just for the sake of writing ballads — for the sake of selling albums, so to speak. In the '80s there was a lot of pressure from labels to write pop/power ballads. I can say very honestly, pun intended, that I didn't succumb to that pressure, nor did I even feel that pressure from Enigma — at least not at this stage in our career. They allowed me the creative freedom to do what I wanted to do as a writer and musician without pressuring me at all. I guess I was spoiled a bit in that sense because I heard horror stories from other bands who received immense pressure from their label to write radio "hits" and it seemed they had no creative control whatsoever.

I write ballads because I enjoy them. I love the big vocal harmonies and that hold-your-lighter-in-the-air feeling you get when you listen to Journey or Styx. "Honestly" was a reflection of my appreciation for their songs.

When I emerged from the garage that day I had no idea this song would eventually become a radio smash. Yes, I felt I had a good song, but that was the extent of it. I also wrote "Sing-Along-Song" on the same cheap keyboard at the same time. I had laid down that signature loop and written the melody and chord progression around that rhythm.

At this stage in my life, I also never wrote songs solely for the purpose of being on the radio. We still had very little radio play, so it wasn't even really on my radar to "write a song for radio." It's not as though I didn't want to be on the radio, I just always assumed we'd be one of those bands that would get airplay occasionally, but that our live show would be our catalyst to success. So writing for radio wasn't something that came naturally to me. I just wrote what I knew and what I was feeling — and some days that was fist-in-the-air metal, and others it was pull-out-your-lighter ballads. I just never really wrote songs thinking "I need to succeed. I must write a song that will make me or us a success." I just tried to write great songs that moved people and hoped that if I did, things would fall into place.

It wasn't until I started writing for *In God We Trust* that I started thinking radio. That entire album was written to mimic the success of *To Hell With The Devil*, which is one of the biggest creative mistakes of my career. I wrote almost every song on *In God* as a direct answer to a song on *To Hell*. Big mistake, at least in my opinion.

What *was* a little more calculated on my part, at least during my writing for the *THWTD* album, were the lyrics. I try to focus not only on my own experience when writing lyrics, but also on the listener. Writing the lyrics for "Honestly" was no exception. I was purposely ambiguous as I etched out the words for this song, wanting the audience to be able to relate to their relationship with God, their wife, girlfriend or boyfriend or whomever. Although writing *certain songs* for me may a bit more inspirationally based, sometimes certain lyrics are much more calculated. I didn't write music for a specific audience, but I always tried (and still do) to put myself in the shoes of the listener when writing lyrics, regularly asking myself if this is a lyric the listener can relate to.

Since the release of "Honestly" barely a week has gone by that I haven't been asked to sing it at someone's wedding and every time that inquiry comes to me, I'm honored. To have written a song that has touched so many lives in very diverse ways is still a huge blessing to me.

You hear a lot of artists talk about how much they hate their big hit and how they wish they would have never written it. Not me. I love that song, still do to this day and I enjoy singing it. Over the years we've done various versions of the song and it always seems to be a crowd favorite no matter what.

I can certainly understand and relate to artists that despise their hit song. It's not so much that they despise the song as it is they wish it wasn't so closely tagged to the definition of their career. I understand this. When you write hundreds of songs over your career you may feel that many of them are much better than your hit, and it can be frustrating to be known the world over for one particular song while your best work is often overlooked. As musicians we progress and mature, we get better at our craft, and we're eager to showcase our work to an audience. It's frustrating to have that audience just want to hear that one song — the "hit."

What I don't understand is hating a song that is as much a part of you and your reason for success as the rest of your catalog. "Honestly" — yes, sometimes I get tired of playing it night after night after night. But more importantly, I don't like the feeling that I *have* to play it, the feeling that I'm letting the audience down if I don't play it, but I think that's human nature. We like to do things because we *want* to do them, not because we *have* to do them. And that's what a hit song will do — it will make you feel like you *have* to play it. But I'm proud of that song and I feel it holds its own.

After the Christmas break we started touring again in February of '86, and continued straight through into May. Our popularity was growing everyday on the road and we could feel what was to come. We were excited to get into the studio and start making the next album. Both the crowds and protestors were growing at each stop along the tour so we knew something big was about to happen, we just didn't know what it would be.

For me, it was more than just a career in music that was on my mind. I was about to go from kid to man in an instant. I was living at home. I was not married. I was in the biggest, most successful Christian rock band at the time, and in May of '86 I found out that my girlfriend was pregnant. Yeah, not really the most opportune time to write a smash-hit Christian rock album. So fortunately,

113

most of the album was written by the time we got off the road because I'm not sure I would have been in the frame of mind to write it otherwise.

Over the next few months my to-do list looked something like this:

Get married, quickly.
Pick a producer for the next record, quickly.
Move out of my parent's house, also quickly.
Make the biggest album of my career, quickly.
And prepare for a new baby in my life, quickly!

Turns out, the choices I would make in regard to my personal life would be the best and most fulfilling ones to date. My professional life however was headed for some turbulence, and I hate turbulence.

TWENTY

Spirits were high in the band upon returning from the *Soldiers Under Command* tour. Whenever we were home we were attending church regularly at Calvary Chapel in West Covina, which was quite the drive from Hollywood but well worth it. Raul Ries was and still is the pastor. We felt at home at Calvary and were always treated like family. The band had a great sense of unity during this time in our career and we were full of hope and optimism as we wrapped up the *Soldiers* era.

Almost immediately upon returning from tour we began meeting with the label about the next album. We knew we wanted to go in a different direction than the previous two albums, and hopefully this one would have a mainstream accessible sound. Theoretically, that would happen largely in part by picking the right producer.

Enigma tossed around several ideas for producers, and we were all in agreement that we wanted someone who could help us make an album that would take us from small theaters to arenas. Initially we were leaning toward a guy named Bernard Edwards. He had produced Power Station and was the bass player from the band Chic. We liked him and thought he was a great option and certainly unique.

Then another producer entered the picture. We had no idea who he was, but the selling point was that he had a hand in a chart topping hit single from the early '80s. I can't say with certainty we were told he *was* the actual producer of that song, but we were led to believe that he was. I can only assume this notion came from the producer himself, or perhaps his manager.

Regardless, we felt he was what we needed—someone who could help us with our sound and reach the mainstream music fan.

We later found out he actually did *not* produce the song that made us want to work with him after all, and to this day it's unclear what role he played on that song, if any.

We hired him anyway and quickly realized this wouldn't be the last half-truth, if not outright lie, we'd get from him. We thought he was a household-name producer. It turned out that he really wasn't well known at all. We felt somewhat deceived about a number of things as time progressed while making the album.

I had eloped with Kyle, so "Get Married" had been checked off my to-do list. I had also moved out of my parent's house so Kyle and I purchased our first home together soon afterward. We had a baby on the way. Life was complicated. I wasn't really concerned about conducting extensive fact-checking on producers, but as time went by we started to uncover some pretty hilarious stuff. Well, it wasn't really funny in the moment, but looking back on it, it's somewhat comical now.

For instance, during the making of *THWTD*, he shared with us that he was one of the character actors in blockbuster movie. We were all standing around the studio talking about that movie and he told us he was in it and that he was one of the three motorcycle cops. As I stood there looking at his face, I remember thinking, "I've seen that movie several times, and I don't recall you being in it."

But I had other things to think about so I let it go. I had to focus on making an incredible record. My suspicions about his acting career would have to take a back seat for the moment.

Several days passed and we were tracking basics at Master Control in Burbank. I had stepped away for a moment to take a breather in the lounge that was equipped with a small TV, complete with rabbit ears. Remember those? Before cable when you received your signal through two long, metal antennas on top of the set?

Despite attempts to watch TV, my mind was wandering to the songs we were recording. I was thinking about Kyle and the baby. I was contemplating how to make the album of a lifetime. And then, as if God had a sense of humor and wanted to let me in on the joke, an add came on that said the movie that he was supposedly in was coming up next. Ha! I couldn't believe it. What a perfect distraction and a great chance to test my suspicions. I went into the control room and said to him, *"Dude! Your movie is coming on right now. The movie you told us you were in — it's on in five minutes! Can you believe it?"*

He turned white as a ghost. He didn't say a word. His silence told me I was probably right. He likely wasn't in the movie after all.

A few moments pass and he quietly leaves the control room to "use the bathroom." As he leaves the room, smiles are exchanged between all the band mates. We were all thinking the same thing: "He's not in that movie!" Moments later, we hear pounding and banging noises coming from the lounge. We didn't think much of it. It was brief. Then he returned to the *studio.*

Curious, I went back out into the lounge only to see that the picture on the TV was nothing but static. At first I thought maybe he just changed the channel. Then I noticed that the antenna had been destroyed. Apparently he broke the antenna to keep us from watching the movie and confirming he wasn't in it.

The *head* tech for the studio, Gary Meyerberg, tried to fix the TV and eventually succeeded. By then, though, the movie was over. Our "actor" turned producer appeared relieved. We knew, at that moment, that he had not been upfront with us. It was a turning point in the making of that record and how we viewed our producer.

Another shady moment came from a piece of rental equipment. We had rented a top-of-the-line Spector bass to use for the record.

When it came time to return the bass, this same producer offered to handle getting it back to the rental company. Come to find out, he never returned it. His brother was a local bass player, and he let his brother use the bass around town for a few weeks, all on our dime.

We obviously began to question our choice in producer. That being said, he did play a role in the biggest-selling album of our career. So that's something. It had the right sound for the time, and I suppose it would be dishonest to say he had *nothing* to do with it. He did play somewhat of an important role in the creation of the album, it just wasn't the role we were expecting. *To Hell With The Devil* became a multi-platinum record *despite* the deception, certainly not *because* of it. If anything, I give great props to our engineer, Dan Nebenzal, who played a pivotal part in capturing the tones and the signature sounds that ultimately landed on the finished product.

Dan was a great engineer with access to one of the best studios in Burbank. We were one of the first bands to use the Mitsubishi 32 track digital machine. When we tracked at Master Control, it was one of the first studios in the world to have a Mitsubishi X-850. Yes, I guess you can say that we were the guinea pigs for the digital recording era. We were skeptical because we had always been told analog was better, warmer, and fatter. I was against recording digitally at first, but I was also in the frame of mind to try something new, to experiment a bit. And digital was that opportunity. As a result, we captured a sound that was definitely unique. It sounded like no other record out there. For better or worse, recording digitally was partially responsible for making us stand out from the other records of the time, sonically speaking.

Dan was friends with Tori Amos, and she was coming around the studio really often. This was before she had signed a record deal, but we did take a break one night to go hear her perform at a small club in Burbank. Our producer went with us to the show, and from that point on we started seeing a lot more of Tori hanging out at the studio. I'm not sure if he had a role in her landing a record deal or not, but it was exciting to have creative, artistic people around. It helped keep the energy level high.

All of this—the fake movie star/producer, the engineer with rising-star friends, and the timid feelings toward digital recording—pales in comparison to what was coming next. We had a bass player we had to tell, "You're not the right guy for this record."

TWENTY-ONE

Everyone has a moment, usually many moments, in life that they wish they had handled things differently. Part of living and growing as a human being, I believe, is making mistakes. If we learn from those mistakes, we become stronger and ultimately, wiser.

Often, we can chalk up the I-wish-I-had-done-that-differently moments to youth and inexperience. I once saw a sign in a store that said "Hire a teenager while they still know everything." I'm afraid there are moments in my teenage and early adult years that would fall under that heading. As a young adult I often felt I knew everything, and nobody was going to tell me differently. At times I was open-minded like a sponge soaking up wisdom and knowledge from anyone I felt had something to offer. Other times I was stubborn and self-assured that whatever decision I was making surely must be the right one.

If I were to list half-dozen things in my life that I wish I had handled differently, one of them would be the way I dealt with Tim during the recording of *To Hell With The Devil*.

The making of this album came about rather quickly, and as I've mentioned before I probably wasn't in the best frame of mind. When recording began, I had recently eloped with Kyle. I was starting a new life in a new world with a baby on the way. I had a record label telling us all the great things going on with our previous albums and that we needed to make another one, fast. Not only did we need to make another record soon, it needed to be a million times better than our previous release.

Pressure to "do the right thing" was upon me daily in the summer of '86.

When we made *Soldiers Under Command,* we had been rehearsing those songs for a few years and taking them out on the road. *To Hell With The Devil, though,* was basically written behind the scenes and not performed in public at all. We had barely practiced the songs, much less worked out the kinks that years of playing in clubs can do.

We started tracking drums and guitars, and next up was bass. Tim came in and laid down his parts. We all felt it was a little loose and wasn't quite what we wanted. We wanted something more "in the pocket," and more locked with the bed of music we already had recorded. Tim has a unique style of playing that comes partially from a jazz influence. This seemingly made it difficult for Tim to approach the record in a straight-ahead, 1/8th note kind of way. I share all of these feelings in the past tense, as he's certainly proven me wrong since.

But the way I was analyzing it in my mind, Tim was going to have a difficult time locking in to the groove we felt necessary for the sound we were trying to achieve. I was hearing bass lines that felt as though they were dancing *around* the groove instead of *with* the groove. I'm sure if you were to ask Tim, he would likely say it would not have been difficult at all for him to lock in like we needed him to do. I should have explained better what I wanted with these brand new songs — songs that, until entering the studio, he had barely even heard, much less rehearsed. And if he were to say that, he'd be right. "Hindsight is 20/20"... "Monday morning quarterback"... all those clichés could apply here.

When Tim first joined the band several years earlier, he and I were really close. We hung out almost daily. I'd go so far as to say he was one of my best friends. We went to the beach, parties, almost everywhere together. We were virtually inseparable. Not only did we have a close personal bond, but we fortunately had a musical one as well. Those were good times.

121

Eventually, however, I believe the creative process began to take a toll on our relationship. I wasn't consciously pushing him or anyone else out of the creative process. I would just write a song because I loved writing songs, and I'd present it to the band. As time went by, I was presenting song after song after song, and eventually I was creating, arranging, and teaching the guys all the parts — mostly, if not entirely, as a result of my love for songwriting.

Tim took an interest in the business of Stryper as well, and he got shunned — again — but not purposefully. He'd eagerly chime in to help out with promotions or business topics and we'd just dismiss it with a quick *"Don't worry about it. Daryn or Mom will take care of it."* He was being told in so many words, *"We've got it covered, just play your bass."*

After all of this, by the time we were making the *THWTD* record, he was basically handed some songs and told to play them. It was certainly not the best way to get the creative juices flowing in a band mate.

So as a band, we made the extremely tough decision to replace Tim on the record. He came in one day and made a pass at a few songs. He laid down parts for, I believe, two to three songs. The rest of us stayed at the studio well into the night discussing our disappointment in what we had heard that day. We decided, as a group, (along with our co-producer) to hire a replacement. Tim came in the next day expecting to record again, and our producer, Robert, Oz and I let him know we'd be using someone else for the album. Understandably, Tim was not happy with this decision.

One of the first guys we auditioned was Ricky Phillips (The Babys, Bad English, Styx) who was, and still is, an incredible player. However, for likely the same intangible reasons we chose not to use Tim on the album, we also chose not to use Ricky. Instead we settled on a guy by the name of Brad Cobb. Brad was a local session player and when he laid down some parts, it just felt right. So we went with our gut and we hired Brad to track all the bass lines for the record. All the while, thoughts of Tim lingered in our minds.

Would that record have reached the success it did had Tim played on it instead of Brad? We will never know. Maybe. Maybe not. But Brad did offer something solid and exactly what was needed for the style of music we were making—a slick and polished rock/metal record. Sonically, I'm happy about our decision to go with Brad, but for many other reasons, I wish we had given Tim more of a chance.

In all fairness to Tim, these were brand new songs and he just didn't have a lot of time to live with them. But we should have given him the chance to work harder. We were a band that wasn't acting like a band. We should have said *"Alright. So it's not perfect. Let's give him some time to work on this."* But we didn't.

From that point forward, I believe Tim felt disrespected, hurt, and offended—all legitimate and warranted feelings.

As if taking him off the album wasn't enough, Tim would get a dose of this treatment twice in '86. We somehow mended ways after his dismissal from the recording process, but then it came time to rehearse for the tour. Once again, we weren't feeling it. So we let him go … again.

This time we brought in a bassist named Matt Hurich. Matt suited up in a custom racing costume, designed by Ray Brown (for Matt, which was later lengthened for Tim), and we took a promo shot that would haunt us for years to come. Matt was in the band less than a month—never even played a show—yet this picture with him in it still shows up on posters and marketing materials to this day. It was as if we took the picture on Friday and by Monday Enigma had circulated it the world over along with a letter stating "This is the only Stryper picture you are to ever use!"

Matt was a good bass player who played in a band called Leatherwolf, but he played more in the style of Steve Harris from Iron Maiden. We sounded like Stryper with the bass style of Iron Maiden. Some of you are probably thinking *"Yeah? And that's a bad thing?"* Let's just say it just wasn't Stryper.

Sitting there one day after rehearsals at SIR Studios in Hollywood, it hit me like a ton of bricks. Stryper is Michael Sweet, Robert Sweet, Oz Fox and Tim Gaines! Somehow when the four of us come together, faults and all, it becomes Stryper. Standing there rehearsing with Matt just felt wrong. Matt's great, and I take nothing away from his abilities. It just wasn't Stryper.

So once again, with our tails between our legs, we called Tim and said, "This isn't working out with Matt. Would you consider coming back?" I wanted him back in the band badly and felt it was necessary for the future of Stryper.

Rob wasn't so easily convinced, however. When Rob sets his mind to something, typically he sticks to it. And he had made up his mind that Tim was out. I had a talk with Rob and Oz and basically shared how wrong this all felt, that we needed Tim back. It was similar to the talk I had when Oz had left the band for a while in the early days. I'm not positive Rob was convinced this was the right move, but I give him credit for opening his mind and agreeing to it.

So Tim, reluctantly I would assume, came down to rehearsals. Before playing a note we all talked and prayed together. We let Tim know that we had made a big mistake and thankfully he rejoined the band.

I think to this day Tim's confidence as a bass player is probably not quite as high as it should be because of those times in 1986, and for that I will forever live with regret.

We just weren't as patient as we should have been with Tim back then. We didn't give him the chance he deserved to learn the parts for the album. Looking back on it, I'm sure he could have pulled it off if we had given him the opportunity and had we shared our expectations more clearly. As proof, I fast-forward to our 2010 release of *The Covering*, an album we did of all cover songs including some that contain the most difficult bass playing in rock music. Tim played on that album and did an incredible job. We had songs on *The Covering* that would be tough for any player, and Tim nailed it with in-the-pocket eighth notes just like we needed him to do. Add to that "Second Coming," which includes re-records of songs from THWTD, and Tim nailed it!

We worked around the clock to finish *THWTD*. We not only had a tight budget, but we also had a stringent timeline from the label. We had Eddy Schreyer at Capitol booked to master the album and we didn't want to lose the session. He was the best of the best and we knew he would put the final "ear candy" on the record. He was booked for months on end, so if we lost our scheduled window of opportunity, we'd have no choice but to go somewhere else—and after all we had been through to get to this point, that wasn't about to happen.

We stayed in the studio mixing night and day. We'd take turns sleeping on the couch and consuming ridiculous amounts of coffee. On the last mix day, when we were scheduled to go to mastering the following morning, Oz desperately needed and wanted a shower. He and I went out behind the studio and he had me hose him down and pour buckets of water over him so that he could at least be semi-hygienic before we had to go to mastering.

The next morning we went to Capitol Records after staying up all night. I was exhausted to the point of feeling nauseous. But we made it through the sessions and Eddy far exceeded our expectations in making our first digital recording sound incredible.

125

When the guys from the label heard it, they were blown away! I remember playing it for them for the first time and seeing the surprised looks on all their faces. I could almost see the dollar signs racing through their heads. We had given them a radio-friendly rock/metal record, or more suitable to the times, an MTV-friendly record. We did get some good airplay. "Honestly" peaked at #23 on the Billboard charts and would become our only single to hit Top 40. But MTV was a different story. They weren't quite ready for us either, but thanks to DIAL-MTV, the fans would soon change and force the minds of the Music Television executives.

TWENTY-TWO

During the *To Hell With The Devil* era, we continued to fuel controversy within the Christian community. More Christians began to support us, but more Christians also continued to protest our shows. Our Christian detractors often felt we didn't preach enough and that we were conforming to the world in order to be accepted. Although our mainstream fan base grew during this period, our Christian message often turned away non-Christians.

We weathered the reactions from both Christians and the mainstream, but I was sometimes frustrated to hear our fans boo the opening act. This happened at the Anthrax show years earlier at The Country Club and I was somewhat bummed that our fans would boo them. Too often, a band would take the stage, singing about whatever, and I'd start to hear booing between the songs, and I would cringe in the dressing room.

I just wish that sort of thing hadn't come from our fans. Instead of booing a band, I wish they had shown respect. It doesn't set a good example and certainly does not exemplify the love of Christ. There are countless accounts in the Bible where Jesus teaches us to be a good example to others. Booing a band, to me, just isn't a good example of exemplifying Christ.

Another incident I recall happened in Greensboro, North Carolina, where we had a band called PKM opening for us. They were a spin-off band with members from the Epic Records act Nantucket who had toured with AC/DC—so they were obviously talented. I was standing side stage and PKM started throwing album covers of their new record into the audience, and I saw people rolling them up and throwing them back at the band, accompanied by boos and questionable remarks.

We always purposely took bands on the road with us that were not Christian bands. We still prefer to operate that way. The reason is twofold: We want their fans in the audience in hopes that we can share our faith, and we want to share with the bands themselves if the opportunity presents itself. And by "share our faith," I mean showing them the love of God and hope that it may have a lasting effect on them.

What band in their right mind would want anything to do with Christianity when the fans of a well-known Christian band are booing them and throwing their stuff back at them? It was disappointing for me to see this coming from our fans, never mind the fact that it made it difficult for us to be taken seriously. What were we supposed to say? *"Yeah, Christianity is great. God is good! Just think, if you accept Christ, you too could have fans that are disrespectful and boo your opening acts."*

I have friends, many of them close friends, who have a regular routine of going out into public places in order to witness to others. They'll go to a mall or a grocery store, not with the intent of buying clothing or milk and bread, but instead to witness to people and share their faith. I've never done this, and I know I wouldn't be very good at it. It's not me at all.

The way I try to share my faith is through my life. I try to let God shine through me by being nice and showing respect to people, by being an approachable and personable guy. I'm more the kind of guy that would be interested in developing a friendship with people, maybe invite them to dinner. Then, only if the door opens widely, I will talk about God. My purpose for developing the friendship is first and foremost to become someone's friend.

People know what I stand for and know that I'm a Christian, so there's really no hiding it. I don't need to boldly say to people in my everyday life, *"By the way, I'm a Christian. Have you accepted*

Christ?" But even if they didn't know me, and I wasn't in Stryper, it's not my personality to operate that way.

If I'm going to speak boldly about Jesus, it's going to be in the songs. *"Jesus is the Way!"* It doesn't get much clearer than when I sing, *"God, I will follow You because You died for me. Gave to me Your life to set me free."*

We have songs that are basically the sinner's prayer summed up in a song. That's how I prefer to share my faith. That's my platform and opportunity to tell the world about God. I'm just not that guy that takes his Bible and goes out seeking others. Even if we didn't have fans worldwide that I could share my faith with, I still wouldn't be that guy going door-to-door.

I don't force my faith on people. Growing up I was around a lot of people that *did* force it on others, and that made me uncomfortable. I don't think you sincerely reach people like that, and if anything, I believe you can push them away. But it works for some, so God bless those who have the ability to "preach" more boldly than I do.

Believe it or not, I'm also shy. That plays a role, too, in my disinterest in sharing my faith in a forward manner. Sure, when I'm on stage, I'd prefer the audience to be focused on the band. But if I'm at a dinner party or a social gathering, I feel more comfortable when nobody notices me.

I'm not shy, however, about sharing my faith. I don't go door-to-door looking for people to talk to about God, but if someone asks, I'm of course upfront about it and comfortable with sharing my beliefs.

There's a lot of disagreement among Christians as to the right way to witness and share the word of God. I'm perplexed when one side can't see the other's side, or doesn't try to understand. "Door-to-door" Christians sometimes get upset because I'm not as forward about my faith as they would like me to be, and lead-by-example Christians are often turned off by those who share more boldly. I try to understand both sides and feel that all Christians should understand this one basic point: God does not call all people in the same way. Some He calls for service in one area and others for service in another. It's always been frustrating for me to see Christians upset with other Christians because they believe God has the same calling for all Christians. He doesn't.

During the *THWTD* era Christians were constantly trying to convince me that I should be doing something the way God called *them* to do it, whatever that might be. I simply wanted to show people that love is the greatest gift, and we're called to love one another. If we lead by example, our faith will shine through just fine.

Being "nice" was difficult during the *To Hell* era when I'd regularly run into protestors screaming at me through a bullhorn, "You're going to hell. You're a wolf in sheep's clothing. Repent." What I really wanted to do was grab the bullhorn and beat them over their heads with it, but of course, I didn't. I tried my best to lead by example. Hopefully a few "protestors" over the years noticed my character and have gone on to throw away their bullhorns and make an actual difference in somebody else's life.

This time in my life was as eye opening as it was confusing. Personally, I had a plate full with my newly found domestic life. Professionally, I was doing everything I could to help Stryper turn the corner into mainstream popularity. Spiritually, I was constantly struggling with the odd clash between the Christians and the non-Christians we were meeting on tour. Going into this era of my life, I assumed the Christians would greet us at concerts with open arms, encouraging us on this path we were taking. Not the case. I assumed Christians would show respect to the non-Christian bands we were taking on the road. Again, not always the case. And I assumed the non-Christian music fans would be our constant antagonists on the road. Also not always the case.

I grew a lot as a result of that confusion, and that growth helped lead us through what was to come.

TWENTY-THREE

New technology and new methods constantly change and challenge the music industry. Some people, usually the old-school folks, hate these changes, and some people wonder how we ever lived without them.

My kids grew up in the Internet Age, a time that forever changed music. Napster made it possible to download music for free. Apple and iTunes made digital downloads the standard for music buyers. Most musicians my age were not happy with the idea of free music when it was introduced. We felt we should be paid for our art, for our work. We also didn't like it because the sonic quality of a download was sub-par by comparison with CDs.

My parents came of age during the proliferation of rock 'n' roll. Turntables made it easy for them to listen to their 45's anywhere there was electricity. Portable radios, car stereos and AM rock radio stations meant they could listen to rock and roll just about anywhere at any time they wanted to. But many in my grandparent's generation saw the new music and the technology that generated it as a passing fad or, worse, evil.

I, however, came of age in what I consider to be a great time in music history—the music video era. For the first time ever fans could not only hear, but also *watch* their favorite bands. An entire network had formed that showed nothing but music videos. MTV was the new radio, and life would never be the same for the music business. All of a sudden it wasn't enough for a record label to make a record and release it—they had to also make a video to accompany the song.

Once again, people on the other side of the fence viewed videos as a passing fad. Given that the video channel YouTube, 30+ years after the unveiling of MTV, is now the most popular outlet by which people discover new music, I'd say the naysayers were once again incorrect about the short life span of music videos.

We had produced two videos prior to releasing *To Hell With The Devil,* but neither had seen much airtime. After making what I and Enigma Records felt was the album of our career, it was time to make videos that would properly reinforce this music. It was time to get on MTV, something all musicians viewed as the ultimate triumph on the path to success. Being on MTV in 1986-1987 was today's equivalent to a video going viral on YouTube and achieving millions of views quickly. It was *that* big, if not bigger. And every band from that era wanted to be a part of the music video phenomenon.

Enigma hired the best of the best to shoot our first video for the song "Calling On You." Wayne Isham, with a company called The Company, had directed notable acts from Motley Crue to Michael Jackson to Bon Jovi to Metallica.

We shot "Calling On You" at The Charlie Chaplin sound stage at A&M Studios, the location where he shot many of those old, legendary silent movies. The enormous sound stage provided a venue for what was often referred to as a "live without an audience" video, basically a performance on a massive stage with pyrotechnics and five trillion lights and cameras and no audience. It's a little awkward at first, but you get the hang of it. This was a common format for rock videos of the 1980s, and it seemed to be working for us as well.

Just walking in to that sound stage at A&M took our excitement level through the roof. We really felt like, for probably the first time in our careers, this was something that would catapult us to a new level of popularity.

The video shoot took one day, with editing taking about a week, and when I saw the final cut I was amazed. I couldn't believe something so big, so huge, so cool *was us*, four "regular" guys from Southern California. Swinging boom cameras covered a stage the size of a football field (or at least so it seemed), and we pulled out every rock move/pose we could think of—all in the quest of a coveted prime-time slot on MTV. Finally, we were going to have the opportunity to really take God's message to the masses. Finally, the years of hard work were about to pay off.

Not so fast.

All the pyro, jumbo stages, swinging cameras, crazy outfits, Maybelline and Aqua Net didn't make up for the fact that we were still viewed as a Christian band—and MTV didn't play Christian music.

After "Calling On You" was submitted to MTV, we heard every excuse for why they weren't going to play it. Although it wasn't said in so many words, the decision was solely and exclusively based on the fact that we were a "Christian" band, and they just didn't want to play Christian music. Where's the ACLU when you need them to yell "Discrimination!" at the top of their lungs?

I couldn't believe what we were hearing. They weren't going to play the video. It was yet another roadblock on the path of Stryper. But the fans came to the rescue.

Begrudgingly, almost miraculously, MTV agreed to play the video in light rotation, but around that time the popular fan-driven DIAL-MTV was the most-watched segment on the network. Fans could call and request their favorite videos, and they did.

It was as if every fan that had stood faithfully by us for the past several years started calling and requesting our video. Almost overnight the video went from light rotation, to heavy rotation, to entering the top 10 countdown. Quickly, we climbed the charts to #1! We went from, "Eh, I don't think we'll be playing a Stryper video," to "Uh, we don't have a choice" and upward to #1. It was an amazing feeling, and I guess you could say that the victory was ours. Also on the chart, below us, were Bon Jovi and Motley Crue.

It was like sweet vindication for all our hard work, but it was also incredibly surprising—a pinch yourself moment. I was simultaneously humbled yet very confident at the same time, humbled to the point of tears and confident in what God had just pulled off.

Our fans from all over the nation rose up and became a huge voice for Stryper and, ultimately, God. It was out of our control but had such a massive impact. The amazing part was that it didn't just peak at #1 and drop off the next week—we stayed at the top spot for weeks on end.

Our second video, "Free," was a live video shot at the Paramount Theater in Seattle in January of 1987. We had played the night before in Canada and were heading to Oregon the next day, so there wasn't a lot of time spent on this video. We did some playback shooting during sound check, without the audience, but the bulk of that video was taken from the live show that night.

"Free" was introduced on MTV while "Calling On You" was topping the charts. The same week "Free" was released, it entered the top 10 at number 10. And just when we thought it couldn't get any better, it did. I recall that day vividly watching the top 10 countdown and hearing the VJ saying that for the first time in DIAL-MTV history a band has two songs in the top 10 at the same time, and it was Stryper. Wow!

Over the weeks and months to follow, "Free" would eventually hit #1 as well.

Our lives were changing rapidly. For the first time we were getting noticed everywhere we went. It was such a whirlwind with everything happening so fast. Touring was relentless. We toured for almost nine months straight to support *To Hell With The Devil* and our newly found fame on MTV.

Next on the list was to start filming the concept part of the "Honestly" video. We set up scenes at the Stryper office, which was a house in Buena Park that we had rented to run all things Stryper. The idea was for this footage to be a pre-text to us going to London for a big international debut. We shot scenes of us saying goodbye to our wives and families. There were a lot of sentimental shots of us with family and even a shot of me holding Mikey when he was a newborn. There were humorous scenes of Robert quickly packing his luggage and his suitcase falling apart as he ran to the limo that would take us to LAX so we could fly to London. We even had an American flag in the footage.

Our first show overseas was performing at the infamous Hammersmith Odeon. We shot all the live footage for the "Honestly" video there. The tour continued through Sweden, France, Germany, Australia, and then back to Japan.

In Australia we saw the birth of our first major tabloid-style rumor about the band. We did an in-store appearance at a record store and were driven there in a limo. Those who have watched the movie *Spinal Tap* recall the scene where the band shows up at a store and nobody is there — not a single fan.

We had no idea what to expect as far as to the number of people that might be there, but we didn't expect many people. When we turned the corner toward the store, planning to enter through a side entrance, there were thousands of people, as if The Beatles were in town. We looked out the window wondering what was going on. It turns out they were there to see us.

For some reason, and we'll never know why, the limo driver decided to plow right through the people and park right beside the store, right in the middle of the massive crowd. We just sat there not knowing what to do. We were about 20 feet from the store entrance and we decided to make a break for it through the crowd. We took a deep breath as if we were jumping out of a plane for the first time, and then we just ran for it. As soon as we opened the car door all hell broke loose. Our clothes got ripped. People were grabbing our hair and we were getting pulled from left to right. It was the polar opposite of *Spinal Tap* and instead more like a scene out of a boy band video. To this day I've never experienced anything like it. Well, there was an in-store appearance in Puerto Rico in 2003 that's a close second to this, but I'll get to that later.

The crowd continued to break windows and climb on top of the limo. They were completely out of control, and it was a total riot.

We made it inside, and for a while made an attempt to sign some autographs through the door, but the tension in the store continued to escalate as people were on the roof of the building and breaking windows outside. Security was light with only a few guys trying to put some order to the chaos.

I began to overhear discussions between security and the owner as to how they were planning on getting us out of there. The tension among the fans was growing by the moment. Surely the thousands of people who showed up knew they wouldn't all be able to get inside for an autograph. It got to the point where we became seriously nervous — for our lives.

They had decided the only way for us to exit safely was in a paddy wagon. The police arrived with sirens blaring. They backed into the entrance of the store and as quickly as we had arrived, we were taken away through the front door and straight to an Australian police station.

Once at the station, we posed with handcuffs on and made the cover page of the news the next morning. In the days to follow, pictures of us being put in the paddy wagon began to surface with headlines reading "Christian rock band Stryper arrested." Not "Christian band draws thousands of fans"… No, that would be too easy. Unfortunately there was no Internet then or surely we would have made TMZ headlines.

The rumors were flying high during this era, but the Australian in-store stands out as one of our favorites.

We returned from oversees and started the battle of getting "Honestly" aired on MTV. It had all the elements of another hit video and when all was said and done, we were happy with the way it turned out.

Previously we had the live-with-no-audience video ("Calling On You") and a video that actually *was* live and captured more of the energy of our show ("Free"). Now we had a video that captured even another side of us with elements of family, country, and unity set to a power rock ballad.

One would think that after two #1 videos on MTV, this one would be a no-brainer for top billing and heavy rotation. Once it was turned in, we got the response, "Oh wait. You have an American flag in the video? That'll need to be edited out. It's too patriotic."

Too patriotic? Is there such a thing? Apparently in 1987 to get time on MTV there was. Once again, we got every excuse in the book on reasons *not* to play a Stryper video.

We caved and re-edited "Honestly" to be less patriotic. They still used some of the scenes shot back in California, but the bulk of it was footage from London.

And once again, it went to #1 on the video charts. I will never be able to thank our fans enough for all they did to prove to MTV, and the world, that there is indeed a place for Stryper in the world of music.

The original version of "Honestly" was eventually included on the release of *In The Beginning*, our behind-the-scenes video about the band and our path up to this point.

To Hell With the Devil went on to become a multi-platinum selling album and, despite all the hardships and hurdles, the battle seemed to have just begun.

TWENTY-FOUR

If I were to point to a time in my life where I graduated from youth to adulthood, it would be during the *To Hell With The Devil* tour. In the middle of this tour, on February 11, 1987, Kyle gave birth to our son, Michael Jr., or "Mikey" as we know him.

I was a new husband and still hadn't come into my own as to what exactly that meant, but I was learning. I was in the middle of unprecedented professional success and suddenly responsible for the life of a beautiful baby boy.

With the birth of a child, life began to come into view through a different set of eyes. I began to question things that I otherwise would never have questioned. Life is precious as I started to realize more profoundly each day, and one of my primary questions was, "Am I doing what's best for my wife and child?"

That question was motivated partially by my eagerness to be a financially responsible father. Was I laying the groundwork for the most financially secure life for my family? Turns out, I was not, but these topics were becoming more and more a part of my daily thoughts.

For example, a few years earlier in 1983 my parents began to talk to Robert and me about music publishing. They taught us basically that most the money in music was primarily in publishing. I trusted their wisdom as my father had experienced some success as a songwriter already in his career. They very lovingly, or so it felt at the time, wanted to help us get our music publishing affairs in order.

Two parties, the songwriter and the publisher basically own a song. I of course was the primary songwriter. The publisher of a song, however, is the company that traditionally helps to exploit and represent the song. In many regards, a publisher is a partner to the songwriter or songwriters of a particular song.

A publisher will typically shop songs for film, television, and commercial licensing. He will ensure proper use of the song with the record label and ensure that proper payments are collected from the record label for the sale and use of the songs. A publisher, at least a good one, is a friend to a songwriter and can be very instrumental in the growth of a song or collection of songs. The publisher also owns part of the song, thus making money off of it as well.

More specifically here's the way it works. A song is 100 percent. The songwriter owns the entire 100 percent until he decides to sell a portion of that to a publisher. If he doesn't sell it, then he owns his own publishing and 100 percent of the song.

A publisher may come to the table with an offering of $50,000 for the rights to half of your songs on a particular album. When the album is released, if it does well, the publisher will make his money back. Furthermore, if the publisher upholds promises to find additional outlets for the song, such as television or film, both the publisher and the songwriter stand to make even more money.

So going in to this situation, as the primary songwriter, I owned most of the songs and theoretically should decide which, if any, publishing company I go into business with.

That's how it works in most cases, in the real world.

But, we don't always live in the real world. I was 20 years old at the time these discussions were taking place, so everything I knew about the business of publishing was based on what my mom and dad had told me and taught me.

And in 1985 they said that they wanted to help Robert and me start our own publishing company. And since they were the smartest people I knew at the time, I agreed.

So, starry eyed and all, I put pen to paper at my parents recommendation and signed over almost 50 percent of my songs. They convinced me that we were forming a company together, the four of us, and technically we did form a company, Sweet Family Music. But in reality, what I was doing was giving away, for free, very valuable assets, assets that at the time I didn't even really know were mine.

I'm almost 50 at the time of writing this book, and I still don't fully understand the complicated business of publishing. I certainly didn't understand it at 20. So when my parents suggested signing a contract and signing over to them part of the most valuable asset in my life, I had no reason not to trust that they were giving me the best advice possible. And perhaps in their mind, it was good advice. But looking back on it, it's certainly not the smartest decision I ever made.

We all had equal shares in this new publishing company, Sweet Family Music. I still owned the songwriting, half of the song of course, but for absolutely no money in my pocket, I just gave my brother, my mom and my dad 75 percent of the other half of the songs, the publishing half. We each owned 25 percent of Sweet Family Music, which in turn owned one half of each song.

Like I said, in the real world, publishing companies would pay big money to own such a large portion of the publishing rights to a national recording artist but again, we weren't always in the real world.

Over the past 20 plus years this topic has obviously come up, almost daily, in my business dealings. Since my days of youth, I've met and worked with some of the most brilliant minds in the

As a young lad and
sporting the stripes,
even then!

At a carnival with Nana
and looking mad as,
well you know . . .

With Nana, Mom, Dad, Robert and
Lisa on Beverley Blvd., Whittier.
Early signs of ADHD?

My first guitar at 5 years old. Let the games begin!

Performing at our first talent show. I played my dad's Fender Jazz bass and it was twice my size. We won 1st place, maybe that's why.

Apparently I was watching too many episodes of *The Partridge Family* at this stage of my life . . .

Singing with the church choir. Dad is leading, Robert (5th from the left), Lisa (far right) and me (far left) singing along. Notice the "In God We Trust" above our heads!

My first taste of Rock and Roll. Dressing up like Paul Stanley of KISS, minus the hairy chest.

Rehearsing with Dad, Robert and Lou Martin. My dad and Lou were the first two guys who taught me how to play guitar.

The band Roxx. Eric, Richard (Odie), Robert and me
with a sun tan and Sun-In . . .

Performing at the infamous Gazzarri's at the ripe old age of 16.

Getting my David Lee Roth on . . .

What? Stripes before Stryper?? Early Roxx Regime
with Scott Lane, Robert, John Vorhees and me.

Stryper's first official tour. The good old days . . .

The gang's all here! With Mom, Daryn, Tom Bruno, Kevin Dugan, Wes Hein and Bill Hein of Enigma Records.

Kyle and I eloping and getting married in Palos Verdes in 1986. Gotta love the 80's, blue satin suits and all.

Proud Papa. It's a boy!

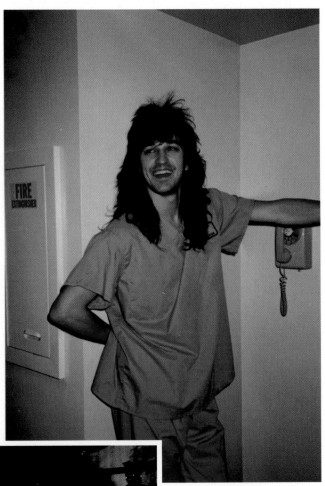

Bonding with my son,
Mikey Jr.

Receiving our first certified platinum award for "To Hell
With The Devil". Wes and Bill were the presenters.

Recording "Time Is Ticking Away" with DC Talk.

The Against The Law sessions, 1990.

Holding baby Lena.
Daddy's little girl . . .

Stepping out on my own as a solo artist. With Doug Beiden, Gregg Fulkerson and my manager at the time, Rendy Lovelady.

The first solo photo shoot, 1994.

Harvesting cranberries at Maple Park, during my "down time" from music.

Shooting the VH1 *Where Are They Now* Stryper episode at Maple Park, Wareham, MA.

Entering the music world again in 2000. Mixing "Truth" at A&M with Bob Marlette.

The last family photo before Kyle was diagnosed with ovarian cancer.

Touring with Boston in 2008. Tom and I on stage (notice Tom's smile). I'd say he was either very happy or laughing at my rock moves . . .

Kyle and I in Las Vegas for the "Touched" photo shoot, not long before she passed.

My friend and spiritual mentor,
Michael Guido.

Not long after Lisa and I
started dating. I don't think
we planned to "match", but
we always did.

The day Lisa and I
heard "Amazed" in
Nashville, with Elvis.

Lisa and I getting married on Jan. 8, 2010, in Boston, MA.

Daryn Hinton and me. She invested in us when no one else would. Thank you Daryn!

My manager and friend, Dave Rose with Melanie, Lisa and Bill Ray Sweet.

Finally meeting one of my biggest influences, Dave Meniketti!

The 4 Tenors—My buddies Tony Harnell, Jeff Scott Soto, Todd La Torre and me. Who knows, maybe someday we'll make a metal opera record?

Lisa and I with the one and only Eddie Trunk. Thank you
Eddie for the constant support!

My friend and
doppelganger, Dave
Amato of REO
Speedwagon.

I'm still waiting for a challenge to get in the ring with this guy, Mr. Chris Jericho. WWF?

"Get Er' Done" — Larry is still air-guitaring to Stryper tunes
before he goes on stage. I've got to see this!

Ringing the closing bell at NYSE with Billy Ray Cyrus. Who's who?

Lisa and I recently in Boston. Thank you Lisa for all you do—I love you . . .

business, all of whom look at me like I just told them I was born on the planet Mars when I share the story of Sweet Family Music. Maybe I *was* born on Mars.

I was 24, and I had a son. I had bills to pay. I had to provide for my family's future. So I began to examine, and question, my business affairs a little more closely in 1987.

There are complications with Mikey's birth. Kyle was in labor for more than 48 hours due to a clinical trial she participated in to induce labor, a situation that ultimately led to many other complications. Finally, despite the extensive labor prep, Mikey was born by Cesarean, and it was a really frightening ordeal. The doctors were baffled by some of the difficulties taking place during labor. Mikey's heart stopped multiple times whenever Kyle was on her right side, so they eventually rushed Kyle in for an emergency C-section. Although it was against protocol back then, I was allowed to be present during the surgery. I even got the chance to show my bravery and look over the "curtain" that separated my eyes from Kyle's incision as they lifted Mikey out of her womb. He was a beautiful, healthy baby boy — eyes wide open, a full head of hair that would make any rock 'n' roll dad proud, and long, expressive fingers that cried out, "I'm playing piano or guitar." Kyle, unfortunately, had postpartum difficulties including deep vein thrombosis, and we almost lost her.

Mikey was born on February 11, and I was scheduled to return to tour in Houston on February 14, which would have been fine except Kyle was still in the hospital with many complications.

I left on the 14th to continue the tour, but I flew home every night before each day off to visit her, then turned back around and flew to the next city on the tour. This went on for about two weeks until she thankfully recovered enough to go home.

I, however, would not see another tour break until the end of April. So Mikey was born on the 11th, I left for tour on the 14th, and I was gone for the next 10 weeks straight. And when I came back, it was only for three weeks before we left again to go overseas.

February 11, 1986 I was single. The sky was the limit and all of life was ahead of me. If I had enough food, money, and happiness, that was all I needed. One year later, however, the world looked considerably different.

With all of this going on, and countless lonely nights in hotels on the road, I couldn't help but ponder everything, especially the music business and whether or not I was making the best of it.

Questions continued to weigh heavily on my mind and heart regarding the entity of Stryper. What are we? Are we four friends making music together? Are we a corporation? If we are a corporation, who owns it? Years earlier I thoughtlessly gave my song rights away for nothing. What about the rest of Stryper? The records, the tours, the merchandise? Was I also giving my rights away here as well? The topic of us incorporating had come up before, but it never really went anywhere. Should I re-address the topic?

These things didn't matter to me when I was 21, but now I was a husband and a father who needed to be a responsible man. And a responsible man examines his business affairs.

I didn't have all the answers yet, and no doubt I was enjoying a hugely successful tour, but I knew that these questions in my head were about to start coming out of my mouth. I needed to start gathering answers, for my family's sake.

TWENTY-FIVE

The *To Hell With The Devil* tour took us through August of 1987. During the second half of that run, we began playing arenas for the first time. Times were changing for Stryper. Our popularity seemed to be growing by the minute. Money was coming in as fast as we could spend it, and that trend would continue over the next year or so.

We took a short break before we were right back in the studio working on our next record, *In God We Trust*.

In our post-tour meeting with Enigma, we shared that we wanted to produce the next album ourselves. Although Enigma gave us incredible freedom and support throughout our tenure with them, self-producing the next record was met with some reservations on their part. Our compromise was to bring in an acclaimed producer, one who had a track record and hit list in pop. That producer was Michael Lloyd.

Michael is a great person and one of the most humble guys I've ever met. Michael was known for having produced groups that were a lot more polished, poppy and slick, like Donnie and Marie Osmond, Shaun Cassidy, The Bellamy Brothers, and The Monkees. And in our meetings with Enigma, it was clear that they wanted our next album to follow in the footsteps of *To Hell With The Devil*, only bigger and better. We did our best to deliver just that.

In God We Trust would become our definition of an over-produced, over-abundant record. I wouldn't go so far as to say it's my least favorite album in the Stryper catalog, but it's certainly not my favorite. There are some great moments that shine through. That album contained some of our very best material and some of our worst. I'm of the opinion that songs like "In God We Trust," "The Writing's On The Wall" and "Lonely" are some of the highlights of that record yet songs like "Come To The Everlife" are some of the low points, at least for me.

In 2005 we did an informal poll with the fans asking what songs they thought we should play for an upcoming tour. We asked fans to rank the Stryper catalog from favorite to least favorite. "Come to the Everlife" came in rock bottom on that poll, and that was no surprise to me.

In general, I think that *In God We Trust* was about as unimaginative as any project we had recorded. I answered almost every shining moment from *To Hell With The Devil* by providing an equivalent. "Honestly" was a hit ballad? Then I'll give you "I Believe In You." A hard hitting, title track opener worked for the last album? I'll give you "In God We Trust." "Calling On You" was a pop-metal #1 video? I'll counter that with "Always There For You."

It was as if I went down the track list of our previous album and wrote its counterpart for this album. I hate to acknowledge it, but that's exactly what I did. What a disservice that was both to Stryper and to God, who has blessed me with the ability to be creative. Honestly, I was as un-creative as an artist could be on this album. And despite all of that, it turned out to be our second most successful album, selling only slightly less units than *To Hell With The Devil*.

I don't blame Michael Lloyd for this record being overproduced. I was the one who really navigated the ship in terms of production. I don't say that to try to win favor with anyone. Had Tim produced it, I would give credit where credit is due. Had Rob produced it, I'd give him the credit. But for all intents and purposes, I was the producer of most of *In God We Trust*. I just didn't get the credit, or the producer's paycheck.

146

It wasn't as if Michael Lloyd sat in the break room all day and collected his check. He did indeed play an instrumental role in helping us achieve a great album.

The album was recorded at three different studios: The Village Recorder, Cherokee Studios, and last but not least, the infamous A&M Studios. We spent more than $600,000 making the album, in comparison to the roughly $200,000 we spent making its predecessor. Most of that $600k was wasted, not on your typical strippers and cocaine that most rock bands wasted money on during that era. It was wasted simply by not managing our time wisely. We'd spend all day working on a guitar solo or a vocal part trying to perfect something that was better on the first take. The $2,500-per-day studio rate added up quickly.

Also, just prior to tracking the lead vocals, I got sick and my voice didn't recover so well. It took me almost a month to get the vocals wrapped. I was facing a couple of hurdles vocally during the process. The most obvious was the physical barrier I faced with my diminished vocal capacity due to illness. But the more prominent underlying challenge I faced was psychological.

These songs were written at the peak of my vocal range. I had a mental war going on inside my head thinking, "I can't sing this stuff. It's just too high." Daily, I struggled to achieve that perfect vocal take. We were purposely trying to get the tightest, most radio-ready recording we could possibly achieve. Eventually, we did, but accomplishing that "polished" sound was difficult.

It is part of the reason we rarely play any of the songs from that album in our set today. Truthfully, it's just too difficult to pull off, and the problem isn't just the vocal challenges. That album is layered and stacked with multiple guitar parts and an exorbitant number of backing vocals, keyboards and whatever else we could throw in. Often as we get together to rehearse for tour, we'll make a feeble attempt to perform acceptable renditions of a few of the songs from *In God We Trust*. *I feel that it's* easier said than done, not without playing to pre-recorded tracks, which is something we haven't done since the tour we did to support that album.

During that tour Robert played to a click track so that we could run backing tracks along with our live performances. Included in those tracks were extra guitars, keyboards, and a lot of extra vocal harmonies. I'm proud to say, that era of our life—the "playing to tracks" era—was short-lived. Even then, we always performed live. It's not as if we weren't playing our instruments—we were. We just had a little help, or a lot of help, enhancing the sound with some pre-recorded backing tracks. Funny thing is, you'd be shocked to learn not only how many bands did it then, but how many bands do it to this day.

In addition to label meetings laying out the sonic goals for this album, we were also coming to a crossroads with the business of Stryper. Dissention was brewing within the band over songwriting. There seemed to be a definitive division starting to build between the band and me concerning songwriting and royalties.

Songwriters usually make more money and this was starting to cause some friction within the band. I began to feel an obligation to split all the songs with the band in response to indirect comments and criticism.

In an effort to keep the peace, I lined up a meeting with our attorney Stephen Ashley to discuss my proposition. I told him that I wanted all the songwriting to be split equally, regardless of who wrote what songs. Oz wrote two songs on that album ("Come To The Everlife" and "The Reign"). I should never have agreed to those songs making the cut (at least not without undergoing some major changes), but in 1988 I was more interested in keeping the peace than ensuring we had the best songs possible on an album.

148

Because I remained silent, "Come to the Everlife" and "The Reign" are now forever etched in the Stryper archives of recorded music. I mentioned previously that I had two major barriers when singing this album: the physical constraints of being sick and the physiological constraints from the high vocal range. But, there was a third—I just wasn't "feeling" these two songs. I sang them, as best I could, but it was difficult as a singer/songwriter to relate to not only the lyrics of "The Reign," but also the music of "Come To The Everlife" as well. I didn't truly believe in those songs, and therefore I couldn't quite sing them with the same passion that it takes to make them believable.

Stephen Ashley privately consulted with me after our meeting on splitting the songwriting and strongly advised me against it. He told me that I would be giving away hundreds of thousands of dollars by doing so. But again, I wanted to keep the peace. I could tell that I was becoming the bad guy, or at least that's how I perceived it. How did that work out by the way? How was I becoming the bad guy? I wrote what I felt—and apparently what the fans felt—were some really good songs that obviously played a major role in our success. Somehow, though, I was feeling like the bad guy.

That's what being in a band can do sometimes. Somehow spending relentless hours alone refining and re-refining songs to become the greatest they can be for the band can be turned around to be a negative thing. What should have been gratitude appeared to be resentment, at least from my perspective.

I allowed mediocre songs to creep into our repertoire just to make everyone happy. I gave away what probably amounted to hundreds of thousands of dollars in songwriting royalties just to smooth things over. Everyone seemed happy for now, except me.

Fortunately Stephen had the wisdom to convince me not to allow my idea of splitting songwriting to stand in perpetuity. After a certain number of years, the songwriting credits would revert to the original writers. So short term, the term when the bulk of the money was earned on a song, we all split the money equally. Long term, the term when minimal money rolls in, I retained the songwriting credit for the songs I wrote. We all agreed to this arrangement and moved forward. For seven years I gave 25 percent to each band member and songwriting credit on songs they didn't write.

Songwriting was and still seems to be the black cloud that hangs over the head of Stryper. I'm a bit of a perfectionist. Well, not a bit—I'm an extreme perfectionist when it comes to music. I want the songs to be brilliant—every single one of them. Unfortunately I seemed to be the only one in the band who felt that way. With the other guys, it was as if it didn't really matter if the best songs made the album, just as long as everyone was contributing and everyone was equal. Who cares if a sub-par song makes its way on the album, as long as everyone gets a fair shake?

That's a fine philosophy for fairy tales, but in the brutal, and fickle, world of music, it's nonsense. And in this ruthless world of music, there are usually managers and labels involved who can tell the band "Look guys, here are the 10 best songs. I don't care who wrote them. These are the ones going on the album." We didn't have that. We had my mom, who just didn't seem to have it in her to say these sorts of things, at least to the band as a whole. Or perhaps equally as possible, she just didn't *know how* to say this.

So, I was the bad guy. I was the one saying "Nope, that song's not good enough for the record." And, honestly, I said that to myself more than anyone. For every good song that I wrote, there were dozens of ideas that never saw the light of day, all because I knew I could do better. It was somehow okay to say to myself, "Michael, you can do better. You can write a better song than what you've got here." It was just very difficult to say those things to my band mates about *their* songs.

150

Even to this day there's dissention within the band over songs, but today it's less about the songs and seemingly more about the money those songs generate. Sadly, today they generate a small fraction of what they once did, but still the black cloud of songwriting lingers in the Stryper camp. Despite my best efforts to deliver the best songs possible to the band and for the band, the songs don't always seem to be a welcomed addition with everyone.

If you're a professional race car driver and your livelihood depends on your car's engine running flawlessly, it would make sense that you would hire a mechanic who had successfully built and repaired many cars in his lifetime. If you were a professional racecar driver, you wouldn't trust someone who had only built three or four engines in his entire life.

The number of songs I've written in my life, not to mention the success that many of them have had, seems as though it should make my input as a songwriter a welcomed asset to the band. Instead, even today, and despite having released seven solo records, several of which appeared on Billboard and radio charts, I feel like the enemy sometimes when I bring in a set of songs for Stryper to record. I'm often made to feel as though I should allow the others to have songs on Stryper records, even though there's no real track record representing their ability to successfully do so.

At times when this has come up for discussion, Oz has been quick to point out "The Way," a fan favorite that he wrote. I will give him that. "The Way" is a good song that the metal heads love, and it's the type of song that would have probably been a number one for Iron Maiden. But those types of songs are few and far between. As talented as Oz is, that doesn't always translate in the ability to compose material that's worthy of making the cut. Hopefully my steadfastness and determination is part of what sets us apart and makes us who we are today.

Next up on the business agenda for Stryper was for us to incorporate. This need for incorporation had been lingering for years. Here it was 1988. We had sold millions of albums and toured the world several times over, and yet we weren't even a legal corporation.

So we set out to finally address this elephant in the room. With our same attorney doing his best to give our mess of a business some structure, we began discussing incorporating. We all agreed to make this happen and when it came time for the final, and merely symbolic, moment of determining the officers of the corporation — president, vice president, secretary, etc. — we once again found ourselves at opposite ends of the playing field. We couldn't decide on a president. Everyone felt like *he* should be president. A simple and insignificant title put the brakes on the idea of incorporating.

Anyone who has ever formed a corporation knows these titles mean nothing. We all would have equal shares in the corporation. Not one of us was going to have more power than the other. The titles were simply something we needed to put on a piece of paper to be filed with the state and in the attorney's file cabinet.

But we went back and forth for weeks trying to determine who would be the president of Stryper, Inc. We simply couldn't come to an agreement, again, even though the title meant absolutely nothing beyond the walls of our attorney's office. At one point Stephen even said "Guys. I don't care if f**king Winnie-The-Pooh is president. It doesn't matter. It's just a piece of paper. Just pick someone and let's write it down."

But we couldn't pick a president. And we didn't. So we continued on with no sense of business structure to our organization. Years later this would prove to be one of our worst financial mistakes as a "business" that we ever made.

Despite our failure to incorporate, it was time to go do a tour to support *In God We Trust*. I was tired. I was burned out. I was worn out spiritually. The brotherhood that we once had was no longer palpable. The peacekeeping was wearing me out. But I needed to set all of that aside for the moment. I needed to go put on a yellow-and-black costume and sing songs that I was creatively, and physically, struggling to embrace. Somehow I needed to rise above the waste and find a way to keep the fire burning.

TWENTY-SIX

Our outrageous spending on *In God We Trust* continued with the two videos we shot to support the album — "Always There For You" and "I Believe In You." We spent more for those two than we had spent on our other five videos combined.

The largest plane ever constructed, with the widest wingspan in aviation history, was stored in an enormous hanger in Long Beach. The plane was the Hughes H-4 Hercules, nicknamed the "Spruce Goose." Disney had acquired the plane and the hanger where it was being stored and subsequently moved the Spruce Goose to Oregon, leaving a ridiculously large climate-controlled hanger completely empty.

We felt that hanger would be the right place to rent for shooting our next video, "Always There For You." "Bigger is *always* better" should have been our slogan in 1988. Bigger hair, bigger homes, bigger cars, bigger shoulder pads, and bigger hangers to stage bigger videos.

I was the guy overseeing our music, and Robert was the guy overseeing the production of videos, album covers, and the image of the band. The problem was that Robert was also really good at spending money. Obviously I was too. We all were, for that matter. I could have lived out many years of my life on just a portion of the money we spent making IGWT. Combine that with what we spent making the videos and we all could have lived comfortably for quite a while. But why do *that* when we could spend it on a helicopter flying us onto a Stryper landing pad for the opening scene of a video? It was eye-catching, no doubt. But was it worth all the money? I don't think so.

I watched the crews building the set for this video and thought, *"God, how much is all this costing? It must be a fortune."* Roughly

$260,000 was the answer to my question. But who was I to argue? Michael Jackson had shot several of his videos here, including his infamous "Dirty Diana." If it was good enough for Michael, it was good enough for us.

The stage in that video lit up from underneath flashing the words "In God We Trust." We had flown platforms that hung from the ceiling. They even custom-made the Stryper logo so that it would protrude from the stage floor. And all of these exorbitant video amenities were accented in the irony that the stage was a replica of a $100 bill. It wouldn't surprise me if that were made out of real hundreds.

As much as I quietly played along with this wasteful spending, in the back of my mind I kept thinking, *"We can't keep going down this path. This is not going to end well."*

The video for "Always There For You" peaked at #1 on the MTV countdown. It was released almost simultaneously with the album, helping to continue the momentum of the band as we prepared to hit the road.

The album was released in June of 1988, but we didn't hit the road until September, kicking off that tour at Disney World. That run took us all over the country playing arenas, back to Japan, Australia, New Zealand and wrapping up on April 9, 1989 in Honolulu.

The spending spree would continue as we toured to support the album. We traveled with three semi-trucks and three tour buses. Granted, in the big picture of rock 'n' roll, that may seem like more than normal, but some bands were taking five, six, or even seven semis and buses on the road. It wasn't necessarily that three trucks and three buses were too much, it was just that our income wasn't lining up with our expenses. We had the income that may have warranted one or two buses, but were spending for three. But that seemed to be the Stryper way. Spend the money and figure out how to make it back later.

The *In God We Trust* tour should have been dubbed *The Practical Joke* tour. It was on this tour, with White Lion as our opening act, where we came into our own as practical jokers.

I loved touring with White Lion. They were an incredibly talented band, particularly Vito Bratta, the guitarist. All the guys were nice, and we enjoyed hanging out with them.

Oz and I discovered CB radios on this tour, and at each arena during the day, we'd walk around the venue talking to each other in trucker lingo. "Breaker, Breaker One-Nine. What's your twenty?" One day as the crew was on stage sound checking, I started into my CB routine and I noticed it was blaring through Vito's guitar amp. So that gave me the wise idea to try it during the show. Right in the middle of White Lion's show I keyed up, "Breaker One-Nine," and it came out through Vito's amps and through the entire sound system. The whole crowd heard it and Vito's head spun around quickly looking at his amp. He kept walking back to the amp adjusting knobs. I eventually confessed and Vito thought it was funny, at least so I thought.

This started a back-and-forth scheme of practical jokes between White Lion and Stryper. The next night of the tour was Rob's turn to be the brunt of the joke. He would climb up to his kit using a striped pole that always reminded me of a yellow-and-black stripper's pole. On this particular night, Rob jumped up on the pole and slid right to the ground. We had an intro tape playing and he had only a moment before we were supposed to start the show at the end of the tape. He kept trying and trying to get up to his kit, but the White Lion guys had smeared Vaseline all over the pole. It got all over Rob's hands and he couldn't get it off. He finally made his way up to the kit using the rear steps, but after the show he was pretty upset. He didn't find it too funny, but that didn't deter the prank war between the two bands.

We decided the next night, moments before White Lion took the stage, that we would peel the backs off the backstage passes that are printed on one side and sticky on the other. We literally covered every inch of the stage with these passes, sticky side up! Have you ever seen a cat when it gets tape stuck to its paws? As White Lion ran around the stage, the stickers kept collecting to the point where they were sticking out several feet on each side of their shoes, and they kept raising their legs and kicking their feet, trying to shake the stickers loose. I don't know if I've ever laughed harder in my life.

This went back and forth for a while until it really started to get out of control. At one point, White Lion ran out during our set and unplugged our mic cables. While the cables dangled from the mic stands, our pre-recorded backing vocals continued to blare.

Now wait a second—don't get righteous on me here. Yes, we had pre-recorded backing vocals during *In God We Trust*. We sang live with them, but we had tracks to help us. And truth be known, we weren't the only ones using tracks. Practically every band was using them in the '80s, or at least most bands that had big vocals and big production.

Anyway, what started out as innocent play seemed to turn into pre-planned sabotage.

We called a truce when Mike Tramp came on stage one night mocking our Bible-tossing by wearing a devil's mask and tossing Penthouse Forum magazines into the audience. It felt like we were all going down a darker path, and it wasn't about having fun as much as it was about embarrassing each other. We spoke and ended the back-and-forth prank war. It didn't stop us from playing jokes within our own band — it just ended the Stryper vs. White Lion battle.

The internal pranks continued on that tour. Sometimes we would put duct tape over a guy's bunk so after sleeping all night and being completely out of it, he'd try to perform the simple task of climbing out of his bunk and he couldn't get out without a fight. Another favorite involved putting shaving cream all over someone's sheets in their bunk, so when they'd climb in it would blend in with the sheets, and they'd splat in a bed of foam.

One time we sneaked into Oz's hotel room before he checked in, and we unlatched the window that was in his shower (you got it, it was a biker motel) and. When Oz showered, we opened the window and dumped all the old food from the bus on his head — yogurt, fruit, deli tray, everything.

Some bands broke TVs and destroyed hotel rooms. We, however, threw lunchmeat on our guitarist's head while he showered.

I enjoyed that tour with White Lion, although I do recall a "what-the-hell-was-that?" moment between Mike Tramp and us. Not long into the tour, Mike came back to our dressing room after he had performed and before we went on and in his thick Danish accent told us what we really needed was to get some style. He shared with us very directly that if we wanted to be big, we needed a new style. He made his point and then left the room.

We didn't really know what to say. It was hilarious to us and we all laughed about it, but it caught us off guard. Whether you liked our sense of fashion or not, it was most definitely memorable. But Mike felt it needed change and wasn't shy about telling us so. The funny thing is I actually agree with him now.

Mikey was two years old at the end of this tour, and for the better part of those two years I hadn't seen him or Kyle much. It was killing me. I was asking God for wisdom and guidance on a regular basis as to what my next move should be with Stryper, if anything at all.

Despite the fun we were having on this tour, there was still some obvious tension among us all. *In God We Trust* had respectable sales numbers, but in the big business of music, respectable isn't good enough. You're always expected to surpass the sales of your previous album—otherwise you know your future with the label is going to be on shaky ground. We had the best label I could have ever imagined for a band like ours. Enigma was incredibly supportive, but still I knew change was coming and at the top of the list would likely be our spending habits.

I had a family at home. I had an album that had not done as well as it needed to. And sometimes I felt like an outsider within my own band.

"What should I do next, God?" was a daily question within my prayers.

TWENTY-SEVEN

Over the years of hundreds of interviews, inevitably I get the common question, "Can you share any crazy stories from the road?" My go-to story happened during the *In God We Trust* tour and is truly a standout moment in my memory.

We were almost at the end of our tour, March of '89, in Sydney, Australia, at the Sports Arena. Little did I know that night would be a topic in interviews for the rest of my life.

The crowd was enthusiastic and the front section was general admission so everyone was packed against the barricade. Our fifth song of the set was "Free." Right in front of me I noticed a guy with a beard, long hair tied back with a red bandanna, earrings, tattoos, beard stubble and missing teeth. A modern-day pirate. He was pointing at my feet. Actually, he was creating a scene frantically pointing and yelling at my feet. He was obviously upset about whatever it was he was pointing at.

I continued to play and sing trying to ignore this guy the best I could, but every time I looked his way, he'd yell even louder and point even harder.

I did however notice something at my feet. It looked like a wadded up piece of gum. It looked as though someone had chewed their gum and spit it out on the stage.

I thought, *"This guy is trying to warn me that I'm about to step in gum."* Still though, that was a lot of effort just to keep me from stepping in gum.

So I glanced at him and gave a thumb up, as if to say, "Okay, I got it. I see the gum. Now stop acting crazy and let me concentrate on the show."

But he didn't stop.

Despite him knowing that *I* knew about the gum, he started yelling even louder, pointing at my feet even more aggressively. This guy just wasn't going to quit until I dealt with the issue at hand.

So I struck a power chord during the second verse of the song and leaned down with my right hand to flick it away. I sent it six or seven rows back into the audience and when I did, my middle finger felt the pain. It was more like flicking a marble then a piece of gum.

Keep in mind we're a loud band — a seriously loud band. But the moment I sailed whatever it was away, I could hear this guy even louder than before. He was yelling at the top of his lungs, so loud I could hear him above everything else.

I tried not to focus on him but he was impossible to ignore. Finally, I was able to make out what he was screaming. "That was my f**king eye!" he shouted as he pointed to his empty eye socket.

At that moment it hit me. I had just sent this guy's glass eye into the crowd! Apparently he had been banging his head so hard that his eye popped right out of the socket and rolled over to where I was standing. I had just destroyed any hope of him getting it back. With a flick of the wrist, it was gone forever.

He was furious. He continued screaming at me throughout the show, occasionally taking breaks to look around the floor in futile attempts to find his eye. I felt terrible, but what could I do? "Hey guys. We need to stop the show for a moment, turn on all the house lights, and take a moment to look for this guy's glass eye that I just flung into the crowd." No, there was nothing I could do.

I tried to focus for the rest of the show, doing everything I could to not look at this guy, which was impossible. Not only was he the biggest guy I had seen in all of Australia, he was the loudest as well.

For the remainder of the night I made one mistake after another. I forgot lyrics that I had been singing for years. I fumbled over guitar parts that normally I could play in my sleep. And in between every single song of the set, that guy would yell at the top of his lungs "That was my f**king eye, mate." He didn't let up on me the entire set. I thought for sure he was going to jump on stage and get a few shots in.

I attempted to speed the set up, noticeably so, going from song to song quicker that normal. Usually I have a few scheduled breaks to talk to the audience where I'll catch my breath as well. Not tonight. The band must have been wondering what was up because I skipped breaks all together, just to get to the next song faster so that I wouldn't have to listen to this guy or face the humiliation any longer. The crowd also must have wondered what was up because I barely took a pause the entire night, taking one song right into the next.

I made it through the show somehow, and I must have washed my hands a dozen times afterward. We had three more shows in Australia on that run. I kept thinking this guy would show up out of nowhere and to get revenge or take my eye. You know, "An eye for an eye." But he didn't.

He lost an eye and I got a weird, great story to tell in interviews for the rest of my life. I never did hear from that guy again, but if he's reading this, I'm really sorry, man! I thought it was gum.

Over the years fans have heard me tell this story so often, they will occasionally throw a fake eye on stage during the show. By the way, please don't do that. I might have flashbacks of that dreadful night!

TWENTY-EIGHT

From the fall of 1989 through the winter of 1991, there were two notably great things that happened. The greater of the two, to which there is no comparison, was the birth of my beautiful daughter, Ellena. The other was the making and release of our fifth record, *Against The Law*, which, despite being considered a commercial failure by industry standards, was, in my opinion, a solid album.

Aside from those two things, most of that time period is somewhat fuzzy. It's fuzzy primarily because, for the most part, I did my best to suppress the memories from that era. They're not particularly fond ones. It may also be a bit blurry because we were drinking a lot during that time.

Allow me to clarify "a lot." I've read other rock-star biographies, and our drinking was mild by comparison. Still, it was enough to cloud my judgment and send me into a downward spiral farther from God than I had ever been since re-committing my life to Christ.

The break between the end of the *In God We Trust* tour and the beginning of the *Against The Law* tour was the longest time we were off the road between tours, although it wasn't much of a break. I went straight into writing mode, only there was one potential problem—the song ideas and creativity coming out of me were very different musically and lyrically.

For the past four years or so we had been beat up pretty hard by the church. There's just so much a band can take from so-called Christians screaming into bullhorns outside their shows, calling them fakes and wolves in sheep's clothing. It can wear you down after a while, and it definitely got the best of me to the point that I had little desire to write spiritually uplifting lyrics. What we really wanted to say to the Pharisees who had judged us for so many years was, "Screw you. We don't live by your laws. Who are you to tell us what we can or can't do, what we can or can't wear or say, or who we can be?" So I did, in so many words.

I knew I still loved God—I just didn't like some of the *people* who claimed to love God too.

I was ready for change in a number of ways. At this point thoughts of leaving Stryper came more frequently, but I couldn't bear the thought of telling the guys. Also, there was still a glimmer of hope in me that the ship just might turn around, that by some miracle I might wake up feeling good about being in Stryper. I felt that maybe we did have one more good record to make.

But things had to change. I began inquiring more into our finances. For the past several years we'd owned this really large (almost 5,000-square-feet) house sitting on a golf course that was used for the Stryper offices. Rob also lived in this house. I eventually found out that he'd been staying there rent-free, and I wasn't too happy with that. I had just assumed he was paying rent to Stryper to live there.

My mom and I seemed to be growing farther and farther apart. From my perspective, it was largely due to my constant questioning of the management of the finances. I didn't think she was stealing from us—I just felt things had been mismanaged for way too long. It wasn't as black and white as stealing—it was more like a grey area of questionable spending habits.

One day I went over to the Stryper house/office and noticed a bunch of new indoor plants and expensive landscaping. Again, I questioned it. Where did it come from? Who paid for it? Come to find out, *I* paid for it. Well, *we* as a band paid for it. Why didn't anyone ask me or the other guys if this was a worthwhile expense? Had they asked, I wouldn't have agreed to it, which is probably why they didn't ask. I could understand an occasional small business expense without our consent, but when thousands of dollars are being spent and it's your money, it's time to say no.

Additionally, we had wasted so much money on the *In God We Trust* tour, there was no way we could be financially sound. I was continually reassured that everything was fine. Still, it was driving a wedge between my mom and me, and to some extent between the band members as well.

Likely through my persistence, we did manage to eventually get rid of that extravagant house. Robert finally moved into a place of his own, and we housed the Stryper offices there. Robert paid for that house, and we rented a portion of it from him to use as office space as we should have all along. I took comfort in knowing that we had made a small step in a positive financial direction by downsizing.

I began to write the music for *Against the Law* and brought it to the band. What came out as I was writing surprised me. We were angry, we were bitter and we wanted nothing at all to do with the part of the church that had given us grief for so many years. So I wrote songs like "Against The Law," "Lady," and "Caught In The Middle." These songs weren't necessarily anti-Christian, but they weren't uplifting songs either. I toned down the lyrics the best I could, but in my heart I was basically flipping off anyone and everyone that had ever given us a hard time for the stance we had taken with the band.

We began rehearsing these songs as a group at Robert's place. That's when the drinking started (at least collectively). We'd come in with a case of beer and before the end of the day our rehearsals were useless, so we'd go shopping for guns (read on). It wasn't as if we were waking up and reaching for a bottle of Jack before breakfast, but each day as rehearsals took place, we started drinking a little earlier. Sometimes, we would just drink and not even get through a rehearsal.

Somehow, with everything going on, we felt for some odd reason that it was a good time in our lives to start buying guns. Yep, firearms. Robert was really into all types of guns, and he had an entire walk-in closet full of them.

We'd rehearse for half-an-hour or so and get bored and decide to go gun shopping.

Kyle thought I was crazy. I'd leave for rehearsals and then come home with a semi-automatic AK-47. She'd say, *"Why did you buy this?"* and I would try to justify it by claiming protection or our rights as Americans or, better yet, "because it's awesome!"

And if that wasn't bad enough, we'd go out into the desert shooting and drinking. Now there's a good match. One time we were out shooting near some sand dunes and this guy comes driving around the side of one of the dunes in his Jeep. Apparently he had been there all along and we almost shot him and his girlfriend. He was ready to kill us, and rightfully so. He said he could almost feel the bullets whizzing by his head. They were probably my bullets.

We just weren't thinking. I guess it was all that pent-up aggression over the years and it was coming out in the form of clichés, booze and guns!

Don't get me wrong—I am a believer in the right to bear arms. I believe the bad guys are going to own and use guns whether they're legal or not. Bad guys are going to do what they do, so I believe every American has the right to protect his or her self. But I believe in sensible and responsible gun ownership. I was neither sensible nor responsible then. I'm surprised someone didn't get hurt or killed during that period.

By the time rehearsals for this album had wrapped, I bet I had purchased more than 20 guns. And, yes, I too see the hypocrisy in all of this. I'm questioning the money that Stryper is spending yet I was putting thousands of dollars into a gun collection? Nothing in my life was rational during this timeframe.

As I suspected, when it came time to take meetings with the label about the next record, our budgets were cut considerably. We would be making this next record for about one-third the budget we had for *In God We Trust*. To me, this was actually a good thing. I was ready for change, in more ways than one.

All within a series of a few short meetings we agreed to drop the yellow and black, change the Stryper logo, change the image and create a project that was the polar opposite of anything we had done in the past. We wanted a raw and in-your-face approach, musically and lyrically.

We chose Tom Werman to produce the record. Tom was partially responsible for getting Boston signed to Epic Records in the '70s and was also known for having produced Cheap Trick, Ted Nugent, Blue Oyster Cult, Motley Crue, and Poison. Tom's a smart guy. He eventually got out of this unpredictable business and opened a Bed & Breakfast called Stonover Farm in Lenox, Massachusetts. In 1990 he was the most sought after producer in town, and we wanted the best. I give equally as much credit to Eddie DeLena, who was the engineer on *Against The Law* and who was responsible for getting most of the tones for that record. There was a solid chemistry between Tom, Eddie, and the band.

As pre-production and songwriting continued on this album, Oz brought in a song called "Not Yo Huggy Guy." Rob and I talked about it and agreed that the title would not make its way onto this record, so I suggested the phrase "Not That Kinda Guy." Oz tried to convince me that the phrase "Not Yo Huggy Guy" would become a popular catch phrase, but I just didn't catch the vision. I never really cared for the song personally, mainly because I was afraid of getting sued by Van Halen for it was too close for comfort to being a replica of their hit song "Hot for Teacher."

Eventually the songs came together and we hit the studio with Tom and Eddie to get this record done. To no surprise, the alcohol consumption continued.

I remember the first night we were in the studio and Tom looked at us and said, *"You guys drink? Well, okay."* Here was this Jewish guy who's probably seen it all from previous bands he had produced, thinking he'd get to take a break from all of that with this Christian band, and we proved him wrong. We had every opportunity in the world to be good examples to Tom and we blew it. I can say with assurance, nobody came to know Christ during those sessions. They came to know Jack and Jim, Bolla and Bud pretty well and that's about it. It's pretty embarrassing—here we were a supposed Christian band being as bad an influence as any band Tom had worked with, or so it seemed.

This was a dark time in my life that I'm really not proud of, yet at the same time it taught me a lot and brought me to who I am today. I look back on it all and wonder, *"How did it get to that point?"* I can tell you this: it didn't happen overnight. It slowly crept into our lives, and before we knew it, we were exemplifying the hypocrisy that drove us to this anger and frustration in the first place. That's the way the devil works. He slowly convinces you that you're not wrong. He convinces you, without you even noticing, that there's no longer a need to hold each other accountable. It must be okay if we're all doing "it," whatever sin "it" may be in the moment.

We were an angry band during this era. We were angry at the church, and we were sometimes angry at one another. We were also angry that our popularity and success had started to slip away.

But we made a record, miraculously, despite all the irresponsibility. And now came time to shoot the videos, again on a much smaller budget than we were accustomed to having.

During the making of that album, I shared with Tom Werman my frustrations with what I felt was mismanagement of the band. I knew we were at a major crossroads with Stryper and if we didn't make some drastic changes, it would be impossible to turn things around. We were changing our sound, look and style but it just didn't feel like it was enough.

After sharing with Tom my interest in seeking new management, he introduced us to Danny Goldberg and Ron Stone of Gold Mountain Management. They were the biggest management company in the business at the time. The two of them have managed some of the biggest and most respected artists in the business, artists such as Neil Young, The Eagles, Bob Dylan, Nirvana, Foo Fighters, Bonnie Raitt, Joni Mitchell and the list goes on.

We took a liking to both of them, and we felt this was the right fit for Stryper. After our meeting with Gold Mountain, they agreed to take us on.

Rob and I agreed it was time to let Mom go as our manager. We met with her, and although it was difficult, we let her know that we'd be entering into a contract with Gold Mountain. We told her that we wanted to try something new and that Gold Mountain would be the best place to start.

Firing a relative, especially your mom, is never an easy thing to do. Rob and I spent a lot of time talking about it ahead of time, wondering how she would take it and how we should tell her. No matter what kind of a job we felt she was doing at the time, she was still our mom. We did, and do, love her. It was a difficult thing, probably more for us than her, to let her go.

I suppose she took it as well as could be expected. Mom encouraged and supported me every step of the way. Her response to the change was fairly typical of the way she usually responds to conflict. She said something along the lines of, "Fine. I was going to quit anyway."

Who knows? Maybe she was thinking about getting out of the business and this was a relief to her. I know it was a relief to me. We also removed our mom of the financial responsibilities by hiring Haber, a business management firm.

Danny and Ron continued to drop by the studio listening to tracks and they seemed to really like what they were hearing. It felt right. No longer were we under mom's management, and we now had a solid professional team in place to help us with the next phase in our career.

Our first video, and single from *Against The Law* was "Shining Star," a song on which we had brought in Randy Jackson, now of American Idol fame, to play bass. I still can't watch that show without thinking of the session we had with Randy, who was a really nice guy.

"Shining Star" was our first video featuring a group of women dressed to kill. That wasn't much of a stretch for the typical rock band of that era, but for us it was a totally new approach. Still, it was tame by comparison. The concept of that video was some sort of futuristic roller coaster loaded with women. We had fun making it, and I'm still very proud of our rendition of that song. The video? I could take it or leave it. But I feel our version of that song really pays proper respect to Earth, Wind, and Fire, and for that we're proud.

We shot two other videos, the most controversial being "Lady." Again, featuring a woman that I was supposedly singing to and singing about. But this time we took it a bit further. We put this girl in a bathtub, bubbles and all, and she gave a sultry performance for the camera throughout the shoot.

The "Lady" video caused some grief between Kyle and me. She was a little hurt that I was a married Christian man singing a song to another woman, or at least that's how it was perceived. In hindsight, she was right. We wound up taking it on the chin from the Christian community for making that video. It's a great song that was somewhat tarnished by a questionable video.

The same day we shot "Lady," we decided to get our money's worth by keeping the cameras rolling and shooting another video for "Two Time Woman." We basically put our hair in ponytails, changed our clothes and kept shooting in the same location. Aside from the extra editing costs, we got two videos for the price of one. But that was the kind of tight budget we were on. Seven years after signing our first record deal, we were just now learning the concept of frugal spending.

Against the Law was released in August of 1990. How we ever got it finished and maintained quality and productivity, I'll never know. God was definitely watching over us, despite us not giving Him a second thought at the time.

Kyle was almost three months pregnant when the record coming out. This seemed like a good time to hit the road and continue a lifestyle of debauchery and sin.

TWENTY-NINE

In support of *Against The Law,* we performed only 23 shows in about five weeks, the least we had ever toured for a release. Part of that run was with the band Bride as support, and the other part with the band Trixter.

I was impressed with both bands. Bride was a great band who crafted solid songs and delivered them with passion. They were definitely committed to their faith, but they weren't too preachy. They were just regular guys that tried to lead by example. I wish their example had rubbed off on us a little more during that tour, but I really enjoyed the time we got to spend with those guys.

The Trixter leg was particularly eye opening and humbling. We were playing mostly small clubs and theaters on this run. Most places we played were roughly 1,000-capacity venues. Planning this tour there were catch-industry phrases thrown around among our managers and agents like "getting back to your roots" and "stepping things up." Sometimes those are proper descriptions of what an artist is doing, but in most cases they're polite ways of describing an artist's declining popularity.

Our first show with Trixter was to about 1,100 people. As I looked out at the crowd, about half of them were young girls wearing Trixter t-shirts. Not only could we not sell out arenas any longer, but also we apparently couldn't even sell out small clubs. We needed the help of a band like Trixter, a band who much like us, was getting little respect from the critics.

The members of Trixter were a great bunch of guys who had just hit it big with their single "Give It To Me Good," so they were living the rock-star lifestyle for the first time. And in some regard, so were we. Until now we had sheltered ourselves in the goody-two-shoes persona, but not in 1990. We were drinking it up right alongside Trixter, and anyone else who cared to join us. I liked Trixter, and I still remain in contact with my friend Steve Brown, the guitarist and founding member of the band.

The first night of that tour was particularly memorable at Rock and Roll Heaven in Toronto. Aside from the many Trixter fans in the crowd, I also noticed Rob Halford of Judas Priest in attendance as well. Apparently Judas Priest was in town performing a few nights later at the arena. It was quite a compliment to see Rob in the crowd taking in a Stryper show. Toward the end of the set, I took a chance and asked Rob to the stage to join us for a song. He did. We played "Breaking The Law," a song we often sound checked with, and it was surreal to stand alongside one of my biggest influences. In my opinion, Rob is one of the best singers and performers of our generation. . For a moment, I was able to forget all the hardships and questions going on in my mind, and I just took in those four minutes with one of metal's most notable singers.

We continued to tour with Trixter, and I continued to see teenage girls in Trixter t-shirts piling into the clubs we were playing night after night. I continued to think to myself, *"We're blowing it. We're not honoring God."* We had always tried to honor Him, but we weren't doing so during this tour. And why would God bless us when we were dishonoring Him by being complete hypocrites night after night? You can't make a mockery of God. Good luck trying if you want, but it won't work. We know this firsthand.

Aside from the traditional live performance touring, we did a promotional tour leading up to the release of *Against the Law*. Robert and Tim went out together and conducted interviews in a portion of the country, and Oz and I went together covering another part of the country.

We would fly or drive into cities and hit every radio station we could. We shook a lot of hands, rubbed a lot of elbows, and did a lot of interviews, all in hopes of this record getting some airtime.

After all the elbow rubbing and hand shaking subsided, we'd go out on the town, sometimes escorted by people from the label or local radio stations. They usually knew the hot spots in town and we were always willing to tag along. We even went to Solid Gold, a strip club in Minnesota, and sat at a booth with the guys in Cheap Trick. I believe David Cassidy was there as well. They said everything about our hypocrisy with a simple glance. I remember when we met Lemmy from Motorhead in a pub in Germany and discussed God as we drank more beer then he did! We were digging our holes deeper and deeper, and the guilt and shame was starting to set in.

One day in particular stands out in my mind. Oz and I met two women at a restaurant/bar who recognized us and struck up a conversation. The drinks were flowing and we talked about getting together later that night. Oz and I, with our two new female friends, continued drinking at the hotel. Oz eventually left with one, leaving me alone with the other.

There's something about booze, a private hotel room, and being hundreds of miles away from home that will allow you to let your guard down and make poor, dishonorable decisions. Within a few minutes after Oz and his companion left, I started kissing this woman. Eventually we found ourselves stretched out on the bed.

By the way, I'm not withholding her name to protect her. I don't remember her name. That's how fuzzy my memory is regarding this time of my life.

But what I do remember vividly is how that night ended so abruptly. I had my shirt off, and she had taken most of her clothes off. We were rolling around on the bed, not thinking about reality. Passion was flowing, as it often does between two strangers alone in a hotel room filled with vodka and gin.

I have no idea what came over me. Well, actually I do have an idea. I'm a firm believer that God speaks to us when we need to hear Him the most. I got up from the bed, half naked, with a beautiful, strange woman lying there staring at me like I was crazy. She asked what was wrong.

"I'm married. I can't do this. I'm sorry," I said, not really even believing the words as they were coming out of my mouth but thankful that they were.

She stood up from the bed, slightly embarrassed, as was I. She started putting her clothes back on after realizing that coaxing me back into bed wasn't going to work. We made some small talk and she left the room within 10 minutes.

Usually when I hung out with women on this tour, it was in the back of the bus. Prior to this moment, I had never taken a woman back to my hotel room alone.

I cheated on my wife, Kyle.

I never had sex with another woman while married to Kyle, but what I did was undoubtedly cheating. We had women around all the time during the *Against The Law* era, usually on the bus. I'm shocked nothing scandalous came out during that period. As a Christian man and a married one at that, I had no business behaving the way I did. For years I had been telling people "You don't need this path," and here I was going directly down the same path I had warned people about for years.

The feelings of guilt were insurmountable during this era. Feelings of wanting out of Stryper were starting to take serious root in my soul at this point, and I think it's partially due to the guilt that I was feeling about what being in this band was doing to my marriage. But I was doing very little to correct it. I wasn't seeking God like I should have. I just continued going down the path of temptation, knowing that I was playing with fire, yet not really caring at all. Well, I'd care for a while, and then I wouldn't, and then I'd care again.

It wasn't as if I was addicted to anything, but I very much compare this sort of behavior to an addiction. You know you don't need, or even want, that next cigarette, but you smoke it anyway. I knew intellectually and spiritually that I shouldn't be living like this, but my actions weren't lining up with my intentions.

That moment with the woman in the hotel room really started to push me toward changing my ways and cleaning up my act.

The other moment that had a profound impact on me during this time was what I touched on earlier in Minneapolis with David Cassidy and the guys in Cheap Trick. There was a promotional event and a party at the biggest strip club in town afterward. Oz and I met David who, at one point early on during the night, turned to Oz and I and said, "Man, I thought you guys were a Christian band." He wasn't being mean or judgmental, just curious and perceptive.

That moment was another sword in my heart. I'm thinking to myself "We *are* a Christian band." But we certainly weren't acting like it. Again, we were the definition of the word hypocrite. I was going on stage night after night singing about Jesus, and yet not giving Him a second thought the other twenty-two-and-a-half hours of the day.

All of this was taking place while Kyle is home pregnant with our daughter and second child, Ellena Rae.

This short-lived *Against The Law* era is what really led me toward the Stryper exit door. I wanted out. And this is where it all began. Now I just needed to figure out *how* to get out.

I wasn't putting any of the blame for this debauchery on Rob, Tim, or Oz. It was all on me. Although we all participated in the lifestyle, the only person to blame for my actions was myself. I felt the only way for me to put a stop to my downward spiral was to remove myself from the situation. I needed to apply the brakes soon and I needed to come to a screeching halt soon, before I destroyed myself and seriously harmed others.

I look back on these times and I'm amazed that my marriage didn't fall apart. Kyle had every right to leave. Tim and his first wife, Valerie, divorced eventually. Oz and his first wife, Leslie, eventually did as well. And Robert was in a serious relationship that also ended. All our relationships took a beating during this period.

It's important to note, at least to me, the comparison between the *Against The Law* era and the earlier years. All the early days were the real deal. There was no questioning in my mind, nor should there be in anyone else's, about our genuineness of our faith and relationship to Christ. We were completely committed to God back then. But somehow the muck and garbage started creeping in and as time went by, it was as if hell was seeping in right behind it. It was almost like it was 1981 on Sunset Strip all over again. We reverted back to our old ways, the old man if you will, and I felt a tremendous amount of guilt over it all.

What is truly a miracle about this weak time in our lives, late '89 to '91, is that it didn't blow up in our face. Call it what you will, but I say humbly that it must have been God's protection — protection that we neither deserved nor were wise enough to ask for. But all of this could have exploded at any time. I'm equally amazed that with all the booze flowing, I never actually ended up sleeping with anyone. I did plenty of promiscuous acts, but somehow it never went beyond that. It had to be God's protection over us, with Him knowing that one day we'd come to our senses. And He waited patiently for us to do so, as only God can and will do.

We were primed and ready for a huge scandal. We were acting like idiots and for years the press had looked for any reason to bring us down and call us out as imposters. Now was the time they could have done so, and we were making it all too easy. Sometimes we wouldn't even try to hide our actions. After many a show, we'd sit at the bar, the same bar we had just played, and drink with everyone. Some fans would look at us with disappointment, and rightfully so. I recall one night after playing Hammerjacks in Baltimore, we sat at the bar drinking and one fan stopped by to talk to us. We were doing shots and obviously getting drunk. He approached with a photo in hand wanting to get an autograph, but as he saw what we were doing, he just turned around and walked away, saying nothing, yet with the most disappointed look it his eyes. It was another sword in my heart.

Yet, somehow, none of this made its way to the press.

This timeframe, about 1990, was filled with religious scandal. Jessica Hahn and Jim Baker. Jimmy Swaggart had just made his infamous "I have sinned" speech about a year-and-a-half earlier after being caught with a prostitute. Religious leaders were dropping like flies, so it would seem only natural that our dirty laundry would be hung out for all to see as well. But it wasn't.

Not to downplay anything we did, because I was truly embarrassed and ashamed by it all, but I do believe there are different levels of scandal. And truthfully, what we were doing probably just wasn't big enough news for the press. There was Jim Baker and his affair with his secretary. There was Jimmy Swaggart and his joyrides with prostitutes. And then there was Stryper, a Christian rock band drinking alcohol and kissing strange women. Again, I don't at all downplay what we did. But in comparison to Baker and Swaggart, we just weren't enough of a scandal perhaps. For whatever reason, God's protection was over this band and I think for that very reason, our actions never really saw the light of day.

The most saddening part this time in our lives was the spiritual break-up of the band happening long before the physical break-up. In the mid-80s we used to encourage one another to do the right thing. We held each other accountable, as Christians should. We were always lifting one another up, really trying to strengthen each other to be better stewards and examples of Christ. Yet somehow, in a matter of just a few short years, we went from that to, *"Hey man. Wanna go to a strip club tonight?"* We'd laugh and say to another member, *"Let's go get another case of beer,"* and we'd always just go right along with whatever was at hand. It's almost as if we were whispering to ourselves, *"Well, if he wants to do it too, it must be okay."*

Once sin creeps its way into your life, it's hard to turn around. You can't pull yourself back up on your own, and certainly not while you're surrounded by people who are helping you dig the hole. This is why we all need Christ. We can't do it on our own. I can't do it on my own, and that's why I've devoted my life to serving God, or at least trying to. I need Him. Michael Sweet can't do this alone. And in 1990, I needed God more than ever to help pull me out of the abyss — but in order for that to happen, I needed to make some drastic changes. God will only help you if you're willing to yield to Him and turn your life around.

After that really short tour, it came time for me to do some serious soul-searching and attempt to take some major steps to repair my life and my marriage. How I was going to do that, I had no idea. I just knew I needed change, and fast.

THIRTY

In November of 1990 when we came off the road from supporting *Against The Law*, we found ourselves without a record label for the first time since 1983. Through a series of industry maneuvers, mergers, and acquisitions, our key-man at Enigma, Wes Hein ended up at Hollywood Records. We had a clause in our agreement that if Wes ever left, we were free to leave as well, a "key-man" clause. But by this time, our sales were plummeting. Capital/EMI had acquired Enigma, and there were talks of other mergers. Enigma was no more and Wes was now at Disney/Hollywood Records. And we were without a record label. The worst part was nobody really seemed to care or even notice outside our inner circle.

I started talking to Wes about bringing us over to Hollywood Records, and he eventually got everyone else on board, as only he could do. They put up a small amount of money for us to do another album. We were going to record two new songs and re-package the hits for a "best of" compilation record.

But I was done, mentally and physically. The idea of igniting that creative fire and touring again made me sick.

I had already started talking to Robert and expressed to him that I needed a drastic change in my life. I was ridden with guilt over my lifestyle, and it was tearing apart my marriage. He knew the writing was on the wall as well, and if change didn't happen, I'd be leaving soon. It wasn't threatening talks that I was having with Robert but instead heart-felt conversations about how unhappy I was. So together we explored options.

Ultimately Rob and I agreed to clean up Stryper. I agreed to stick by Rob and he agreed to be supportive in getting Stryper back on the right path. It wasn't as if Rob was resistant to cleaning up our act — I think he wanted to as well. But if I'm being perfectly honest, what I think he wanted the most was to keep the band together, and he could see that changing the scenery was something incredibly important to me so that made it important to him as well.

Throughout our career it's always been kind of a "Robert and me against the world" mentality. The saying that blood is thicker than water holds immensely true in our relationship. I appreciated Robert during these times for wanting to get on board with my idea of change. I think deep down Rob wanted it, too. We probably all did. It was exhausting being who we were, or who we were pretending to be, on the *Against The Law* tour. Aside from the obvious physical exhaustion that our lifestyle provided, it was also spiritually exhausting trying to be something we weren't.

From the days at Whittier High when Oz's outburst got us into trouble, we had seen reoccurring patterns of defiance from Oz. We can all be a little defiant at times, but Oz seemed to take it to a new level. I recall in the early '80s Oz getting punched by Tommy Lee's bodyguard/bouncer outside the Troubadour in West Hollywood. After a few drinks, Oz decided to moon Tommy and started mouthing off about something. A few seconds later, Tommy's fist came flying through the crowd in full force, past my face and Robert's face, as he tried to punch Oz for his "body language." A few moments later, Tommy's hit man came over and started punching Oz. That incident was a blur and one of those moments you look back on and think, "How did that happen?" I guess if you show your backside to someone for no apparent reason, you'll most likely find out.

So aside from being exhausted from all that was going on in my life, it was uncomfortable for me to consider the idea of discussing change with Oz.

I couldn't, and still sometimes can't, approach Oz with my thoughts like I can my brother Robert. At least that's the way I perceive it. I'm sure Oz might say otherwise and probably even say that I'm difficult to approach. It certainly isn't the case all the time but from my point of view, it can be a little uncomfortable talking to Oz about issues that he doesn't agree with, no matter the magnitude or significance of the topic. I can open up to Robert, and although we may not see eye to eye, he will at least understand my point of view—but I feel Oz can take a bit more of a defensive approach. Don't get me wrong, Oz and I have been the best of friends over the years and often he's been the only one I felt comfortable talking to, but when it comes to certain issues, discussing them with Oz can be a challenge.

At this time, I was entering a chapter in my life where I wanted to get my act together. I wanted to regain my spiritual composure and really focus on my marriage more than my music, and I could talk about these things with Robert, and I did. Robert is even-keeled, slow to anger and a good listener, so I chose to share my concerns with Rob for fear of rebuttal.

I knew I wanted out, but perhaps there were solutions I hadn't considered. Robert provided a way for me to share my feelings in hopes that just by talking things through, I might find the answers myself. Maybe it was our bond as brothers and growing up together.

We had agreed, through Wes and Hollywood Records, to record two more songs. Rob and I were discussing doing this without Oz. It was the easy way out with less stress and fewer complications. I wasn't ready to deal with the situation so Robert had a phone conversation with Oz and they eventually settled on Oz playing on one of the two songs we'd be recording. Oz played all guitars on the song "Can't Stop The Rock," and I played all guitars on the song "Believe."

On February 17, 1991, our beautiful daughter Ellena Rae was born. Ellena's birth helped me to see what was important and what was not. Daily, my focus grew less about Stryper and more about my family. I'm not sure if it's the same emotional bond for every dad that has a daughter, but Lena's birth brought some sense of structure to my life and helped me to realize the importance of family first, music second.

Although Kyle and I weren't supposed to have any more children, Lena's entrance into this world indirectly brought stability and healing to a broken marriage and a wounded relationship. When Lena was born, it took the doctors an exceedingly long time to revive her and get her breathing on her own. We prayed earnestly for her, and not long after, she cried out and gasped for air. We almost lost her. It was a miraculous moment that seemed to bind our family together in a way like never before. Mikey and Lena both seemed to be miracle babies, and each separate experience of seeing my children born drew me closer to God and ultimately, closer to my family.

Soon after Ellena's arrival into this world, the band completed recording and on July 20, 1991 we released *Can't Stop The Rock*, a collection of hits with two new songs. Only a handful of tour dates were planned to support this album. None of us was really in the mood to tour, at least not relentlessly as we had done in the past. And I had a beautiful new baby girl at home who was now the focus of my life.

But in August we scheduled to do a show at The Whiskey in Hollywood, which would be followed by two dates in Germany. I was feeling sick at the Whiskey show and couldn't figure out what was wrong. The next morning I was feeling worse, much worse. I went to the doctor and discovered I had pneumonia.

As we were scheduled to go to Germany soon, I notified our agent and the guys that we'd need to cancel those two shows. The doctor said I'd be out for at least two weeks. I thought that was optimistic because I felt like I was on my deathbed. Within an hour or so after I notified everyone of my condition, I was down for the count. I got a call back from Rob saying that they felt it would be best if they went over to Germany and fulfilled their obligations. He said this hesitantly, knowing I wouldn't be happy.

He was right, I wasn't happy — but not for the reasons they may have assumed. Although I applaud their commitment to the shows, I felt betrayed, not to mention belittled. Was my contribution so insignificant to this band that they felt they could go and do shows without me, and that the fans wouldn't care?

I couldn't believe that the guys were going overseas without me while I felt as though I was breathing my last breath in bed. Maybe I was getting a taste of my own medicine since I was so dismissive of Oz's involvement with the recent recordings. But somehow it felt different. I was the front man for Stryper, but I felt as though they were saying "*Eh. You get your rest. It's no problem. Nobody will even notice you're gone. We'll go play these two shows and be back before you know it.*"

That was it. That was the turning point for me. If there was any doubt in my mind whether or not I would remain in this band, this moment sealed the deal. Ten years together and it came down to this — me sick with pneumonia and my band saying, "*Hope you feel better. Get well soon. But you know, the show must go on.*"

By this time there was so much animosity and distance between all of us, I didn't really care what happened.

They returned from the Germany run. I read reports that many fans were disappointed. No kidding. I don't blame them. If I paid to go hear my favorite band, that's exactly what I want to do — hear my favorite band, not 75 percent of my favorite band, with the missing 25 percent being the primary voice of my favorite band. I'd be a little upset too. The shows could have and should have been postponed.

December rolled around and we hammered together a string of dates that started in the Northeast and took us through the Midwest and down into Texas. Oddly enough, despite our declining popularity, we sold out two nights in a row at The Union Bar in Minneapolis. This 13- show run wrapped up on December 22, 1991 at the Celebrity Theater in Anaheim, California. I didn't know it at the time, but that would be my last show with Stryper for almost 10 years.

Believe it or not, as 1992 came around, somehow talks of a new record crept into conversation. One thing leads to another, and we actually started setting up to rehearse songs for another album at our warehouse.

Kyle knew I was unhappy and that I wanted out. She and I regularly discussed the pros and cons of leaving Stryper. To both of us, the pros column was much larger than the cons column. But still, the reality of actually leaving the band was somewhat frightening. It was all I had ever known. Playing music with Robert, Oz, and Tim had seen me tour the world over, appear on radio, television and MTV, get married, have two kids, and witness first-hand God changing lives through Stryper.

Was I really ready to give this up?

Yes! A resounding "Yes" was the answer every time I asked myself that question, and a resounding "Yes" every time I prayed and asked God for answers.

Finally, one day I said to Kyle, *"I'm gonna do it. I'm gonna quit. Tonight is the night. When I go to rehearsal tonight, I'm quitting."* I went to the Stryper warehouse that night with determination. That day would be my last in Stryper, I was sure of it.

But that night I wasn't feeling quite so brave, so we just jammed and worked on some song ideas. I returned home that night only to have Kyle ask how it went, and I shared that I just couldn't do it today.

A few days went by and I got my courage up again. *"Seriously. I'm quitting, today,"* I said with a smile to Kyle as I exited the door headed once again to the dreaded Stryper rehearsal warehouse. As I was leaving, she smiled back with a glance of encouragement and love. *"Good luck. I love you!"*

"How'd they take it?" she asked when I got home. My head bowed with embarrassment, again. *"You couldn't do it, could you?"* she said in a supportive tone that made me appreciate her even more. She said, *"That's okay. You'll know when the time is right."*

See, that's the thing about Kyle. As much as Stryper was the catalyst to potentially ruining our marriage, she still wasn't pushing me out. She didn't like me being in Stryper at the time, but only because she knew the kind of man I was becoming in that band. She also saw how desperately I no longer wanted to be that man. So instead of getting mad and saying, *"Why can't you just do it? Quit, you idiot!"* she embraced me, knowing that this sort of thing — conflict and change — didn't come easy for me.

The next week it was the same routine again. Leaving the house, I was convinced this was my last day in Stryper only to return home without results because I just couldn't find the right words. By that point I started making excuses, not so much to Kyle — she didn't need excuses — but more to myself. *"Someone stopped by. It wasn't a good time to talk."* or *"Robert was feeling a bit sick. It was a bad time to break the news."* Excuse after excuse.

This went on for a while. Eventually Kyle stopped asking, and I stopped making empty promises. Before too long Kyle's departing words became more perfunctory than encouraging, *"Have a good time at rehearsal. Drive safely."*

One day, there were no mentions of the forgotten exit plan, and I went to practice as usual. This time though, before I even picked up my guitar, I just started spilling my heart. I'm not good at this sort of thing. I don't just come right out and say, *"I quit."* Instead I lead the listener on a long journey of explanations leaving them guessing where the story is going.

I talked. Rob, Oz, and Tim listened, and surely they wondered where I was going with all of this.

I talked about how I wanted to put my family and marriage first. How I now had *two* children and felt as though I was not the father and husband I wanted to be. I talked about how I missed the old days when we, as a band, were spiritually unified. I spoke of wanting to get back on the right path and that I was finding it difficult to do so with the way things were going. I said I was ashamed and embarrassed about how we had been acting as a band. I discussed our declining popularity. I shared that I wanted something new, something fresh, and something exciting.

Now looking back on it, after 30 minutes of pouring out my heart, I suppose one of two things could have come out of my mouth as a conclusion to my rambling, either *"Let's pull ourselves up, get ourselves right with God, and make Stryper the best band it can be with new songs, new energy and a renewed vow in our faith."* or *"I quit."*

I chose the latter. And although I didn't say the exact words, *"I quit,"* I do believe I concluded with, *"I've decided it's time for me to leave the band and work on my own life and my family."*

It was a somber conclusion. There were several attempts, mostly by Rob, to try and salvage things. Rob's the eternal optimist. I love him for that. He would have done almost anything to keep this band together, and I think that's what broke my heart. I felt as though I was letting him down, that I was breaking off with my own brother. I *was*, in a professional sense. The thought of letting Rob down tore me to pieces. At moments during the evening, I looked at Robert with his head bowed. He knew this wasn't going to end well. At one point he glanced up and caught my eye. I had to look away for fear I'd start crying.

Despite knowing that I needed to get out of this band, I felt guilty for letting Rob, Tim, and Oz down. Mostly Rob. Actually, that is the only reason it took me so long to do it. I didn't want to let them down. I wanted out, I just didn't know how to go about it.

As we wrapped up the evening with small talk, we grabbed our gear and headed out to our cars. I put my guitar case in the trunk of my Sterling, waived to Rob as he was driving out of the parking lot, and I headed home for the last time from a Stryper band practice.

On the drive home I was filled with equal parts of sadness and joy. At moments during the drive I couldn't help but smile. I was free! And as quickly as that smile came, I could feel myself tearing up. I never questioned that this was what I wanted—I just wasn't sure how I'd feel about it once it actually happened. Now I know—joy and sadness. Stryper was done, or at least I was done with Stryper.

When I got home it had been so long since I first began making promises of quitting, Kyle didn't even bother to ask. *"Oh, hey honey. Mikey and Lena are asleep. I put some leftovers in the fridge if you're hungry..."*

"I quit," I said interrupting her in mid-sentence.

"What do you mean you quit? Seems she had already forgotten. Or maybe she just didn't want to seem hopeful that it was the band I was talking about.

"I quit the band. I'm no longer in Stryper."

She didn't say a word. She walked over and put her arms around me. Not because she was happy, although I'm sure she was. She knew I wanted this. But she also knew I would be a mess. She hugged me and didn't say a word. She knew that I must be filled with an array of emotions and what I needed the most weren't words of comfort. I just needed love and encouragement—and she gave that to me unconditionally.

That night she didn't ask me questions like, *"What's it feel like? What's next? Are you going to do a solo album?"* nor did she attempt to slander the band by saying anything negative. All those things you might think a wife would say on a night like this, she said none of them. She was just there for me. If I wanted to talk, she would listen.

But I didn't want to talk about it. I wanted to know every little detail of what Mikey and Lena did while I was gone. It was my first step toward genuinely wanting to rebuild our family and be more available for them. I didn't want to re-live the conversation with the guys. I wanted to help pick up the kids toys and do chores around the house. I wanted to be a dad. I wanted to be a husband.

I went to bed that night in February 1992 for the first time as Michael Sweet, father and husband, with not a single care as to what my future might hold professionally. I went to bed that night with no regrets. I was committed to giving my life completely to God, my wife, and my children. Finally, I was free—free to do what I wanted to do. And it felt great! "Thank you God. My life is back in Your hands again. Use me as You see fit. I'm Yours."

THIRTY-ONE

What now? I'm out of Stryper.

And did I mention that I'm also broke and bankrupt?

Throughout all the debauchery and inner-band turmoil, there was also the financial stress. We were the classic story: rags to riches and back to rags.

If VH1 were to do a "Behind the Music" episode on Stryper, I could hear Jim Forbes as he would likely say in his signature voice, "*Stryper was a band that had it all and broke down barriers doing the unthinkable in taking their yellow-and-black religious message to the mainstream. But ultimately, they would choke on their own financial excess. Less than a decade after shocking the world with their seminal debut, they would find themselves back in the very place they started, without a record label or a bank account. The righteous rockers have lived the dream, as well as the nightmare, of the rock 'n' roll roller coaster.*"

Throughout this haunting narration would be footage of us in private helicopters, setting up our elaborate and expensive stage, and numerous semis full of equipment would be parked next to a limousine. The upbeat background music would turn to somber stringed instruments and the "lifestyles of the rich and famous" footage would segue into melancholy shots of me sitting on the front porch of my dilapidated house in the ghetto, smoking a cigarette donning a seven-day unshaven beard with an empty bottle of whiskey in my hand—although the latter part of that scene would not be true, it *would* make for good TV, wouldn't it?

In 1992, not only were we without a record label, I received this news: "Oh, by the way, we're almost $2 million in debt."

191

Two million dollars? How does that even happen? I know exactly how it happens. I let other people make financial decisions on my behalf, and I didn't pay any attention to my own business affairs. All those times I would quietly question the overspending, I should have spoken up and demanded answers.

Even more damaging, we still had never incorporated, which meant we had to file bankruptcy as a partnership, therefore individually. When I received the news, the words of our attorney from years earlier rang in my head, "I don't care if Winnie-the-Pooh is president of the corporation. Just pick somebody to be president and let's form this corporation so you'll be protected."

We of course didn't listen to him. Our egos and stupidity got in the way of us choosing a president for our corporation, again a position that meant nothing more than a title—and our way of solving that issue was to just ignore the issue. Now we're all personally bankrupt as a result.

As high as we might have gone with this band, the unraveling of the business deals that had been going on were of the lowest of the lows. We were now the cliché of musicians who made money. We didn't know what to do with it, and we were now penniless.

Experiencing the explosion that took place with Stryper's popularity was quite a whirlwind. We rose quickly, and were not prepared to handle it all in a financially responsible manner.

All of a sudden we went from having nothing in 1982 to flying first class and staying in five-star hotels. We were making a lot of money and driving nice cars, but we weren't putting any of our money into long-term investments.

Up until this time, my mom had been the primary manager of the band. The bankruptcy period was on her watch, and I would imagine that didn't set well with her knowing that she was in the driver's seat. I don't put all of the blame on my mom, or even most of the blame for that matter. Yes, she was not only managing the band and handling our finances, but it was all of our jobs to keep an eye on what was happening – to boldly question anything we didn't agree with. We didn't. We gave her free reign for the most part, and in that respect, it's our fault.

At our peak, we might have been making $100,000 a night, but we were spending more like $125,000 a night. And when you operate a business like that, you eventually wake up two million dollars in debt. If you look back at the production we would take on tour – the "no devil", "no 666" and "Stryper" signs, the elaborate and enormous Stryper flashing backdrop, the rotating, 1000 light dual drum kits, the expensive means of travel – it all just added up over time and none of us was keeping tabs.

It was our attorney, Stephen Ashley, the one who wisely advised us to incorporate many years ago, who had the unfortunate job of calling a meeting between all the band members and my mom. Our tax accountant was also present. We sat across from one another at a large conference table when Stephen delivered the news. Everyone had already gathered when I entered the room and from the somber atmosphere I almost thought someone had died. I knew we had a serious meeting planned, but I had no idea what was about to come out of Stephen's mouth: *"We've studied this every way possible, and unfortunately there doesn't seem to be any way out but for all of you to declare bankruptcy."*

It was a wake-up call and I was furious – at my mom and at myself. All Rob and I could do was shake our heads in disbelief. Every "Would of, Could of, Should of" imaginable ran through my mind. If only I had paid more attention to what was going on.

My mom, at the time, dismissed it, blaming "overspending" as the cause. You think? What I really wanted from her was an apology or at least a partial admission of fault. But instead I got reasoning and explanations. *"Of course it was overspending!"* I thought but didn't say it.

Again, I didn't put all, or even most of the blame on her. I just wished she had accepted a little more of the responsibility.

We owed a lot of people money, two million dollars worth. So aside from the shame of having to declare bankruptcy, we had a lot of debtors angry with us, including the management company we had signed on with, Gold Mountain. We were so deep in debt by the time they took us on, we didn't have the money to pay commissions—so they weren't too happy when they found out they wouldn't be getting some of their money as well.

Shockingly, I escaped that bankruptcy with few repercussions other than bad credit and angry debtors. I didn't have to give up a lot of my assets such as my house, car or musical equipment. But with two young children and a wife, not to mention no more band as my primary source of income, a bad credit score weighed heavily on me.

I'm pleased to say that over the years I have rebuilt my credit (it's better now than it was then), and I've risen above the bankruptcy cloud that consumed us. I've learned I never want to have to go through that again.

As horrible as that whole financial mess was, it is a big part of why I am who I am today. It's helped me to be a better steward and to be more responsible with everything that God has loaned or given to me. He wants us to be good stewards and to be responsible and I wasn't doing that in the '80s. I still struggle with it at times, but I'm a lot better with money today than I was then.

I should set the record straight. Personally, I have never been rich by the world's standards. I've certainly never been a multi-millionaire. I probably would have been a millionaire had I been more frugal with our spending. I've also never been one for extreme extravagance. Yes, I've owned a few nice cars and several nice homes. But I didn't have a garage filled with Bentleys, Lamborghinis or Maseratis. I didn't have six homes scattered throughout the world. I spent money that I shouldn't have spent, and that I didn't have in the bank, but it never got to that extreme. Most of our frivolous spending was on stuff that, at the time, we thought we needed to make the band better.

I've never really even understood the extravagant way of living. Even in my most immature days, I didn't see the purpose in owning a fleet of cars or multiple mansions.

My house in Fullerton was a modest 2,000-square-foot, flat-roof home. It was my only asset to speak of and, fortunately, I didn't have to give it up in the bankruptcy settlement. But I had no stocks, bonds, or retirement funds. We just weren't that business savvy at the time.

If I were blessed with fortunes to the level where I could buy a house on the coast of France, or a fleet of exotic cars, private planes, and yachts, I would like to think I'd behave responsibly. People are dying in our own country, in our own backyard, of starvation and homelessness. Even in my most reckless days with money, I can't imagine not giving freely and generously.

On days when I find myself thinking of money, and wishing I had more of it, in my heart-of-hearts the reason I would like more is so that I can help more people. Maybe one day I'll have that opportunity.

But then in 1992, I had no money. I was bankrupt. I had no band and, of course, no record label. Yet somehow I was the happiest I've ever been. I had my family, and I'd given everything back to God.

I wasn't completely without a plan, though. For the past year I'd been working on some demos with Brent Jeffers, and my future looked promising, even though I didn't have any sort of business structure in place. No manager. No label. No agent. But I was making music that I thoroughly enjoyed. And I had a strange sense, a gut feeling, that it might just go somewhere new.

THIRTY-TWO

After leaving Stryper, I took a little time to breathe. I was going to church regularly at Calvary Chapel in West Covina and really growing in my faith. I credit Pastor Raul Ries for giving me a solid foundation in my walk with God. Many times during the *Against the Law* period I longed for a day when I would get back to regularly attending church. I felt freer than I ever have before.

I was the happiest I'd ever been in my marriage and I was now able, for the first time, to play a more active role in the lives of my children. It was priceless to be able to watch them grow up. Although I missed out on so much time with my son, I wasn't about to make the same mistake twice. I took time just being a dad, and it felt long overdue.

It didn't take long for me to get the music bug again though. I started writing new material and recorded some demos in San Bernardino with bassist Terry Usler. Tony Palacios from Guardian, whom I respect immensely, played on some of those songs as well. We tracked five songs, and although nothing immediately happened with them, I eventually self-released them on a CD called *Unstryped*.

At church I began talking to Raul's son Shane about the demos I had been making, and he offered the church studio that he engineered to me as well. Shane has a great sense of music and is incredibly talented and he was recording some amazing stuff at the church. We tracked some newer songs that I had written, "Tomorrow Tonight," "All I Wanna Do Is Love You" and "I Think You Hear Me Knockin'." The songs felt like they were really coming together, and I was excited about music again. I met a well-respected manager named Stephen Prendergast, who had managed the Canadian band Honeymoon Suite, and we worked together for

197

a short while. There was no ceremonious breakup between us — we just never really got things off the ground.

I continued to write and record and eventually had some cassettes pressed. I shopped the tapes around to industry people the best I could and those songs eventually caught the ears of Troy Van Leer at Benson Records. Troy was a friend and a fan and liked the songs, but wanted to hear more.

Around that same time, someone had sent me some demos created by Gregg Fulkerson, the singer/guitarist for the band Blue Tears on MCA. Gregg was a talented writer/producer.

I really connected with Gregg and flew to Nashville to do some recording with him. We co-wrote a few songs, "Together," "All This and Heaven Too," and "Ain't No Safe Way" and recorded them at his house on a Fostex, 1/4 inch, eight-track machine. We sent the songs over to Benson, and I headed back to California.

I could feel the momentum building. Sometimes in this business you can just tell you're in a lull, and other times, often for no apparent reason, you just have this feeling that things are coming together and taking shape. That's the way this felt. But the best part was — I didn't care. Sure, I was hoping to continue in music, but it was nice to be making music again just for the sake of enjoyment and honoring God with the gifts that He had given me. I was giving it all back to Him, and the songs seemed to be pouring out of me. It felt great, and whether or not they achieved commercial success was not important to me. What was important was getting God's message back out to the people.

Back home in California, things were slightly awkward. I would still visit my parents and, occasionally, I'd land in the middle of a conversation between Rob and my mom talking Stryper business. After all, Stryper was technically still together.

After I quit in '92, the band did a short run in Germany and Sweden with Oz covering vocals. Although Oz can sing, I know Robert wanted someone who could not only sing better then Oz, but someone who could also take the front-man role. You have to have someone leading the band live, and Robert knew how important that was. The band performed one show at Knotts Berry Farm in May of '92 in which they brought in Dale Thompson of the band Bride to sing lead. Dale is an amazing singer, one of the best in the genre in my opinion, but I was hearing from the fans that it just didn't work. Fans weren't buying it and, for whatever reason, Dale didn't stick around long. Sometimes things don't gel, and my guess is that was the case here. Likely, both parties knew it wasn't going to work out.

Stryper went back to Sweden, Denmark, and Switzerland as a three-piece in '93. Meanwhile, I was in my zone making solo music and spending time with the family. There was no animosity in my heart, and I was genuinely wishing the guys well. More truthfully, I wasn't giving Stryper much thought at all. People would ask me, *"Stryper's doing a run as a three-piece. Does that bother you?"* It didn't at all. I was actually rooting for them to find a singer and continue finding success. I was happy and content with my place in life, so I really did want the best for the guys moving forward.

Back in Fullerton, I continued writing and enjoying the process of creating music. Unexpectedly, I received a call from Troy at Benson Records. On the phone with him was Jerry Park, the president of Benson. I sat down hoping and praying that this conversation was heading where I thought it would go.

"We love the new songs," Troy said. *"We'd like to talk about moving forward and signing you to Benson Records!"* Jerry confirmed those sentiments. By the fall of 1993, I signed a lucrative recording contract with Benson.

I set out with Gregg Fulkerson and engineer Doug Beiden to produce my first, nationally released solo album. Working with Gregg and Doug was exciting. I could tell I was heading in the right direction musically, although as we were recording, I couldn't help but feel the record needed more. We had already recorded eight or nine songs including "Together," "All This And Heaven Too," "I Think You Hear Me Knocking," "All I Wanna Do Is Love You," and "Ain't No Safe Way," but I felt that the record was lacking certain aspects and lacking, believe it or not, me.

Gregg's production style was very much in the vein of Bon Jovi and Def Leppard, so I flew back to California, where I would write and self-produce two more songs—"J.E.S.U.S." and "Take Me Home"—and record them with Doug.

Benson introduced me to an industry guy named Rendy Lovelady, who was just starting to get into artist management. I met with Rendy and we began working together. He's an amazing guy and dear friend and still, to this day, we remain in touch. Rendy was instrumental in the success of my first solo release and solo career.

Benson got behind the record in full force, and it was released in April of 1994. We shot videos for "All This and Heaven Too," "Someday," and "Ain't Not Safe Way," a video with an intro that featured a teenage couple contemplating sex. Although it was quite possibly one of the corniest videos I've ever made, it was somewhat of an edgy video for the Christian Music industry in the mid '90s.

Back home in California, I put together an all-star band consisting of Jamie Wollman (from the band Surrender) on drums—Scott Harper (from Whitecross) on bass—Dennis Cameron (from Angelica) on guitars—and the fiercely talented keyboardist/vocalist, Paul Huesman. John Huie, a friend and former Stryper agent, booked the solo band, and we set out for almost three months in the summer of '94 playing festivals, theaters, clubs and malls. Yes, malls.

We did something really different during this tour. The intention was to play an acoustic set at Christian bookstores across the country, but many of these stores were located in malls. Often the turnout would be so large that we'd have to move from the bookstore itself to a common area in the mall, which was even better for us and those attending.

Benson pulled out all the stops in support of this album. When someone purchased the CD, they also received a free VHS that featured the three videos and some behind-the-scenes interview footage. The label also created life-sized standup cutouts of me. It was a little strange walking into the bookstores and seeing these cutouts standing at the front entrance. I still have one of them in my basement. The first time Benson did this, it was flattering—but the second time, for my next album *Real*, some executive decided that they didn't like the expression on my face. They said my eyes, and I quote, looked too "sexy," so they photo-shopped new eyes on my face. I remember walking into the label and seeing it from about 100 feet away and saying immediately, "What did you do to my eyes?" I looked like Michael Sweet's cross-eyed doppelgänger!

The tour for that first solo release was a blast, and the brotherhood within the band was a much-needed breath of fresh air. Rendy was still learning the ropes as a manager, but he was a mover and shaker. He was constantly on the phone working hard for me. During the process, he was calling in a lot of favors, sometimes without my knowledge.

One of those favors was with a lighting company. They traveled with us on tour and brought out quite an elaborate system. Although I was much savvier business-wise as a result of my failures in Stryper, I failed to ask questions about the lighting. I just assumed it was all covered in the tour budget.

We arrived home after that tour and soon after, I received an invoice for almost $25,000 from the lighting company. I called the company to get to the bottom of it, and they said they had a signed contract for this amount. I knew I hadn't signed anything, so I asked them to fax me a copy of the agreement. Sure enough, I didn't sign it, Rendy did. I was considerably upset and called Rendy. I told him he needed to deal with this because I wasn't going to pay for something I didn't know about, and had I known about it, I certainly wouldn't have agreed to it. What's more, when I did inquire about the lights early on, Rendy assured me it was not a problem and that he had worked it all out.

To Rendy's credit, he owned up to this and somehow took care of it. I don't know if he paid it himself or what, but I did know that coming off the heels of financial ruin with Stryper, I was not about to fall back into that world. Had this been several years earlier, I probably would have buckled and just added it on to our ever-growing debt pile, but not today. I wasn't going to roll over and let someone else's business decisions effect me personally and financially.

My marriage was strong at this time, and Kyle was becoming much more involved and active in my career.

When you turn everything over to God, I believe He opens doors. He wasn't just opening doors for me—He was breaking down the entire doorway. I was back on stable ground, solid ground. And to top it off, my first solo album went on to achieve five #1 singles and it sold in excess of 300,000 copies, more than the previous two Stryper albums combined.

I was back. Mentally, spiritually, and financially, I was back in a way that felt great.

As 1994 came to a close, however, something strange was happening in Orange County, California—the county in which

Fullerton, and my home, sits. I couldn't believe what I was seeing in the news. My home county may be declaring bankruptcy. Allegedly Robert Citron, the county's treasurer, had made some seriously bad investments, and the county was heading for ruin. In December, the entire county did in fact declare bankruptcy. Home values plummeted as a result, including mine.

We decided the best thing for us to do was to sell the house for what we could get and move back east to my mother-in-law's home in Buzzards Bay, Massachusetts. We sold the house for a loss and moved back into Kyle's childhood home on Cape Cod. Her mother was still living in the house, so Kyle, Lena, Mikey and I all moved in with Marion. It was not quite the rock-star set up, but I'll admit it felt good to be out of Southern California and on the path to a new life.

By this time, grunge music had consumed the world for a couple of years, and it was making me nervous about the next album I was contracted to record for Benson. I decided on doing something completely different from my previous album, or really any album I had ever released. I went for more of a stripped down, acoustic sound.

The album was called *Real* and it was released in October 1995. By industry standards, it didn't do nearly as well, but I did manage to squeeze three #1 songs out for Christian Radio, including a video for the title track. I only toured for about three weeks around the release of this album, mostly festivals and clubs.

Soon after that I got the news that Benson was going under, and they eventually sold to Provident Music Group. Yes, yet another financial disaster in my life.

I was starting to feel a bit deflated musically as 1996 rolled around. *Real* didn't meet my or the label's, expectations in terms of sales. Shortly after its release, I would find myself without a record label once again. And it wasn't as if Buzzards Bay was the hotbed for music. I was as far away from my comfort zone of Los Angeles as I possibly could be, and I was faced with the harsh reality that this might be the end of the line for my musical journey.

THIRTY-THREE

With no record deal in place, I found myself 32 years old and feeling like this might be the end of my life as a musician. But some interesting things were happening in 1996 — most notably, the Internet. It seems strange to talk about an era with no Internet, but I lived through the commercialization of this technology.

Thanks to the Internet and a handful of faithful Stryper fans, I would eventually jumpstart things again, but prior to that happening, I honestly thought that maybe God just didn't want me to do this any longer.

After Benson had shut their doors, I started recording some demos at home. I had a few digital 8 track machines synched together and a drum machine that I programmed and I started recording basic ideas and sending them out to all the labels and people that I knew in the industry. I seemed to keep hearing the same exact phrase when I'd follow up with people I had sent music to — "Sorry Michael, we're not interested." This went on for months on end.

Danny Goldberg, Stryper's manager during the *Against The Law* period, had gone on to form Artemis Records. He politely passed when I sent him some material. Eddie DeGarmo was running Forefront Records, and he also passed. I don't have a favorable memory of Eddie's "pass", however. In our initial phone conversation, he asked me how old I was. I told him I was 32, and Eddie proceeded to explain that they were only signing artists a lot younger than me. Ouch.
Yeah, right Eddie. You're never "too old," buddy....

After hearing "No thanks" many times, eventually I packed up all my gear and put it in a large storage area in the basement. *"Maybe I'm just not supposed to do this anymore,"* I thought as I packed my guitars and equipment neatly behind the closed doors.

Soon afterward, I threw myself into working the family cranberry and camping business. I was making a whopping $250 a week, if that. Kyle worked in the office and made a little more than me, but not much more. During harvest season, I worked in the bogs, wearing waste-high hip waders. And during the camping season, I was known as "Ranger Mike." My duties involved driving around in a jeep, showing guests to their campsites and making sure all the campfires were out at midnight. I promise I'm not making this up.

This was all documented in a show on VH1 called "Where Are They Now?" That's right, my life now consists of hip waders, campfire curfews, and cameos on "Where Are They Now."

Several times during my stint as Ranger Mike, I would on occasion run into Stryper fans. One guy in particular was blasting "To Hell With The Devil" as I walked up to tell him and his 20 some odd guests that they would have to put the fire out. He glared at me with frustration and then began to recognize me. "Aren't you Michael Sweet?" he asked. "Who's Michael Sweet?" I responded and then confessed to the accusation. I wound up letting them burn the fire for another hour because I took a seat and hung with them for that hour. It was humbling but always interesting, and I was okay with it. My walk with God was stronger than ever, and I was learning to be happy with my place in life and accept the path that I was on.

I was focusing on keeping my priorities straight — God and family. For a while it felt great not having the pressures of the music business hanging over my head. At the end of the day, I'd come home tired and dirty from working outside, but it felt great to work hard and then spend time with my family in the evenings. Somehow it felt good to be physically exhausted at the end of the day.

My life was in God's hands and if this is what He wanted me to do, I was going to make the best of it. I wanted to give my best, no matter what I was doing. It also felt good to not have record executives telling me they were going to "pass" or that the single wasn't charting, or that sales were declining and they might not be able to work the album much longer. The pressure was off, in the corporate sense anyway.

No more suits telling me whether or not my music was good enough or marketable enough. I knew that as long as I was working hard, honoring God, and providing for my family, things would work out.

But as I drove around in the Jeep all day, worked in the bogs or cleaned out campsite cesspools, inevitably song ideas would creep into my head. After almost two years of working in the family business, I had dozens of songs in my head but nothing to do with them. I had no outlet for them to be heard.

In 1997, though, some interesting doors began to open. For years the unofficial band historian had been a guy by the name of Brett Christensen. Brett knew Jeff Wollschlager who, for a school project, had developed The Michael Sweet website. I, along with a large majority of the world, was still not Internet savvy, but Brett told me about this website Jeff had developed and I eventually took at look at it. I was really impressed with what I saw, and I contacted Jeff about making MichaelSweet.com official. On my $250 a week salary, I certainly had no money to hire a webmaster, but Jeff offered his services for free and launched MichaelSweet.com in 1997.

I had been attending a home church that I and a few other people had formed called Cornerstone. Pastor David Johnson led the church, and we met in different homes each week, ours being one of those homes. I led the music. I felt better about my faith than I had in years and I looked forward to church every week. A couple by the name of Russ and Ria Berg were also members. They owned a business that supplied home-schooling curriculum, and eventually they helped in getting Mikey and Lena what they needed. It was an amazing group of eclectic and exciting people, including my dear friends—actor, director and writer David Wall and his wife, Kerry. The Bergs and the Walls were from California as well and we instantly bonded. It was a small group, but we had the energy and passion of a mega-church.

On New Year's Eve of 1997, the Bergs invited Kyle and me to their house for dinner. Also at that party were brothers Justin and Joel Christian and Rob Graves. Justin would ultimately help in writing many of the lyrics for my next album. They told me about a guy they knew, Kenny Lewis, who had a small recording studio in Middleton, Massachusetts. I was intrigued. I had all these songs in my head from working at the campground and had no way of recording them.

A few days later I met with Kenny and he offered to record my songs for free. He was a believer as well and just wanted to help me out. Kenny and I have remained lifelong friends, and Kenny has also been instrumental in helping to launch not only my career but Stryper's career as well. Kenny was an incredibly positive turning point in my life.

Whenever time permitted, I would drive to Kenny's (90 miles each way) and record, all the while learning of growing interest in my music from around the world through the website Jeff Wollschlager had set up. Fans were contacting Jeff through the website asking about me. This gave me an incredible passion to continue recording with the hopes of one day sharing my music again..

Still, I continued to shop songs to labels, and I continued to get turned down. So in 1998, with no help from a label at all but with all the power of the Internet, I self-released the songs recorded at Kenny's under the title *Truth*. Shockingly, I sold almost 25,000 copies on my own, stuffing packages from the basement each day and night for months on end.

Every time I hear musicians complain about the Internet, and sometimes being one of those musicians, I try to remind myself of 1998 when it was one of the best things that ever happened to me. I no longer needed the validation of a record label. I no longer needed a label to say, *"Yes, we will release your music."* I, for the first time ever, had the ability to reach the fans directly and bypass the labels completely, and I have to say it felt awesome!

Up until this point, I had so many doors slammed in my face I was almost beginning to believe myself that possibly nobody cared if I ever made music again. But thanks to Jeff's website and Kenny's recording studio and both of them willing to offer their services for free, I was able to release music directly to the fans. For that, I will forever be grateful, and to the 25,000-plus fans that purchased that CD.

I continued working part-time at the campground, and in 1999 I self-released *Unstryped*, the demo I had recorded back in '92. I put it out mostly as a means to subsidize my income, as I never have been particularly fond of those recordings.

That same year I reconnected with Bill Hein, from the Enigma days, now with Restless Records. He heard the album and loved it and ultimately signed me to a deal to re-make *Truth*. Bill was behind the project 100 percent. We got Bob Marlette to produce it and Kenny Aronoff to track drums. Rob Graves co-produced part of the original record, and has since gone on to produce many albums as well, including RED and Pillar. I even brought in Oz to do a solo on the song "The Ever After."

That recording came together perfectly. To this day, it's one of the records that I'm most proud of as an artist. I poured my heart and soul into the making of those songs.

Within what felt like days after the album being released, Restless Records' parent company, Regency Films, pulled the plug on funding for the label. *Truth* was released on October 10, 2000 with all the power and force of a Kleenex being tossed across the room. It was basically dead upon release, which is sad because I feel it was some of my most artistic work ever recorded.

I'm beginning to see a pattern here. I got signed to Enigma, and they closed. I got signed to Benson, and they disappeared. I got signed to Restless — they went under. Most artists can go their entire life and never get a record deal. I, on the other hand, by the age of 37 had somehow managed to successfully help three labels close their doors.

Truth having never seen the light of day is one of the saddest moments, if not *the* saddest moment in my career. I put everything I had into making that record and artistically it was unlike anything I had ever made. I wrote those songs working in the bogs — out in the cold with blisters on my feet and hands. I had tearful crying sessions with the packing and unpacking of my musical equipment. So much incredible work and patience had gone into the making of this album, only to have it fall by the wayside in what seemed like an instant. It was heartbreaking, and I couldn't believe it was happening. Recovering from this would not come easy.

THIRTY-FOUR

I did not get into music for the money. And, I'm still not in it for the money. But I need money to live, just like anyone else. Yet with me there has always been this awkward dance, a fine line I've had to walk, between needing money and being mindful to not do something *for* the money.

Because I'm a Christian this can get even more awkward than it might for other musicians. The general public would likely be shocked to see the incredibly high number of requests we get from people asking to send them free music or to perform for free. The sometimes stated and sometimes presumed assumption is that because we are Christians, we should do things for free. And when we're unable to do so, it's equally as alarming the backlash and cries of outrage we receive. *"You should not charge us for a performance. You're a ministry, and we're trying to raise money for our church. Shame on you!"* is a typical response when we politely explain our inability to travel across the country and perform for free at the Main Street Christian Church of Home-Town USA.

This has always fascinated me. I won't say that it angers me because it doesn't. I completely understand their intentions. It's just a little baffling.

They are asking *us* to perform for free, to raise money for *their* organization. And why do they need the money? To pay for the contractors, plumbers, and electricians that of course will not work for free to build their new Sunday school wing at their church.

So why not just ask the contractors and plumbers to work for free? Well, because they won't. They too have families to feed. They too have mortgages and utility bills to pay. So instead, they ask, and often expect, us to perform for free to raise money for whatever expense-of-the-month might be on their budget calendar. Why is this? Why do people so easily ask us to perform for free but rarely ask the builders to work for free? Are our skills as musicians less difficult or less valuable than those of the contractors and plumbers? Because we're in ministry we should perform for free, but the contractors shouldn't work for free?

Don't get me wrong, not everyone who asks us to perform for free gets upset when we can't. A lot of them understand that we just simply cannot afford to do so. But the ones that don't understand sure do get vocal about it.

It's tough, because truly if I could, I'd play every request we get and charge nothing for it. But if I did that I would be an irresponsible husband, father, and bandleader. So we have to ask for money whether we, or the people asking us to play, like it or not.

At this point in my life I have two basic choices: Get paid to make music or get paid to work at Home Depot. Either way, I need to get paid. I need to provide for my family.

So for my entire life I've walked this fine line between music and ministry. I do it because I love it. I get paid for it so that I can provide for my family. But somehow, when you're a Christian musician, getting paid is often taboo.

As I started to dance with the idea of playing with the guys in Stryper, I was once again reminded of this fine line. Yes, I needed money, but I didn't want to do it for the money. It's a tough balance that I've always struggled with.

In 1999 I was a weekend warrior, working a day job mostly and playing out on the weekends whenever possible. One of those gigs was in Puerto Rico, where I flew down to sit in with Oz and Tim performing with their band, Sin Dizzy. I came out and played with the guys, and we even did a few Stryper tunes.

212

The morning following the show a longtime fan, Rich Serpa, met with us at breakfast to discuss an idea he had been working on for a Stryper Expo. The thought was to bring in Stryper fans from all across the world to meet, trade collectibles, and to ideally have us perform. I was skeptical, for a number of reasons. For starters, I knew something like this would be an enormous undertaking physically, logistically and financially. Lots of Stryper fans over the years have come to us with grandiose ideas only to have them fall by the wayside after realizing the time and money that would be involved.

Rich seemed sincere, motivated and smart, so I was interested in exploring this idea. But my other reservation would be—could Stryper bond together as a band again?

I continued conversations with Rich, and eventually I agreed to be move forward with and perform at the Expo.

Brett Christensen and a guy named Greg Hayes had already started Stryper.com, so we promoted the Expo through that website mostly. Still, as the date approached, I was skeptical that anyone would even show up.

Since we had no infrastructure to take ticket reservations, Rich had convinced a local bookstore in New Jersey to take orders and run them through the stores credit card processing in exchange for a small percentage of the sales. After the first week or so of being on sale, Rich went in to the bookstore to check to see if we had sold any tickets. The owner of the bookstore was polite but said they were having second thoughts about handling the orders. He said they had been getting calls from all over the world and that he had to bring in another person just to handle it all. Fortunately, the bookstore owner stood by us and continued taking calls and processing the sales.

Ultimately, all the stars aligned and on May 21, 2000 we held the first Stryper Expo at the Sheraton Tara Hotel in Parsippany, New Jersey. About 1,500 people attended from as far away as Japan and Australia.

For the first time in nine years the four of us—Robert, Tim, Oz, and myself—performed together as Stryper. It wasn't really much of a performance, though. It was a small stage set up in the hotel ballroom. I wore Adidas sweat pants, if that gives you any indication as to how seriously I took this. Yes, I loved seeing everyone, and I enjoyed the camaraderie and "hang time," but an actual rock show it was not. At best, I viewed it as a jam session with former band mates. Still, it was fun, and the reception was incredible. We didn't get paid for performing at the Expo. Although it was a success, Rich was financially only in a position to cover our travel and lodging expenses.

Jeff Wollschlager had come out to help with the event and after it was over, he drove me back to my house in Buzzards Bay, about a five-hour drive from Parsippany. During the drive he asked me what it would take for me to want to put Stryper back together. The list was too long to consider. I had enjoyed one night with my former band mates and was content leaving it at that.

A few days following the Expo, however, I received word that there was interest in Stryper playing a show in Costa Rica in December of that same year. Rafael Richards ran a cable access show and had come to the Expo to interview us. The minister of a church in Cartago, Costa Rica, had contacted him about trying to bring us down, who in turn contacted Rich, who in turn contacted me.

Again, it came back to the fine line between wanting to do Stryper for the right reasons yet also needing the money. I never have been involved in Stryper for the money. It has to feel right. Over the years leading up to this we've been offered a lot of money to reunite, but it just never felt right. But I was coming off the heels of the Expo, and that felt great. The outpouring of support from the fans blew me away, and I had a great time jamming with the guys. That situation led me to become open to the idea of playing another show. I negotiated the deal and we accepted an offer of $30,000 — quite a bit more money than any of us had seen in a while. Rich went as our tour manager and the show took place on December 16, 2000. We played to almost 6,000 fans.

We flew down to Costa Rica a few days prior to the show to get a short rehearsal in and to do some press.

Getting in and out of any foreign country is never easy, so we put it in Rich's hands to help navigate the visas, work permits, and customs forms in order for us to bring some gear and merchandise.

Robert had become involved with a company called World Gone Mad Entertainment, a one- or two-man operation funding Robert's solo project, Love Trash. I was a bit apprehensive about the guy who ran that company, Mike Reynolds. Something just didn't feel right about what little I knew of him.

Stryper was not a band, so there was no official Stryper merchandise to speak of. I went down there with a bunch of Michael Sweet merchandise. Tim and Oz brought some Sin Dizzy stuff, and this guy Mike Reynolds brought some Robert Sweet merch, but he also took it upon himself to print and bring Stryper merchandise as well.

The government in Costa Rica at the time was a bit sketchy to say the least. Getting in and out of customs and even conducting basic business was risky and often resulted in behind-the-scenes payoffs. Rich was working with a missionary to get our merchandise through customs, so Tim, Oz, and I had no problems getting it through. Mike Reynolds however didn't go through Rich's suggested missionary and instead went at it alone. As a result,

Mike's merchandise got detained in customs, and he had to pay some pretty hefty fines to get it out. He eventually made his way into the country with Stryper t-shirts in tow.

Oftentimes throughout the history of this band, I'm fully aware that I get the "bad guy" rap — and by that I mean that I'm the one who speaks up when I see something I don't like. As a result, I'm always seen as the bad guy of the bunch for doing so.

It didn't set well with me that Mike Reynolds had just taken it upon himself to print Stryper merchandise. If someone was going to make money off the Stryper name, it's only fair that the rest of the band participate in the profits. After all, it's our name and likeness!

After many problems Mike encountered in customs, when the day of the show arrived, the police were on site. They were planning to shut down the merchandise sales or at least get paid under the table for allowing the sales to go on. Tim, Oz, and I didn't want the hassle, so we closed up shop and just didn't sell any more merchandise. Our merch stands had only been open for a short period of time when the police arrived, so we didn't sell much of anything. But Mike Reynolds had invested tens of thousands of dollars in printing Stryper merchandise, not to mention the fines he had to pay to get it in and out of customs, so he wasn't about to shut down. Unfortunately he had no choice. The police made him shut it all down and he was stuck with thousands of dollars in Stryper merchandise that he likely was not going to be able to get out of the country. Needless to say, he was furious.

Part of my reason for wanting to go to Costa Rica was for a young teenager named Andreas who was part of the church bringing us down. One day after leaving the church, he and his brother were in a horrible accident. His brother died instantly, but Andreas barely survived.

When we arrived in Costa Rica, Rodolfo Arias, the minister of the church who had arranged for the concert, picked us up at the airport. On the way to the hotel he asked if we could go by Andreas's house to lift his spirits. Of course, we agreed without hesitation.

We went to his house on the outskirts of town where Andreas was still bedridden in casts, braces and a neck sling from the accident. He could barely move. It was a really sad scene. The family was obviously really poor. The house was run down, and the Christmas decorations that adorned it were made of Popsicle sticks and yarn. Yet the spirit of God was there.

Andreas didn't even know we were coming. As we all piled into his small bedroom, not much larger than a walk-in closet in most American homes, he lit up the room with his smile. He was thrilled to see us. He was so badly injured his family had to help lift him up so that he could sit upright in the bed. We had brought a guitar and handed it to Andreas to play a few chords. Tears ran down his face as he strummed out some chords.

Everyone in the room was asking me to sing. I wasn't sure I could keep it together long enough to sing a few lines. It was so sad to see Andreas, crippled in bed yet incredibly thrilled to see us. The house they were living in most likely would be considered condemned by all standards in the United States. Yet here he was propped up against some pillows strumming away the best he could with this guitar.

I started signing "Honestly." Basically I was singing a cappella, as the guitar was electric and wasn't plugged in to an amp. Tears were flowing. Parents and relatives gathered around. Even I was getting choked up. I managed to make it through the song, or at least most of the stanzas, and it seemed to really lift his spirits. If ever I had felt God's Spirit in a room, it was then.

We said our good-byes and went about the evening and doing interviews. The next day, we held a press conference in a Burger King, which may seem strange, but believe it or not the restaurant chain was one of the sponsors. Inevitably, the press wanted to know *"Will Stryper be reuniting?"* It was a fair question given this would be our first real performance since 1991. Yes, we had played the Expo, but I wore sweatpants at that show and therefore, I wasn't really dressed for a "real" show.

Regardless of how they would reword the question, I'd give my standard answer that I had been giving for years: *"If we were to get back together, it would have to be for the right reasons* and God's hand would have to be on it.

After the press conference, Rich pulled me aside and in his thick New Jersey accent said, *"You keep saying it has to be for the right reasons. Did you not feel God's Spirit in the room at Andreas' house? If that's not the right reason, what is?"*

He had a point. But little did Rich know there were deep-rooted years of animosity and heartache between the band members. I never have questioned what God was able to do through this band, but I wasn't sure I was ready to put myself back in a position of reliving the past. I compared the idea of reuniting with Stryper to that of getting back together with your ex-wife after a divorce. Sure, it was great at the time, but something happened to make that marriage end. Why try to relive that all over again? Let it go and move on to other things, I told myself.

No doubt, I did love the idea of once again feeling God move through our music and touching people's lives. But I wasn't sure that I was strong enough to knock down the walls that had been built between the members of Stryper. I just wasn't ready to go back to that place in my life.

Throughout the times, when I would question getting back together with Stryper, it seemed that every time I took one step forward, something would happen to set me two steps back. Prior to the show, I was feeling a little drained so I asked for a doctor to come to the hotel to inject me with a B-12 shot. Vitamin B-12 helps boost my energy levels and can often get me through a show when I'm feeling under the weather. Unfortunately while on site, I got word that Robert had made a request from the Doctor as well, only it was for a supply of prescription Vicodin. Whether it was true or not, it was enough to send me two steps back on the path to a Stryper reunion.

The show went on as scheduled, and despite us sounding pretty rough, we managed to entertain an enthusiastic crowd. It felt good.

After the show, Rich informed me that Rodolfo and his church had lost money. All the unexpected expenses and payoffs had put them in the red.

Upon checking out of the hotel the following day, I was greeted by an enthusiastic Rodolfo who hugged me and thanked me for doing the show. He said he felt many lives were touched and that Costa Rica needed this show to help bring back the peace of God to the community. He didn't mention the money he had lost.

I pulled him aside and handed him my enormous suitcases full of Michael Sweet merchandise that I was obviously unable to sell due to the police intervention. I told him to take it and sell it for whatever he could get to help offset his financial losses. He was tearful as he hugged me and reluctantly took the merchandise. Despite his financial hit, he didn't want to see me take a loss either. I felt he needed it more than I did, though.

I have fond memories of Rodolfo, Andreas, and the beautiful people of Costa Rica.

Talks of the second Expo were already in place to be held this time in Azusa, California, in May of 2001. Rich Serpa again was leading the charge. The plan for round two was to be bigger and better than the first, with other bands performing and more vendors selling and trading Stryper collectibles. There was a state-of-the-art sound system and staging in place at Azusa University for what would become Stryper's second "official" performance as a group. I would not be wearing sweatpants this time around.

Unfortunately after our return from Costa Rica, things had started to go south between Robert and Mike Reynolds of World Gone Mad. Mike had purchased and controlled RobertSweet.com at the time, and I assume Mike anticipated promoting Robert and his new solo project.

In April of 2001, about six weeks prior to the second Expo, I had gone over to my friend Chris Ragucci's house to record some promotional videos with Rich Serpa to help promote the Expo. While there, Rich received a phone call saying that he needed to look at RobertSweet.com. I could see from the look in Rich's eyes that this wasn't going to be good.

Together we went to Chris's computer and pulled up the website. Wow! Apparently something happened that angered Mike Reynolds, and he hijacked Rob's website and posted some disturbing comments — most notably that Robert was not actually married to Victoria (or Starri, as we call her). This shocked me. For all I knew, Rob and Starri were married. They had led me to believe, and anyone they talked to, that they *were* married, and I had no reason to doubt that.

Robert later posted a statement on Stryper.com that he indeed was not married. He was apologetic to everyone and said he had hoped to keep this matter private.

It continued to get ugly between Mike and Rob. It even got to the point where Rob filed a restraining order against Mike.

Two big steps backward.

I was out at that point. Any thoughts of ever wanting to reunite with Stryper were thrown out the window, much less performing at The Expo. I was not about to go back to the *Against The Law* days of standing on stage proclaiming "Jesus Is The Way" and at the same time having this sort of thing going on within the band.

I only share this story from my perspective. If Rob ever writes a book I'm sure he can share the intimate details of what was going on behind the scenes in his life. There's probably much more to the story than I know. But what I *do* know is that I saw Rob admit to not being married, and I saw an ugly and public battle going on between him and Mike Reynolds. I didn't even want to know how much, if any of it, was true. The drama alone was enough to make me want to not be a part of this.

I told Rich I was not going to play the second Expo. Rich put a halt on all promotions that included me performing, and considered cancelling the Expo all together. Just a few days before the Expo, however, Rob followed through with getting married, which was honorable. Rich asked me to reconsider. Reluctantly, I did change my mind, but by then his entire marketing campaign was in the toilet. He had only a few days to recover from that blow. It ultimately hurt him, and the Expo, financially.

I went to California and played at the second Expo, but it wasn't like the first time around. There was an impressive crowd of almost 4,000 people, but it was very uncomfortable to me.

Aside from all the drama going on, when I arrived at the Expo site, it looked like a three-ring circus of people selling Stryper merch, including my mom. My mom had not gone to the first Expo.

According to Rich it was because he wasn't willing to pay her or cover her travel to attend. But she managed to make it to this second one, and she brought out the entire attic's worth of memorabilia to sell off. Brett Christensen also had an enormous booth of Stryper collectibles that he was selling, as did many other people. The whole thing just didn't feel right.

Throughout the years there have been a lot of people who have tried to capitalize on the Stryper name. Rich, by the way, is not one of them. When Rich first approached me about the Expo he made it about Stryper, not about him. Even in this circus atmosphere, he seemed to be doing things with a pure heart.

The vibe was not good at the second Expo. I didn't want to be there, but unfortunately I had already planned another Stryper show to take place two months later in July at The Cornerstone Festival in Illinois. I did my best to put a smile on my face and go through the motions of a show.

I left the second Expo with an extremely sour taste in my mouth. Whereas the first Expo led me toward considering a reunion, this second one sent me running in the exact opposite direction.

Those feelings remained as we went to Cornerstone. I put on the game face and played the best show I could, ironically to the biggest crowd ever to attend a Stryper show—more than 30,000 people. And once again, we got paid really well.

But I don't care how much we got paid. After the last few months of this soap opera, I could say with great certainty that I would never be playing in Stryper again.

I'm done. It was a good thought while it lasted, but the last nine months have reminded me of exactly why I left this band in the first place.

THIRTY-FIVE

In 2002 Michael Sweet Productions was a do-it-yourself operation, and I was beginning to not only feel comfortable but also happy in that role. I felt in control of my life. I still worked part-time at the campground, but most of my time was spent making phone calls trying to book solo shows. At night I would fill orders that had come in through MichaelSweet.com. It wasn't glamorous, but I was happy.

I would set up shop in the basement and get an assembly line going of stuffing CDs, cassettes and T-shirts into envelopes, addressing the packages, and getting them ready for tomorrow's mail. I enjoyed the work and the process, and once I had a system down, I actually looked forward to my daily routine. Although it wasn't what I had envisioned, I took it seriously and did my best to get things out on time, sometimes making multiple post office runs in one day.

Over the years so many good-intentioned people have offered to help me. Some of them turn out to be godsends, but most of them turn out to be folks with big ideas, lots of excitement, but with very little follow through. Nonetheless, anytime someone comes knocking on my door with ideas or interest in helping out, I try to hear them out the best I can. You just never know when you may run into the one or two few people who actually will follow through with an idea.

So in the spring of 2002 when I received a letter from a manager in North Carolina offering to "help," I took it with a grain of salt. But like with the others who have come and gone with big ideas, I decided to follow-up and give him a call. I will say this, the letter I received wasn't the typical *"Let's get Stryper back together and you can make big money again and be on top of the world. You should be playing stadiums!"*

223

Yes, letters and emails like that were a regular thing. But this one was different. There were no promises of stardom or riches. It was just a simple letter stating he was a fan and willing to help if I needed anything.

His name was Dave Rose, owner of Deep South Entertainment. We talked on the phone for a while, and while I liked his enthusiasm I had seen first-hand that enthusiasm can only do so much. I was scheduled to be performing in Charlotte, North Carolina, for a Christian festival produced by Richard Young, a promoter who had been (and still is) a longtime supporter of Stryper. I invited Dave and his business partner, Andy Martin, to the show.

When Dave arrived backstage, he introduced himself briefly and I went on with my pre-show routine. As he walked away I asked Kyle "Who is that again?" The combination of my bad memory and me receiving an overwhelming amount of requests from people willing to "help" made it impossible for me to remember the details of names, and because of that, I was embarrassed.

Dave spent most of the time talking with Kyle, but later in the day we all talked for a while in the catering area backstage. He shared with me his passion for my music, but what I remember most is that he seemed sincere in wanting to help, all the while not offering promises of world tours and guaranteed placement back on the charts.

I got a good vibe from him but I was comfortable with my "less is more" place in life and in music. I wasn't ready to complicate it with business people. Based on past experience, I was pretty much done with managers.

We continued to stay in touch, and in fall of 2002 Dave flew out to Massachusetts where he, Andy, Kyle and I went to lunch at a local Applebee's. We talked more seriously about some ideas for my career and the possibility of working together. We also spent several hours talking about shopping my music to record labels and trying to get some momentum going again with my solo career.

Just to gauge his reaction, but also in the interest of being honest, I said to him at that meeting, *"Dave, I'd like to work together, but I need to tell you that I will never play in Stryper again."* He seemed genuinely okay with that. Normally when I would share my disinterest in Stryper with someone I would see the look of disappointment in their face. Or they would turn the conversation toward why the band should get back together. But Dave seemed unfazed by the statement, which made me even more comfortable.

After our meeting, he sent me a marketing plan and a management proposal. I remember in that proposal, as part of his closing sales pitch on why I should work with him, he wrote, *"I'm probably the only guy in the business who has managed Grammy-winning artists and also owns an original cassette of the Roxx Regime demo."* His love for my music and knowledge of my career was evident.

We began working together that summer. Dave starting shopping my material to labels and, just as I experienced, he was met with minimal interest.

Not long prior, I had met Jonathan Harris, a guy who seemed fairly well connected in the industry, and eventually I hired him as my part-time tour manager for the solo shows. Jonathan owns a hat company where he makes custom painted cowboy hats for anyone and everyone. He seemed to know a lot of people and have some good connections. He also had lots of promising ideas. Jonathan had connected with a booking agent, Andrew Goodfriend, and like many conversations when my name comes up, the idea of a Stryper reunion tour was discussed immediately.

I was apprehensive for all the reasons I've previously stated, but I agreed to let them put their feelers out and see what kind of interest there might be.

Simultaneously, as these insider talks were going on about a reunion, Dave was continuing to run into closed doors with my solo career. Labels and agents just weren't as interested as we had hoped. One day on the phone with Dave as we were discussing the frustrating hurdles we were encountering with my solo career, he said to me, *"I know you don't want to do Stryper again, but it just may be the best way to let the world know you're alive and well and still ready to make music. Maybe doing a one-time Stryper reunion tour would create the buzz we need to get labels interested in you as a solo artist."*

I desperately wanted to kick-start my solo career again, but it seemed that the only way I could do it would be to get back in the spotlight with Stryper again. This was not at all the solution I was hoping for. I didn't want to get back in Stryper.

What if I just did a one-time reunion tour with no promises of the future? What if I mended ways with Rob, Oz, and Tim? Maybe that is *just* what I need to get something going with my solo career again. Maybe it had been too long since Stryper and I needed some sort of spark to get things going again.

I knew, however, in order for a reunion to take place there would need to be a lot of true healing, and without that I wasn't about to head down this road — solo career or not at stake.

In 2002 I had reached out to Hollywood Records about the idea of a 20th Anniversary Greatest Hits CD, with a couple of new tracks recorded for the album. I wrote two new songs, "Something" and "For You," and for the first time in almost 10 years the original members of Stryper recorded together. That album, called *Seven*, came out in March of 2003.

The idea of a reunion was becoming stronger, but I knew a lot of damage repair needed to happen before this could go any further. It started with me calling all the guys. One by one I called and shared my heart about the idea, and my reservations, of a reunion tour.

You often hear bands that reunite talk about putting the past behind them. I took just the opposite approach. Rather than putting the past behind us, I felt we should confront the past. If we put it behind us, it would only show up at our doorstep again. But if we faced the past, dealt with it, and healed from it, perhaps God could work through us again. I wanted to talk about the past and mend the things that broke us up in the first place. We needed to give this band back to God completely. Through these phone conversations with Tim, Oz, and Robert, I began to feel the possibility that we may actually be able to forgive one another and turn this band around.

Andrew and Jonathan had been reaching out to promoters to see if there would be interest in Stryper shows. *Seven* had been released with a favorable response. Dave was also encouraging a reunion in order to possibly get my solo career back on track. Most important, I felt God's hand was in all of this. The toughest part of all of this would be convincing Kyle that it was meant to be. She, of course, and rightfully so, was apprehensive about a Stryper reunion.

I prayed about the situation, and I was beginning to feel that God was calling me to give this a shot—the idea of a one-time reunion tour.

I gave the green light to Jonathan and Andrew to put together a short reunion tour. We would support *Seven* and start the process. Through it all, I was honest in letting everyone know that this was a one-time deal. This was not Stryper reuniting on a permanent basis—this would be a one-time only reunion tour.

As things started to ramp up, I also began to realize we were going to need some serious help in getting this off the ground. Jonathan was a real go-getter, but I felt he lacked the experience within the industry to completely handle putting together a tour of this magnitude.

I called Dave and asked if he'd like to manage the reunion tour. His response was an enthusiastic *"Yes, of course I would. But I need to ask – do you even have the authority to appoint me as manager? Are there still agreements with your Mom? Do the other members need to sign off on this?"*

I told him that I did have the authority. I said if I was going to do this reunion tour, I was going to lead it. For the most part, Robert had always led Stryper. After all, I joined Robert's band as the singer. But if I was going to come back to this band, it was going to have to be under terms I was comfortable with such as personal and spiritual terms and business operations.

Looking at it from a business point of view, Stryper was failing toward the end in the early 1990s. It did fail. We went bankrupt. So if you have a business that fails and you decide to reorganize or re-launch it, you don't go back to the old ways of doing business. You do something new and try to right the wrongs that happened in the first place.

I was already skeptical about the idea of putting Stryper back together, even short term. But if it was going to happen, I had some basic conditions that I needed the guys to agree to, and one of those was that I would be running the band. This was not a power play for control but rather a desire to make absolutely certain that we didn't fall back in to our old ways—ways that had obviously broken us apart. I said, *"The only way I'm going to do this is if you let me take care of handling things the way I feel they need to be handled, including the people we do business with, the songs, the show, and the overall operations of the band."*

I spoke with the guys about Dave, and they were hesitant but supportive for the most part. I think they all just wanted to reunite so badly that I could have told them anyone would be managing the band and they would have gone along with it. I was determined not to slip back into the old routine of letting others handle our business. I knew that with Dave driving the car, I would be able to give the directions — and I needed that for my sanity of knowing we'd stay on course.

We began rehearsals for the tour, which consisted of a series of reconciliation meetings. Most of them happened in hotel rooms where the four of us would gather and just go around the room pouring our hearts out. We held nothing back and spoke openly and honestly about what was on our minds. We spoke specifically to one another about deep-rooted pain whether it was between Tim and I, Rob and Oz, Oz and I, or whomever — we just opened up and told each other exactly what we were thinking. There were a lot of feelings of resentment that came out in those talks. It was some heavy stuff, but the wounds needed to heal.

I would express myself and why I left the band and why I didn't want to rejoin. They shared with me why they were upset at me for doing so. We talked about the *Against The Law* issues, the drunken days and all that went on during that time period. By doing this, a lot of tears were shed and a lot of forgiveness was granted. We prayed together. It was like we were starting all over again. And we were — friends and brothers again from the beginning.

We had lots of these prayer and healing sessions during rehearsals. After years of animosity and tension, it felt as though we could breathe again. We had laid the weight at God's feet and we stopped trying to carry it ourselves. And on October 2, 2003, we began the first tour together in 12 years. Our first show was at Jaxx in

Springfield, Virginia. That tour took us coast to coast, and we played to capacity or near-capacity crowds nightly.

We got off to a slightly rocky but comical start with this tour. Jaxx had agreed to let us come in a day early to do a full rehearsal. We needed a practice run outside the confines of our small rehearsal space. Rob's drum tech had set up his kit on that first day, and I immediately noticed what was painted on the kick-drum head facing the audience. It was a picture of Rob from the '80s painted on the drumhead for all the audience to see.

Oz, Tim and I felt that it came across somewhat vein and out of place. But that was Rob—the consummate showman always willing to push the envelope. I wasn't quite ready to push the envelope quite yet.

It was the classic *To Hell With The Devil* era picture where Rob has one hand raised behind his head. It was sometimes referred to as the Farrah Fawcett shot because of Rob's hairdo and obvious pose. So how do you tell your drummer, and brother, that he shouldn't have a picture of himself painted on his kick-drum head? Well, the right way would probably be to sit down and have a conversation about it. Nah, that's no fun. So when he wasn't looking we cut some of Oz's hair and taped it to Rob's armpit to make the picture more lifelike.

Rob saw it and wasn't too happy. We ultimately told him in a respectful manner that we just didn't feel it set the best tone for the show being our first time back in 12 years. He understood, I think. Honestly, I'm not even sure it was Rob who had it done. His drum tech may have taken it upon himself to do it. Either way we all got a good laugh out of the armpit hair.

Michael Guido came out for a while during that tour and really helped to get us back on track spiritually. We continued to meet on the bus nightly as we prayed together and continued to work on rebuilding trust. We humbled ourselves again and as a result we began to see a lot of things happen that we had not seen since the early to mid-80s. Lives were being touched with a whole new generation of Stryper fans. Older fans were bringing their kids to the shows, and it was great to feel God working again. Almost nightly I'd end the show in a prayer. It was amazing to be performing at clubs where only God knows what took place the night before or the night after—but at the end of the night of the Stryper show, we would ask the entire place to take a moment and pray with us. We still do it to this day, and it's always a special part of the show.

We played to a capacity crowd at Irving Plaza in New York, and in an attempt to stay on course with promoting my solo career, I would take meetings before and after the shows. In New York, for example, I met with Danny Goldberg of Artemis Records the day after our show. He had previously passed on me, but this mention of a sold-out Stryper show seemed to spark his interest. We played Rocketown in Nashville, and the day prior to the show I took meetings with a lot of industry folks from my past. Everyone seemed to be excited about possibly working together. And in St. Petersburg, Florida, at Jannus Landing, an A&R guy from Big3 Records named Jim Beeman came out to the show and took an interest in a possible future together.

Maybe this *was* what I needed. Maybe if I gave it all back over to God and truly surrendered, and truly asked for forgiveness both of Him and my band mates, He would bless my life as well. That's my experience with God. When you give it all to Him, He does the same in return. I was feeling good about being back in Stryper, all the while reminding the audience nightly that this was not a permanent reunion. It was a one-time "celebration" tour.

As the tour wore on I began to feel less excited about it. Maybe it was being on a tour bus for seven weeks with these guys for the first time in 12 years. That was partially it, but I did start to feel some of the old ways creeping back in slowly. When there's as much deep-rooted animosity built up between members, it's just hard to regroup from that, no matter how much you try to do so.

The tour ended in Boston on November 19, 2003, and the love we felt from the fans throughout the tour was moving.

Financially, it was our first profitable tour since *Soldiers Under Command*.

In March of 2004 we picked back up and played an unforgettable show in Puerto Rico at the Tito Puente Amphitheater to a sold-out crowd of 7,000+ people. It was the most enthusiastic crowd I had witnessed in a long time, possibly ever. We filmed that show for a DVD, and I'm glad we did because it was great moment to capture in Stryper history. It wasn't so much our performance, although I felt we played well, but the energy level of the fans in Puerto Rico is like no other.

While in Puerto Rico we did an in-store appearance at a mall. It was held at a record store in San Juan. Thousands of people showed up as if we were reliving the days in Australia when the police had to be called out for crowd control.

As we were leaving the store after the event, I decided to take a detour to a coffee shop. I quickly got some coffee and we all headed for the mall exit. As soon as we opened the doors to leave the mall, I heard someone yell, *"There they are. Stryper."* I turned around and saw a mob of fans, hundreds of them, who were running toward us. We all took off sprinting toward the SUV that was waiting outside to drive us back to the hotel. The driver was in the vehicle. He could see us running toward the car and the sea of people behind us, so he jumped out of the driver's seat and opened all the doors so we could get inside quickly.

I ran at full speed toward that car, spilling coffee everywhere, then literally dived through the open doors into the back seats. The driver sped off with the doors still open but the forward momentum slammed them shut just as the crowd approached and started banging on the sides of the car. Our fans in Puerto Rico are passionate about Stryper — *and for that* I'm forever thankful to them.

During the tour in the States we recorded many of the shows, and in May of 2004 we released a collection of those recordings called *7 Weeks, Live in America,* our first-ever live album. We released that project and the Puerto Rico DVD on our self-owned label Fifty Three Five Records. Surprisingly, as a self-released album without the backing of a major label, we charted on three different Billboard charts, hitting #2 in the Internet charts, just behind Hillary Duff. That live album also charted on the Christian and Independent charts as well.

It was a nice reunion run but I was happy it was over. I walked away from that tour feeling equally as good about its success as I did about its conclusion. I enjoyed seeing the fans and playing to incredibly enthusiastic crowds, but I felt the same as when we started the tour. As far as I was concerned, it was a one-time deal and we would not be permanently reuniting.

In 2004, I recorded some songs at my home studio with the intention of shopping for a solo deal. Jim Beeman from Big3 Records, who had seen us the previous year in St. Petersburg, took an extreme liking in the songs. He played them for everyone at the label, and they were impressed with them as well, including the label president and owner, Bill Edwards.

In the meantime, we had been offered another show as Stryper that we decided to take in September of 2004. It would be at Night of Joy held at Disney World in Florida. We had played Night of Joy before, and it was always a positive experience so we were excited to come back. There was only one problem. We had reservations about continuing on with Tim again and likewise, Tim had reservations about staying in the band.

Coming off the heels of the Puerto Rico show, things just didn't feel right. Tim didn't seem happy, and we weren't completely happy with him either. We had all grown over the past 12 years, and it was unrealistic to think we'd all be at the same place mentally or as I often put it, on the same page.

We scheduled a conference call for the four of us, along with Dave Rose, to discuss the future of Stryper. On that call we were planning to let Tim go. We had called Dave in advance and discussed the best way to break the news. There's never an easy way to break this sort of news, so it's always helpful, at least for me anyway, to talk it through with someone else in advance.

As the conference call began we told Tim that he seemed unhappy in the band and from there we let him have the floor. He talked for a while and ultimately admitted to indeed not being happy within the band. He said that the "rock star" lifestyle just didn't seem to be for him any longer, and within a few minutes of the call he suggested that he step down from Stryper.

Well, that was easier than I expected. Here I was nervous about how to let him go, and he lets himself go. It was for the best. At the time, he seemed miserable in the band and if there would be any chance for Stryper to continue, although we were still somewhat uncertain of that future, it would need to be without Tim.

We hired Tracy Ferrie to take his place for this show. Tracy had been in several Christian bands prior and had toured with me for my solo stuff as well. It seemed to make sense that he would make the perfect replacement.

While in Florida, I shared with the guys my interest from Big3 Records, and in the rental van I played the songs I had recorded.

Oz loved them. He really took an interest in the songs, and I could tell he was genuinely impressed. After a couple of listens he spoke up saying *"These are great songs. This should be a Stryper record!"*

That statement and excitement from Oz planted the seed in my heart and head.

I went back to Big3, who was already offering me a deal as a solo artist, and asked if they'd be interested in turning it into a Stryper deal instead. Bill Edwards was thrilled about the idea and got totally on board with it. We signed an agreement to do three albums with Big3 and to tour in support of those albums.

Well, it looks like Stryper is back together after all on a permanent scale. Tracy joined the band as a full-fledged member. We all went back into the studio to overhaul the songs I had previously recorded with plans as a solo release. Although many of the initial tracks remained on the Stryper version, all the guys came in and laid down their respective parts and it slowly transformed from a Michael Sweet solo album to a Stryper album. We called it *Reborn*, a statement of our renewed faith in God and in ourselves.

Reborn was released in August of 2005 and debuted at #111 on the Billboard top 200. I was impressed with that given it was our first full-length studio album in 15 years.

Stryper was back, but would we be able to grow our fan base, or would we become just another nostalgic touring act? We had a renewed energy and were eager to give it all that we had, with God leading the way.

THIRTY-SIX

The honeymoon was over by the time we set out to tour in support of *Reborn*. Our attendance had dropped slightly on this tour, which was to be expected given the "newness" of us being back together had worn off, never mind the fact that this tour consisted of only 75 percent of the original line-up.

Reborn continued to garner press and attention but the most enlightening developments to me were the sporadic comments from fans saying, *"Eh, this is just another Michael Sweet solo record."* This surprised me. Word had spread that I had previously written and recorded these songs and then turned the material into a Stryper record. Keep in mind it was Oz who suggested the idea of this becoming a Stryper record (and Rob agreed), yet there was this spin on it within the Stryper community that I was somehow forcing my solo material into becoming a Stryper record.

These comments from fans were eye opening for a few reasons. First, they were from the same people who for years had been complaining *"Why don't you put Stryper back together?"* and now were quick to pass judgment that this was just another solo album. My knee-jerk response to the naysayers was *"Look, it was YOU that wanted me to put Stryper back together. If it weren't for this album, Stryper wouldn't be back together. Which would you prefer? Us back together or not?"*

Secondly, what exactly *is* a Michael Sweet solo album versus a Stryper album? I've always written most of the songs for Stryper. I've always led the band musically. It's the same songwriter, same singer and same guitar parts. Sure, there are subtle differences between a Stryper record and a Michael Sweet record (mostly in the style of songs and edge), but certainly not major ones, especially regarding *Reborn*. And lastly, the accusation of this just being another solo album was simply wrong. The guys come in to record their parts. It was a Stryper record created in a similar fashion to all the other Stryper albums that have been created.

The reviews of *Reborn* were overwhelmingly positive, but within the tight-knit circle of Stryper fans I got a solid lesson in *"You can't please everyone."* They wanted Stryper back together, but apparently only on their terms. I'm not exactly sure what those terms would have been. Did they expect us, now in our 40s, to all move into a house together in Southern California, write songs collectively during the day and drive around Sunset Strip at night in our yellow-and-black van tossing demos to everyone we passed? What did the naysayers want? The reality was that this was the real world, where we were all living in separate parts of the country and living separate lives. Basically, we made the record the same way we had always made albums, but it was difficult for some people to believe that.

We started the tour in August of '05 in Puerto Rico, and we toured the U.S. through the end of November doing what I call a "House of Blues" tour. Essentially, we were playing at House of Blues and similar-sized venues throughout the country. We toured overseas the following year, in 2006, playing primarily festivals.

In August of that same year I released another solo album, *Him*, a collection of traditional hymns on which I rearranged and wrote new music. It would be my fourth full-length studio album (fifth if you count the two versions of *Truth*). It was a small independent release through a company where my friend Jamie Warden was working. I went to the Gospel Music Association (GMA) week in Nashville and did some promotion and interviews to surround it but it never really got the push it deserved. I presented a lifetime achievement award at the televised Dove Awards (part of the GMA week), alongside my friend Bryan Duncan and gospel music icon Andrea Crouch.

We were on a limited budget with this release, but thanks to one of my best friends and publicist Brian Mayes, we managed to get that album some solid attention in the Christian music world. In a business where publicists come and go regularly, Brian has been a solid rock. He's always been there for me, even when I didn't have the money to pay a publicist. He's always quick to jump in and lend a helping hand. He worked hard getting *Him* as much attention as possible given its limited budget on a small label. I'm proud of that album, and I still think it holds its own as a creative and respectful approach to some of the greatest hymns of all time.

The year 2006 was tumultuous in my personal life. Kyle and I had been going through a stressful legal battle with her brother, Brock. The cranberry bogs where I had been working had been in Kyle's family for more than 100 years. They were one of the top cranberry producers in the state, selling to Ocean Spray from the very beginning.

Kyle's father, Paul Tucy, had married into the family business when he married Kyle's mother, Marion. Unfortunately in the '80s they wound up divorcing. In the divorce, Paul purchased the 800+-acre piece of property (one of the largest privately owned lots in Massachusetts) from Marion for a ridiculously low price. Still, Marion got some money and the house they had built together overlooking Buttermilk Bay. Paul got the cranberry business and the campground.

Kyle became estranged from her father in the '80s and moved to LA to pursue a career as a make-up artist in the film industry. Although she had graduated with honors from Colby College with a degree in child psychology, she decided to become a make-up artist and wound up being one of the most successful ones in LA. When we moved back to The Cape in 1995, Kyle mended ways with her father, and he eventually hired us both on to work at the campground. Brock didn't seem to like this, as he had been working there throughout her time in LA and, in my opinion, viewed us as a threat. Brock and Paul had a really odd relationship. They were constantly arguing and yelling at one another, or so it seemed to me. It was obvious Brock didn't like Kyle and I being a part of the family business.

Paul eventually became ill with prostate cancer. As his health was deteriorating, Brock somehow managed to obtain power of attorney for his father. Paul signed over the campground and cranberry business to Brock, who became the sole owner. Paul eventually passed away, and by this time Kyle and I were not working there much at all.

Paul's intentions were to always leave the business to Kyle and Brock, collectively. But as time passed, Brock refused to give Kyle her half of the estate. For months Kyle patiently waited for Brock to do the right thing. We eventually consulted with our pastor who suggested that we hire an attorney and proceed with legal action. So we did. It was a spiritually, mentally and emotionally draining battle, to the point where I had to rush Kyle to the hospital multiple times due to exhaustion and borderline breakdowns. Barely a day went by throughout this process that Kyle wasn't in tears or close to it. It took a significant toll on her, and I witnessed it first hand. Stress can weaken your immune system, and I believe it to possibly be the primary cause of many major illnesses.

Eventually we won the long and drawn-out lawsuit, but we were beaten up pretty bad. To fight with your own brother like this, over something that shouldn't have been a fight in the first place, made Kyle an emotional wreck. Unfortunately, it wasn't as easy as *"Judgment in favor of Kyle Sweet"* and we'd move on with our lives. After the judgment, we received a payout from Brock, but later we discovered that the IRS had accessed the value of the property to be substantially more. That meant more taxes were due on the property, and now we had to pay a large portion of the bill to Uncle Sam. It was one mess after another. Eventually, Brock declared bankruptcy and after more than a century, the banks would now own the family business.

As we moved in to 2007, the plan was for Stryper to begin working on the next studio album for Big3, but Kyle got sick and life got complicated.

She had been complaining of bloating and cramping, and she began putting on some weight. Her doctors passed it off saying she was nearing the stages of menopause. Believe it or not, this went on for more than a year. On the night of February 9, 2007, as we settled in to bed, I noticed a protruding lump in her abdomen. Kyle was becoming more and more uncomfortable, so the very next morning we went to Jordan Hospital in Plymouth where they ran some inconclusive tests and an ultrasound. They discovered a large mass near her ovaries, but they were uncertain as to what it was until they performed a biopsy. Kyle and I didn't want to admit it, nor did we say it out loud, but we had an idea what it could be. We prayed and hoped for the best, though.

The following day she was transported by ambulance to Boston's Brigham and Women's hospital, which is ranked among the best hospitals in the country. As a result, it's difficult to get seen on short notice, but they rushed Kyle in and began testing, including biopsies. It was a sad time as it was Mikey's 20th birthday and approaching Lena's sweet 16, plus Valentine's Day right in the middle. We spent those birthdays and Valentine's Day in the hospital.

Thankfully, I had Pastor David Johnson with me. He was a rock and incredibly helpful with things both small and large, from helping with the kids, running errands, and he was there with sympathetic and unwavering spiritual guidance.

The biopsy came back and revealed ovarian cancer. The hospital scheduled surgery immediately, and we were able to get one of the best surgeons, Dr. Colleen Feltmate, at one of the finest medical establishments in the country.

Throughout all of this the days and nights were much longer. I slept every night in a chair in Kyle's hospital room. The operation was scheduled to take about two to three hours, but instead it was lasted more than five hours.

David Johnson and I sat in a waiting room. We were the only two there. We talked and prayed and also sat in silence. I told myself everything would be okay. David told me everything would be okay. But, intellectually, I knew the possibilities of a bleak future were very real.

The doctor finally emerged from the operating room exhausted and drained from an unusually long procedure. *"I got everything I could, all that was visible,"* were her words to me. She went on to share with us the details of the procedure, and how the cancer had spread. She told us it was Stage 4 ovarian cancer due to it having spread to other organs. She shared with us some of our treatment options available and that we would be closely monitoring her progress over the coming weeks and months.

Even though Dr. Feltmate had taken the time to share so much, I heard none of it.

I only heard *"Stage 4 ovarian cancer."* After that she may as well have been speaking German. Fortunately, David Johnson was there to help me sort it all out. I knew I needed to be strong for Kyle and for the kids, but all I could do was cry. One thing I did take away from this post-surgery briefing was the doctor telling us that from here on out the future would not be about the quantity of life – it would be about the quality. Basically, beating around the bush, she was telling us Kyle's time here on earth was limited and all we could do was to give her the best quality of life possible until the end.

After a long process, Kyle healed from the surgery and weeks later she started treatment. During the process, it was the first time I had heard the term CA-125, which is a tumor marker used in ovarian cancer staging, and it would become a term I'd use hundreds of times daily in the coming months. A normal, non-cancerous reading typically has a value ranging from 0 to 40. Kyle's marker was 6,000+ when first diagnosed.

After much thought as to which drug treatment to use, Kyle began chemotherapy. In the months that would follow, I'm not even sure how she got out of bed every day. It was overwhelming and exhausting, but she was a fighter. She would pull through each day with optimism and hope.

I was wrestling with all sorts of unwanted thoughts and questions in my head, as was Kyle. *"How could You do this, God?"* was a common one. I had all of these thoughts and I just couldn't control them. I kept asking God why this was happening. *"We've served You our entire lives and this is what we get? We have two kids and Kyle doesn't deserve this, we don't deserve this,"* I would think regularly. I'm surprised we were able to hold it together. As difficult as it was, we continued going to church but we were committed to fighting and working hard on what would surely be a long road ahead.

In the meantime, we were visiting dietitians and spending time shopping for anything and everything that could possibly get her body in check and her immune system strong enough to fight this dreaded disease on its own. We prayed a lot. We also questioned God a lot. It was an up and down, all-around roller coaster ride emotionally and physically. Miraculously, after only a few treatments her CA-125 number began to drop and eventually, in the safe range, below 40!

For all practical purposes and according to the numbers, Kyle was cancer free. The doctors called it "remission." We called it a miracle. To say we were ecstatic with joy would be a gross understatement.

Our good friends Matt and Laurie Crouch invited us to be on their program *Praise The Lord*, which airs on TBN. It was a segment about miracles, and man did we have one to share. We announced to the world that Kyle was cancer free. For a moment, life was amazing. We were so incredibly thankful and happy.

But as quickly as the cancer left, it came back, with a vengeance. Her CA-125 number rose again, and we began the journey that would test our faith and our family.

Just a few weeks after Kyle had surgery, in March of 2007, one of my favorite singers of all time died. It was Brad Delp, lead vocalist of rock band Boston. Maybe I had a heightened sense of just how fragile and precious life was during this time. Whatever the case, I felt the need to publicly express my feelings about Brad's untimely and tragic passing. Brad had committed suicide. Here I was dealing with life being so uncertain for my wife, and one of my childhood rock hero's had taken his own life. The world was a confusing place for me at the moment. Why was all this happening?

One of my friends, Brian Dixey, was Brad's guitar tech. Brad's and my path had come close to crossing many times, but I never had the pleasure of meeting him. But ever since I first heard Brad sing when I was 13 years old, I admired him. Boston was a huge influence on me. It wasn't just the vocals, but I would work for hours trying to achieve a better guitar tone because of that band. I've always loved Brad's voice, and from what I heard from friends that personally knew him, he was one of the nicest guys you'd ever want to meet. I heard he was very un-rock-star like and an incredibly humble person.

I wrote a few paragraphs online about Brad and what he meant to me. From what I understand, Tom Scholz and his wife, Kim, had read what I wrote and were deeply touched by it.

Feeling alone and confused after finding out Kyle's cancer was back, I was out in the yard one day doing some work, trying my best to cope with everything at hand. Yard work was my therapy. It gave me a chance to think without all the congestion of phone calls and emails going on. I remember feeling abandoned by God. I felt as though He was nowhere to be found. I continued to ask, *"How could God do this to a woman who has devoted her life to Him and given up everything for Him? Now she's stricken with Stage 4 cancer and has to suffer."* Not that God owes me, or anyone anything, but those were just the honest thoughts going through my head at the time. It was a tug of war between all that I knew and all that I thought I knew.

At a time like this you want to have hope. You want to have faith. But you're faced with the statistics that less than 5 percent of women with Stage 4 ovarian cancer survive longer than two years.

With all of these thoughts going on in my head, my yard looked immaculate during this time. I mowed, raked and cleaned the yard regularly.

Kyle came out on the back deck one day and motioned for me to turn off the mower. *"You've got a call,"* she said. I didn't want to take any calls. *"It's Dave Rose. He says it's important."* Dave, my manager, tells me that he had just heard from Kim Scholz—Tom's wife—and they had asked if I would like to be part of the last-ever Boston show, which was going to be held in the city of Boston. It was a show to honor Brad Delp and to raise funds as a benefit to Brad. They were calling it their last show ever and their intention was to bring out a variety of guest singers to participate including Ann Wilson, Mickey Thomas, and Sammy Hagar.

Almost immediately, my stomach turned and all the questions you would assume might run through my head did. "Maybe I'll *get to sing 'More Than A Feeling' or 'Peace of Mind' or 'Rock and Roll Band'! It would be awesome to sing one, two or even three of those classic Boston songs."*

Not long afterward, I had that conversation with Kim who suggested I sing a song called *"Higher Power." I had to Google that song.* It wasn't necessarily one of their hits. I could only assume they chose this song because I was a Christian and they thought this would be the most suitable song. She didn't say that of course, but it was the only thing I could imagine at the time. Inwardly I was slightly disappointed but on the phone I said *"Absolutely. Anything you want me to sing. Count me in."*

A few days passed and I continued my daily yard work routine when again the phone rings, this time my cell phone. I looked at the screen and it read "restricted." I never answer restricted calls, ever. I don't like talking on the phone in the first place, never mind to people I don't know. Since I'm not aware of any friends who have a restricted number, surely it must be a sales pitch. For some reason I shut the mower off and answered the call. It was Tom Scholz, obviously calling from a private number.

I tried to be calm and collected, but I was talking to Tom Scholz! I was floored and nervous. We talked for a while as I paced back and forth in my backyard. He admitted to having never heard me sing prior to reading my post, so he had gone out and bought some Stryper records. I don't know how many he bought or specifically which ones other than he did mention purchasing our most recent album, *Reborn*. He shared with me that he was really impressed by the songwriting and my singing.

To be told that by Tom Scholz was beyond huge to me. Boston was a band with one of the best singers of all time, and a band with some of the best rock songs in history. So I'm on the phone with Tom in my jeans and tee shirt with a smile on my face thinking, *"Wow. This is unbelievable. I've probably just heard the biggest and best compliment I've ever received in this business."*

And then it got better. Because Tom had heard me sing and had heard my songs, he said he wanted to open up the opportunity for me to sing more than just *"Higher Power."* I mentioned how it would be amazing to sing more, and he said he would also like me to sing *"More Than a Feeling"*, *"Rock and Roll Band"*, and possibly *"Peace of Mind."*

I couldn't believe what I was hearing!

After reality set in, I realized how much I needed to rehearse and prepare. "More Than a Feeling" is a tough song to sing, and I don't think any singer would dispute that. I had a lot of work to do.

I went into my studio and started learning the songs both on guitar and vocals, as I assumed I would be playing guitar at the show as well. I learned these songs note-for-note, or at least to the best of my ability, rehearsing for hours on end.

Rehearsals with Tom and the band had been scheduled for a few weeks prior to the show. In my first rehearsal it was just Tom, Gary Pihl and I. I was a nervous wreck, but it all hit me like a ton of bricks when I went to plug my guitar in. I walked over to the pedal board that controlled my amp and written in black Sharpie on a piece of tape it read, "Brad." I was playing through Brad Delp's rig.

We didn't do any singing on the first song, which was "Rock and Roll Band." We just played. I could see in my peripheral vision that Tom was pleased. We paused after part of the way through the song and Tom was grinning ear to ear. He said to Gary that he had never heard the guitars sound this good. He told me about

246

previous encounters with players and that this just felt better than he could imagine. He was really excited about the guitars and for that, I breathed my first sigh of relief in months.

Honestly, I was surprised by how little singing I did the first few days of rehearsals. I had just assumed that my voice would be the deciding factor. Fortunately I had practiced those guitar parts relentlessly in the week's prior.

The first full band rehearsal for the show, with drums, had me a bit nervous as well. We started with "More Than A Feeling." I sang that song my own way. Aside from me sounding nothing like Brad, I had my own style and interpretation of that song, so I was a little apprehensive with this being the first song that we'd rehearse together as a band. But as we got through the song, I could see it was working. Tom was smiling, and everyone in the room seemed to be doing so as well. After it was over there were high-fives being passed around and real sense of celebration in the air. They seemed to genuinely approve of my interpretation of the song.

Show day came on August 19, 2007. The show was taking place at the Bank of America Pavilion in Boston. It was a sold-out show. I had never had so many knots in my stomach. I was so nervous, and I couldn't seem to overcome it backstage. I had Dave Rose there. He's always been a great support. He was giving me lines like *"I feel like a proud Papa."* He was really encouraging. Kyle was also there, and she helped sooth my nerves as well. I think she was partially just happy to see me doing something other than Stryper and on such a grand scale.

Showtime came and I went to strike the first chord on my guitar and nothing came out. I hurried to the side stage and said to the guitar tech that I was getting no signal. He already knew it and was equally as shocked. If you see footage of that show, you can see guys frantically running around on stage trying to figure out what was wrong — why I wasn't getting any signal.

It was not the best way to start the show of a lifetime. "Peace of Mind" would be the first song I'd sing, and despite my guitar still not working, I was ready—nervous, but ready. I recruited the crowd to raise their hands and sing along. They did. It was magic. A sea of Boston fans, mostly there to pay tribute to the band's recently deceased singer, were joining me, singing along to one of Boston's biggest hits. For a moment I truly did feel at one with the audience, and as odd as it may sound, I felt Brad's spirit among us. It was no longer as if I was singing *to* the crowd—it was as if I was singing *with* the crowd. Together we were singing for, maybe even with, Brad. We were like a group of friends gathered to pay tribute to a lost friend. My nerves went away the moment I realized that the crowd and I were in this together. Together, we were going to sing Brad's songs.

My dear friend to this day, Tommy DeCarlo, also had his debut with Boston that night. He sounds like Brad. Kim had discovered him through a myspace account, when Tommy was working at Home Depot. Tommy had never been on such a professional level before, so I'm sure his nerves were just as shot as mine, if not even more so. He did a great job that night and it was really cool to see a "regular guy" singing these songs so perfectly.

After the show Tom was incredibly appreciative and excited. We talked for a while afterward, and I could sense his excitement about what had just taken place onstage. He shared with me that because it went so well, the band was considering doing more performances and that maybe this won't be the last Boston show after all. He said my performance exceeded his expectations, and he indicated that if Boston did any more touring he would like for me to be a part of it.

"What? Did I just hear that right? More shows and me a part of it?"

That's when I felt a little nudge from God. Not that it's about being rewarded from God. It's not. God doesn't owe me a thing. But all

248

my days of mowing the lawn wondering where God was and what He was thinking, this moment was as if God was tapping me on the shoulder and saying, *"I haven't gone anywhere, I'm right here by your side."*

THIRTY-SEVEN

Anyone who has followed the career of Boston knows that it's a band that doesn't move at a swift pace. The band's first album came out in 1976 and the guys only had a total of six studio albums spanning 35 years. They've never been known as a band to turn out releases in a timely manner or regular pace. So when Tom (Scholz) mentioned the idea of me possibly touring as a member of Boston, I was hopeful but not exactly optimistic. This was okay with me though, as I knew Kyle would need me to be home, not to mention I wanted to be home with her.

While I was on tour overseas with Stryper in November of 2007, I received a call from Troy Blakely of APA (the agency for both Stryper and Boston at the time). Troy told me that Boston was going to tour in 2008 and they'd like me to be a part of it. I accepted the invitation, although I did find it odd that the phone call came from the booking agent and not directly from Tom. Regardless, I was thrilled at the possibilities. Simultaneously as I felt excitement, concern set in over how I would possibly be able to pull this off. I couldn't leave Kyle while she was sick — the thought was just too much for me to bear. The what-ifs were racing through my head and it was overwhelming to say the least.

Soon after I accepted the position over the phone, word had traveled fast. Boston had issued a press release, and I began getting asked about my involvement with Boston almost immediately during Stryper interviews. Being alongside my band mates while talking about possibly touring with Boston wasn't the easiest of conversations to have and often it was uncomfortable.

Whether it be a new band I'm producing or an opportunity to sing or play on another record, or in this case tour with another band, I don't always talk in depth to the guys in Stryper about these moments. I've just never felt much of a congratulatory vibe from the guys when these types of opportunities arise. Perhaps they view my other projects, and particularly one as grandiose as touring with Boston, as a threat to the longevity and sustainability of Stryper. Speaking openly and honestly, they're probably right. So as a result, we just don't talk too much about this stuff when we're together.

Sure, they said they were happy for me, and I believe they were to some extent, but it certainly wasn't jubilation. I can understand that.

When I returned from the short run overseas, I spent a lot of time talking to Kyle about the idea of touring with Boston. She encouraged me to do it, as I suspected she would, but I wasn't so sure. I was her primary caretaker, and the thought of leaving her alone was more than troublesome to me. Frankly, it consumed my every thought. I was doing all the shopping, most of the cooking, most of the chores around the house and even bathing and cleaning her when she was really weak. I also administered her medications often and helped to keep things in order there. The thought of leaving her seemed impossible due to the day-to-day details of life. But Kyle encouraged me to press on. She knew this meant a lot to me, and as a result it meant a lot to her.

Stryper performed only one show in 2008. It was at the Dunkin' Donuts Center in Providence, Rhode Island, as part of the Station Family Fund benefit concert. A solid line-up of notable acts played including Twisted Sister, Gretchen Wilson, Dierks Bentley, Tesla, and us. Tom and Gary Pihl sat in with us as we performed the Stryper version of "Peace of Mind." Musically it was a sub-par performance to say the least, and even more unfortunate it was forever archived in VH1 footage as they filmed it for broadcast.

But that night wasn't about me, or Stryper, or any of us on stage. It was about the families of those who lost loved ones in the tragic fire at the Station Nightclub in West Warwick on February 20, 2003. I met people that night that really touched my heart. Some were children whose parents had gone to the show that night of the fire and they sadly lost both of them. Some were survivors who were horribly burned in the fire. Many were under incredible financial distress due to the lack of insurance or loss of work. It was a moving night, and I was honored to be a part of it. So Stryper's sub-par performance didn't seem like such a big deal in the grand scheme of it all.

I was appreciative of Tom and Gary for sitting in with us. Like the good sports that they were, they even wore yellow-and-black attire. It wasn't quite the leather pants and studded puffy shirts we often donned. It was more like yellow button-down oxfords and black jeans. Tom and Gary aren't known for their fashion and I say that with the utmost respect. So to see them come out of the dressing room ready to play along with Stryper wearing their button down oxford and pale yellow sleeveless tee, black jeans, and tennis shoes — it was very cool and thoughtful of them.

That night backstage I noticed our bass player, Tracy Ferrie, spending a lot of time rubbing elbows with Tom and Kim. He seemed to be laying it on thick attempting to get to know them better. It was embarrassing for me as Tom was there because I had asked him to participate, so to have a band member of mine hovering around him like a used car salesman made me uncomfortable. By the end of the night, Tracy had even mentioned to Tom that if he ever needed a bass player to give him a call. Really? We're at a fundraiser event, and I've invited my new band mates from Boston to be a part of this show, and all that my Stryper bass player seems to be concerned with is getting himself a new gig? Funny thing is, I predicted that he would do just that on the ride up and even had a small bet going with Kyle. I won the wager, and we laughed about that on the ride home.

Rehearsals for the Boston tour started in April of 2008, and thankfully Kyle was showing some signs of getting better. She was not as weak as she was earlier in the year, but we continued to do all we could to improve her health. Rehearsals were exciting yet intense. Tom and I seemed to form a quick, deep bond and friendship.

Lena and Mikey really stepped up in a big way to take care of their mom as the date of the first Boston show approached. I wanted to be there for them anytime I could, but I knew in the back of my mind that I couldn't be of much help thousands of miles away on the road. Lena basically became her mother's caretaker and if it weren't for her, I'm not sure how we would have gotten through the summer of 2008.

Kyle continued to show signs of improvement though, and this is what mentally got me through the idea of leaving. The first show of the Boston tour was outdoors in Thunder Bay, Ontario Canada on June 6, 2008. It was windy and stormy to the point where we were fearful at times that the stage or lighting truss might collapse. I hoped it wasn't an omen for what was to come, but the show turned out just fine — more than fine. It was a pinch-myself moment knowing that I was a legitimate member of Boston and officially on tour with the band.

I was definitely prepared musically by the time the tour started. Actually, I think I was prepared before the first rehearsal even began. When I commit to something musically, I give 110 percent, and this was no exception. Prior to the first rehearsal, I had put in hundreds of hours on my own. So by the time we got to the first show in Canada, I was as prepared as I could possibly have been. I was still nervous, but then again I'm always nervous before I go on stage. I wasn't nervous necessarily because it was Boston — I just get nervous before going onstage period. This definitely wasn't my first rodeo. I had played to sell out crowds in amphitheaters and large arenas many times before in the past, so this was really nothing new to me, it was just with a new band — a band I had admired as a kid.

Nobody will ever be able to fill the shoes of Brad Delp, nor should they try. Wondering how the crowd would react to someone singing these songs other than Brad caused most of my nerves. Throughout the tour, I was relieved by the crowd's acceptance.

It took two of us on this tour to even come close to singing what Brad once handled by himself. Alongside me they had brought in Tommy DeCarlo to sing lead vocals on half the set as well. Tommy's one of the nicest guys I've ever met, and I really enjoyed working with him. To this day he's still a close and dear friend. Night after night we'd stand alongside one another and sing the songs that we both grew up hearing on the radio and on our stereos.

When you work hard at something your whole life, it feels good to be recognized and acknowledged for that work. Whether you're a plumber, a banker or a musician, it feels good when someone notices and says, *"Nice job."* I was getting those pats on the backs from within the band, but that seemed to be the only place I was getting them.

The publicity for this tour leaned heavily toward Tommy DeCarlo and the Home Depot connection. This bothered me a little. It even bothered Tom at times because he apologized to me for that very reason. Discovered on myspace and employed by Home Depot, Tommy DeCarlo was getting a lot of attention and publicity. I understood it—a regular guy who works at Home Depot and then turns rock star makes for a great story. At times, though, I felt somewhat slighted by it all. I had worked my whole life trying to become a better singer, guitarist and performer and when I finally receive a moment to shine in one of the greatest rock bands of all time, Home Depot gets the spotlight.

Occasionally I would find myself in a conversation with someone and the topic of what I did for a living would come up. When you have long hair and a soul patch you get the *"Are you in a band?"* question a lot. And I did. But when I would explain what I do, that I play and sing in the band Boston, I would regularly receive responses like *"Oh, are you that dude from Home Depot?"*

Aside from feeling under-appreciated, or at least under-noticed by the public, the Home Depot publicity angle bothered me for other reasons. For starters, it felt corny. Boston doesn't need Home Depot. Boston doesn't need a gimmick, and to me this started to feel a little gimmicky. When we played Atlanta, hometown to the megastore, there was a sea of orange Home Depot aprons in the audience. There were many times when Tommy would get introduced as *"from Home Depot."* You would have thought the company was paying Boston to endorse them—but in reality it was quite the opposite.

From what I understand, when Tommy inquired as to whether or not he'd still have a job when he returned from the tour, they informed him that he would no longer be employed. What? Boston through its publicity and onstage mentions must have given that company millions in promotional value, and they weren't even going to give Tommy his job back upon returning from tour? That was it for me. To this day, my stomach turns when I enter a Home Depot because of all of this. I felt bad for Tommy. It's not like Boston tours every year and Tommy could rely on the band to make a consistent living as a musician. He needed a job when he returned. Home Depot was happy to have him strap on the orange apron to do interviews. But when it came time to give him his job back, what does he get? "You're on your own, pal." It just didn't seem right: the publicity, the hypocrisy, and the goofiness of it all. After that tour I vowed to shop at Lowes and not at Home Depot. I'd be a liar if I said I haven't been to Home Depot since, but man it was upsetting to me. Still is.

Spiritually during this tour I felt like I was slowly coming out of a deep dark hole. For months on end I had been questioning God.

255

But during the time in Boston I was surrounded by love and support. Kyle had begun to feel strong enough to fly, and in July she and the kids flew out to Denver to see us perform at Red Rocks—not exactly my best night, but I was happy to have her there.

Tommy got sick at Red Rocks to where within a few songs he couldn't even talk, much less sing. The crew and even the band turned to me hoping I could pull it off. I didn't know the lyrics to some of the songs Tommy was singing, never mind he was partially singing them because they were songs more suited for his vocal range and style. We made it through the night with everyone stepping up to the plate the best they could, but for the first time I felt a little unprepared that night. It's not as if they had asked me to be ready in case Tommy couldn't sing, but I wish I would have considered this as a possibility ahead of time. Maybe I could have risen to the occasion and filled in with his parts. So on the same night that I experienced the joy of seeing my wife and kids for the first time in over a month, I also felt disappointed in myself for not being ready to take on the extra vocal parts when the band needed me most.

The friendship between Tom and I continued to grow and strengthen. Tom had lost Brad, and I was faced with the very real possibility of losing Kyle. We had a kinship of sorts in that pain and misery. I had read the stories of Tom for years about how he was reclusive and somewhat untouchable. He didn't let many people into his world. He even told me on occasion how few people he had let in over the years, and I was one of the few. I felt honored that he let me get so close, but it also felt very natural—I think for both of us. In many ways we're a lot alike, particularly in our perfectionism and approach to music. It can drive those around us crazy, but we understood one another in a lot of ways. At times he would refer to me as a long lost brother, and I felt the same.

The crew referred to me often as "Glue" on this tour. When I asked where they came up with that, they said I was the glue that held the tour together. I'll admit, we all were often on pins and needles. Sometimes Tom wouldn't like the way something sounded at rehearsals or sound check and he'd just walk out or off the stage. Some people on the tour would often say they'd wake up every day wondering if this would be the last day of the tour—feeling as though Tom may just cancel the whole thing I suppose. After all, he had done so before.

I felt that way too, but for different reasons. I tried to keep the spirit of the band a little more lighthearted. I would always try to loosen things up during sound checks and crack a smile from a smile-free zone. Most of the time it worked. But Tom and I had grown so close that he began to share with me how important he felt I was to this band. On occasion he'd tell me that he wouldn't want to tour without me. Again, this was very flattering, but it was also nerve-racking. What if Kyle got worse and I had to go home? Would he cancel the tour? I didn't want that sort of pressure on me. Or what if I got sick and couldn't perform? What would happen then? I appreciated the confidence Tom bestowed upon me, but it was a bit unnerving at times not knowing what the future may hold.

The morning of July 25, 2008, I awoke frantically as I realized Kyle's birthday was the next day and I had done nothing to prepare. I didn't so much as have a birthday card ready. I was a wreck. We had a show that night in St. Charles, Missouri, and I had absolutely nothing! I scrambled in putting together some gifts, and I managed to get them to the local FedEx just before they closed at 7p.m. I felt horrible. I had just done what I'm so good at doing—procrastinating and forgetting. I had known her birthday was coming up for a while, but I did nothing about it.

The thought that this might be Kyle's last birthday crossed my mind, and the guilt laid heavy on my heart for having allowed the time to get away from me. Time was a precious thing in 2008. I knew it was limited and for me to let the hustle and bustle of a tour get in the way of me remembering Kyle's birthday — well, it really put me into deep depression for a few days. But again, the love and support that surrounded me, and the prayers for Kyle pulled me through one day after another.

The tour ended on August 31, 2008 in San Juan, Puerto Rico. We had performed over 50 dates in all, and it was an experience for which I'd be forever grateful. The years of feeling as though there might be something for me outside of Stryper had come to fruition. Wanting to feel as though my hard work was appreciated outside the comforts of the yellow-and-black zone was something I had always sought. I'm eternally grateful to the Boston fans for accepting me like they did, and to the band members for being so encouraging and supportive through such a tough time.

When I returned home a couple of days later, I had found out that Kyle had gotten much worse while I was away. She and the kids had kept all of this from me. I suppose they didn't want me to worry. Either way, I was once again reminded of the selfless love Kyle had in her heart. She wanted me to do this Boston tour, even if it meant keeping from me the extent of her illness while I was gone.

I happily and quickly fell back into the role of caretaker and was more than relieved to give my kids a break from what I knew to be an extremely time-consuming, but often rewarding, job of being there for Kyle 24/7.

My friendship with Tom didn't end with the tour. Kyle and I would visit Tom and Kim at their house for dinner. We would watch American Idol together and enjoyed a deep-rooted friendship between the four of us. Kyle and Kim continued to grow close, as did Tom and I. The fall and winter of 2008 was a special time in my life. I had successfully toured with one of my favorite bands. My wife, although still sick, was living life with a smile as often as she could.

The future was uncertain at best and catastrophic at worst. The days were a struggle and the nights sleepless, but through it all, in that moment, I was at a peaceful place in my life.

THIRTY-EIGHT

As 2009 rang in, there was a feeling of defeat and despair in the Sweet household. Kyle was becoming weaker by the day. Her pain and suffering was unbearable and extremely difficult for all of us to see. Many times I would pray for God to just let her have one day without discomfort and pain. I would have taken all the pain from her body into mine if she could have had just had a moment of comfort. It's so incredibly discouraging to see someone you love so much suffer every minute of every day. I cried a lot, mostly in private and while talking to family and friends. I wanted to be strong for Kyle, and I was doing my best but it was difficult if not impossible at times.

On March 2, 2009, Kyle had become so weak and sick that she was transported to hospice. I followed the ambulance from our home to hospice. Shortly afterward, our pastor, David Johnson, arrived to be by our side.

By this time Kyle was barely coherent and on a lot of pain medication. The medical professionals drained Kyle's lungs multiple times throughout her battle, and her lungs were filled again with fluid. She had lost all of her strength and lost a lot of weight as well. David, Kyle, and I would sit in her room and read scriptures and pray. It's all we could do to bring some sort of peace to this horribly frightening and uncertain time. The kids would have been there too, but Kyle didn't want them to see her like this. Although that was a tough decision, I abided by Kyle's wishes. It was hard because understandably the children wanted to see and be with their mom.

Before Kyle had moved to Los Angeles in the '80s, one of her close friends was Mary Kaldis. When Kyle got sick, eventually Mary came back into our lives. She was a nurse and was a godsend in helping to care for Kyle during this time.

260

Hospice is not really the ideal place for visitors. The patients are rarely in a condition to see people, and in Kyle's case she didn't really want people to see her. Although it was hard to explain this to loved ones, I understood why. The time seemed to pass so slowly. I rarely left Kyle's side, and David Johnson was there as much as he could be. My only solace was when Kyle would sleep peacefully, with no apparent pain. I took comfort in those moments of silence when I knew she was comfortable and resting her frail body. I'd hope that she was thinking or dreaming of pleasant thoughts. I'd pray for her to wake up feeling better than when she had fallen asleep. I'd read magazines and drink coffee, but all I could think about was wishing Kyle would find just a brief moment of peace.

Although visitors were few, the outpouring from around the world was beyond moving. Friends we had not connected with in years reached out with their prayers, thoughts, and concern. I will never be able to thank the countless people who offered prayers and support during this dark time, but if you're reading this—thank you and God bless you!

I reached out to a lot of people as well. There's no book that teaches someone how to go through this. It's difficult on so many levels and to so many different degrees. There are no step-by-step instructions on how to navigate the road of terminal cancer. I'm sure many books have tried, but no amount of planning or literary education can prepare you for the emotional extremes one feels during these times. It's a different journey for everyone.

I knew what was coming. Kyle and I both knew, but we didn't say it aloud. We just held hands, prayed, and did our best to believe that in all the madness, God still had a plan. It was hard to believe, but we kept faith despite the fact that many prayers were not answered in the way that we wanted them to be. It was a difficult test of faith and trust.

I stayed by Kyle's side almost nonstop while she was in hospice. I was doing my best to take all the calls that were coming in and making calls to keep everyone informed. Some friends had called and asked if they could stop by. When they arrived, I met them out in the lobby. Very few words were said, as there was so little to say. We sat and prayed. It was the early evening of March 5.

Down the hall a nurse came running toward me saying, "Come quick. She's taking her last breath." I immediately jumped up and ran down the hallway. I had never run so fast in my life. A million thoughts raced through my head in the few seconds it took me to run to her bedside.

I grabbed Kyle's hand and starred at her, hoping she was still breathing. I was hoping she would know I was there for her until the very end. I held my breath while I held her hand. I waited. And waited. As she took her last breath, I squeezed her hand to let her know I was there. I wanted her to know that she was not alone. I wanted her to have comfort. Whatever fears she might have at this moment, I prayed silently for them to go away. I squeezed her hand again.

"I'm here for you Kyle. I love you," I said as I knelt by her bedside.

She gasped and didn't breathe again.

My wife and best friend died on March 5, 2009.

I didn't cry. I just sat there in silence. I stood up beside her bed and, after what felt like an eternity, I turned to walk back out into the hallway. I looked back one last time and saw her lying there peacefully.

I had two years to prepare for this moment, but I realized I wasn't at all ready. I didn't know what to do. It was difficult for me to focus on gathering my thoughts and deal with providing the information hospice needed to prepare Kyle. I tried my best to regain my thoughts and to cope with the idea of breaking the news to Mikey, Lena and Marion. Eventually Pastor David drove me home.

When I walked through the door of our house that night, the kids were home. It was as if there was no sun and no moon. The sky was never darker. The earth was never quieter, and it felt like the end of the world had come. I felt as though I would be giving my kids a hug and the world would end two seconds later. My heart was so heavy and my mind was diverted, like nothing I had ever felt before.

I didn't know what to say when I came home, or what to do, or where to go. I was lost. I tried to collect myself to tell the kids. It wasn't easy and actually caught them by surprise. They knew mom wasn't doing well, but I think they had hoped that she would return home. We all did. So I just came out and said it. *"Mom passed away tonight. She's with God now. She's gone."*

That's when the tears came. They had just lost their mom and no amount of comfort I could provide would be enough. We slept together on the couches in the living room. We wanted to all be together that night. And I'm not sure I was ready to sleep in our bed alone. I missed the uncomfortable chair in the many hospital rooms I had slept in over the past few years. Although it was different rooms at different places, that uncomfortable chair seemed to remain the same — a symbol that my discomfort in that chair paled in comparison to what Kyle was going through. That chair represented my ability to remain connected to my wife. As long as I was in that chair, I would know that I had another day with Kyle. So to go from that to a nice bed — I just wasn't ready. We got some blankets out of the closet and Mikey, Lena, and I all slept in the living room that night. We didn't go to sleep until very late that evening.

Surprisingly I felt a sense of relief after Kyle passed. I knew she was in heaven and that I, and the kids, would see her again. Kyle was with God and no longer had to deal with fluid in her lungs, vomiting, pain, or discomfort of any kind. Knowing this gave me incredible peace. I even had brief moments when I would smile. I knew with full confidence that Kyle was in a much better place. There was no doubt that this woman who had dedicated her entire life to God was indeed in heaven. I was sad of course, but selfishly. I was sad for the kids and me but not for her. She was better off — I had no doubt about that.

After the sense of peace wore off, fear set in. Kyle had always taken care of the details of day-to-day life, the kids, and almost anything that required focus and attention. This was all on me now and how would I handle it? How would I handle life without Kyle? I had always leaned on her for so much — in all aspects. I was fearful that without her I'd crumble. Aside from the emotional stress of helping everyone deal with the loss, I had to deal with everything Kyle dealt with, and I realized just how big a job that was. It was all on me now, and I feared that I couldn't handle it.

Lena and Mikey helped me pick out Kyle's clothes for the burial. That was a tremendously sad moment going through Kyle's closet knowing that she once stood in this very spot debating on what to wear for the day. Never again would I be able to see her fumble through the hangers of clothes to decide on something to wear. Today, the kids and I had to make that decision.

The funeral took place in Wareham, Massachusetts, and the huge number of people who attended from all over the country was overwhelming. It seemed every friend Kyle and I had ever known came to her memorial service. It was touching and spoke loudly about who Kyle was. The line wrapped around the funeral home for friends and loved ones to pay their respects to a woman who was admired by every person with whom she came in contact.

The days and weeks that followed were miserable. I didn't know how to deal with this loss and how I was ever going to get over it or get through it. So I dealt with it the only way I knew how.

I went back to work.

I called Dave Rose less than a month after Kyle's passing, and I said, *"Let's tour. I'm ready to hit the road."* I felt that we needed to stay active as a family in order to rise above the storm, so I did something really unconventional. Mikey had been working on some new material with his band, Flight Patterns (5-6 songs or so), and I walked into his bedroom and said, "If you guys can pull together 45 minutes of material by August, you can open the Stryper tour." Mikey looked as though it was April Fools and couldn't believe what I was saying. I arranged for Flight Patterns to be the opening act, and I also arranged for Lena to work selling merchandise. Together we would hit the road as a family. I look back on that time, and I wouldn't change a thing. We needed to heal, and I felt this would be the best way to do so. The kids agreed and so it was.

Our life with Kyle was something we cherished every day. She touched all those that knew her, and when all the tears dry and the sadness of her loss subside, we'll realize how fortunate we all were to know and love Kyle Rae Sweet.

THIRTY-NINE

Throughout my life I have been amazed by God as to what He can do, *when* He decides to do it, and just how little I understand His plan. Sometimes it confuses me. I do my best to pray faithfully and follow His lead, but often, when I least expect it, He throws a curve ball and I don't really know what to think.

Stryper getting a record deal. The unexpected pregnancy that led to my son Michael being born. Charting, touring, and selling hundreds of thousands of albums as a solo artist, and just when I thought I had seen it all, becoming a member of the band Boston. All curve balls that I never expected.

In most of these cases, the unexpected gifts from God come along at the most inopportune of times. I'm usually not ready for them. But somehow, He shows me the path, if I'll just listen and follow His lead. God is amazing that way. To even try to understand His plan is futile. We as humans like to think we're in control over our lives, that we have complete say-so on how everything will fall into place. For a believer, that couldn't be further from the truth. We don't always like to admit it, and we're not always fond of when He decides to do what He does, but we know deep in our faith that God has a plan for our lives and if we'll just open our hearts and minds, He'll lead us down the right path, the perfect path.

A couple of weeks after the funeral we received an outpouring of gifts and cards from many people. I was touched by all of them, but one in particular arrived that really caught my attention. It was a really unique gift basket. It was distinctive in that I could tell a lot of thought went into it. It contained gifts for Mikey, Lena, Marion, the dog and even a gift certificate to one of my favorite restaurants, Inaho—a Japanese restaurant in Yarmouth Port, Massachusetts.

It was from Lisa Champagne.

She had been a friend of Oz's for about a year, and our paths had crossed a couple of times through Oz, but I didn't know her well at all. I sent Oz a text message and asked for her phone number so I could call and thank her. It was such a thoughtful gift, and I wanted her to know how much it meant.

I eventually dialed Lisa's number. She answered, and we had a short but pleasant conversation. While wrapping up the call, I asked her if she'd like to help me use the gift certificate and have dinner sometime. I made sure to mention it would not be a date, just a simple, friendly dinner. From what little I knew about Lisa, she was coming out of a long relationship that had not turned out as planned and was in no position to start dating, nor was I, obviously. But I did want and need someone to talk to, and Lisa seemed to be a great listener. Come to find out, I had mentioned once in passing that my favorite restaurant was Inaho. She actually listens to people when they talk—a skill I've yet to perfect.

To say that I enjoyed the dinner would be an understatement. To say God was throwing me another curve ball would be true, but it would also be an incomplete description of the night. I felt a connection with Lisa I didn't in the least expect. We drove separate cars and we met at the restaurant with full intentions of this being a simple, friendly dinner. What happened instead was as inspiring as it was confusing. It was as exciting as it was terrifying. Within a few short hours over dinner, I felt a strong connection with Lisa that I wasn't sure I'd ever feel again. With no disrespect to my late wife Kyle, it was a type of connection I'm not sure I had ever felt before. It was uniquely different in so many ways. It was all its own.

Lisa was like a female version of me. Similarly, I was like a male version of her. We had so much in common yet I couldn't help but continually reminding myself *"There's no way this can be happening. It's too soon! Or is it?*

Almost four hours after that dinner began, we went our separate ways. I knew I wanted to see her again, but I certainly was not planning to rush into anything. Her ex-boyfriend was still living in her house at the time. They had already made the decision to end the relationship but being the person that Lisa is, it was difficult for her to ask him to move out. At that time, they were in the process of trying to figure out the logistics of going separate ways. Lisa was planning on selling her house and her ex would be moving elsewhere, so it was somewhat complicated.

A few days later, Lisa invited me over to her house for a dinner party. I went but didn't stay long — not because I didn't want to stay — I just didn't want to overextend my welcome. It was a little uncomfortable as her ex was there as well as many of his friends. I think everyone there could sense that Lisa and I had some sort of connection and there was no denying it. I left shortly after eating dinner and went home.

Lisa and I talked on the phone that night and a few times the days that followed. I enjoyed every moment of getting to know her. Those who know me can appreciate the fact that I'm not a phone person typically speaking, so to actually *want* to talk to anyone more than five minutes is certainly a sign that I'm enjoying the conversations. Often we would talk for hours.

I was absorbing every ounce of every moment, and I didn't want any conversation with her to end. Lisa's love for life was infectious, and her compassionate heart for others was endearing.

Later that week we met for lunch at Trevi, a Mediterranean cafe in Mashpee Commons and once again, we didn't want the conversation to end. After a late lunch that day, I walked Lisa to her car. We embraced as it began to rain, and we held each other as if we didn't want to let go.

All the while, we were not romantically involved. We both thought it was odd, yet exciting, that we had taken such an instantaneous liking to one another. As a result, we remained cautiously aware of our feelings in an attempt to not let things move too quickly.

On April 10, 2009, Lisa had tickets to see Chris Cornell at The House of Blues in Boston, and she invited me to go with her. This time we drove together. Upon arriving we had dinner in The Foundation Room, a VIP lounge in most House of Blues venues. We spent a lot of time talking with Bob Dougherty, the GM for the venue, and after dinner we got a glass of wine and continued talking, just the two of us, like we had done so effortlessly in the weeks prior. No topic was off limits. We talked about God, my kids, her life, and her work. We shared our dreams and our fears. Time stood still when I was with Lisa — so much so that we missed most of the show and we didn't even care. We were in our own world that night, and it was magical.

If I were to pick a day as our first date, it would be that night. We kissed for the first time. I was happy, scared, and nervous all rolled into one.

Six days later on April 17, I sent Lisa this email, word for word, typos and all:

> **From:** Michael Sweet
> **To:** Lisa Champagne
> **Sent:** Friday, April 17, 2009 11:27:22 AM
> **Subject:** What you mean to me.......
>
> Hello My Darling,
>
> I'm sitting here at my computer and I wanted to take a moment to let you know what you mean to me. You are precious and priceless. You light the darkness within my heart and you have made me believe in the

beauty of loving someone again from the depths of my soul. Everything you are is exactly what I would ask for in my prayers to God. The amazing thing is that God knew this already and I didn't have to ask. There you were, my hearts desire in a friend, a companion and a soulmate. I see how much you want to serve The Lord and it inspires me to do the same. You are a gift from God and I want you to know how eternally grateful and thankful I am to know you, and for you to love and trust me! I am yours, Always......

Michael

That's exactly how I felt, and still do feel. I could no longer fight the plan God had put before me. From this point forward, we considered ourselves a couple.

Several times a week we would meet at The Cape Cod Canal to talk and read the Bible together. It was soothing for me as well as for Lisa. She had been yearning for a closer relationship with God. Our time praying and reading the Bible together on the canal really helped in establishing a strong foundation for our relationship. I eventually ordered a personalized Bible for her and a few other books that we read from often for guidance and direction. Whatever was to happen from here on out, we knew we had to put God first.

If you had asked me in June of 2007 what my life would look like professionally in a few months, I would never have in a million years dreamed it would include being a singer and guitarist in the band Boston. Even if you had said to me matter-of-factly, "Michael, in just a few months you will be a member of the band Boston," I would have recommended that you see a psychiatrist. And in March of 2009 if you would have told me that by the summer of that same year that I'd be in love with a woman named Lisa, I again would have recommended you see a doctor immediately, because you must have some sort of psychological disorder.

This is how God works. *His* plan is not *our* plan. His plan does not abide by the rules of business or the rules of society, or even the rules of love. His plan for all of us is perfect and beyond our comprehension, if we will just open our hearts and trust Him.

I spoke to Mikey and Ellena about my relationship with Lisa and explained how things were getting serious. Of course, I wanted their blessings, yet I understood the sensitivity of the matter. The last thing I wanted to do was to hurt my children. Lisa felt even stronger than I did about this. She often was brought to tears when we would discuss Mikey and Ellena's feelings and even suggested putting things on hold for a while. I felt that if we loved each other, it was okay to move forward.

After speaking with Lena and Mikey, I encountered different reactions. Mikey questioned our relationship and felt that we were rushing things, while Lena expressed that she wanted me to be happy. Lisa eventually spoke to Lena and told her that she didn't want to hurt her or Mikey. Lisa even said that she would walk away from our relationship. The last thing Lisa wanted was to hurt my kids. She really cared for Mikey and Lena and would never do anything to hurt them.

I also spoke to a number of dear friends and family members from Guido to Daryn to my band mates to Kyle's personal friends (many of whom accepted Lisa from the start) and my parents. They all expressed their love and gratitude for Lisa and were sincerely excited about the decision to follow our hearts and take our love to a new level.

On June 30, 2009, Lisa's birthday, I asked her to marry me. There was not a doubt in my mind by this point that I would be incredibly happy and eternally grateful if this amazingly beautiful woman would take my hand in marriage. Thankfully, she said, "Yes."

Lisa is undoubtedly one of the most incredible human beings and accepts everyone with an unconditional and loving spirit. She can walk into a room of 1,000 people and instantly light the place up with an atmosphere of joy and friendliness. She works with disabled and special needs people and has done so most of her life. She is so giving of her time and of herself. She's the ultimate hostess on every level imaginable. These are the qualities that made me fall in love with her and ask for her hand and her heart.

We chose the song "Amazed" by Lone Star to be "our" song and the date of 1/8/10 to be our wedding date. We chose that date based on it's meaning—"1" representing the beginning of a new year and one God, "8" representing new beginnings and "10" representing the number of perfection or completion of "God's divine order." It just so happened to have been Elvis Presley's birthday as well, which was pointed out to me by Oz. Lisa and I thought that was pretty funny since my dad was at one point an Elvis impersonator, and I grew up in a home where Elvis was a daily subject if not the sixth family member. Now what were the odds of that?

One day while in Nashville and walking down Broadway, Lisa and I were discussing whether or not the date we had chosen for our wedding was right, and suddenly we heard our song, "Amazed." As we looked around to see where it was coming from, we noticed a statue of Elvis on the sidewalk, in front of Legends Gift Shop. As we walked across the street, we discovered that "Amazed" was blasting from a speaker next to Elvis. We were blown away and at that moment we knew in our hearts that this was a confirmation!

On January 8, 2010, Lisa and I were married at a relatively small ceremony in Boston with our families and friends present. It was surreal and beautiful. I wrote a song titled "How To Live" for Lisa and sang it for her that night. Aside from not getting to eat my meal (which I ranted and raved over for days), the night was perfect.

Prior to our wedding, Stryper toured in support of the album *Murder By Pride*. I wanted my family to be with me, so as I mentioned earlier, we took Mikey's band Flight Patterns out as the opening act, and Lena traveled with us as our merchandise girl. Lisa came to as many shows as she could, and I think this was a time that we were all able to bond.

It was a grueling tour logistically that kicked off in September 2009 at the House of Blues in Boston. Immediately upon arriving for sound-check my heart felt comfort remembering my first date with Lisa there just a few months earlier.

By this time in my life, I was losing touch with some people who were really close friends. My relationship with Lisa was difficult for a select few to understand, both fans and friends alike. Some made brutally vicious comments toward Lisa and me. Others took a more subtle approach to their disapproval by simply choosing to remove us from their inner circle. Occasionally it would make me angry. Sometimes it would make me sad. But it always surprised me as to how little people would take into account that perhaps God's plan for me was not something that could, or even should, be analyzed or scrutinized. It shocked me as to the sense of entitlement some people felt they had over my life and how I should live it, as though they knew better than I what was right for my life. I had served God the better part of 34 years, and it was bewildering how anyone that really knew me would think I somehow wasn't seeking complete wisdom and guidance from God through this unique stage in my life.

I bit my tongue a lot. I turned the other cheek a lot. I said very little, and certainly didn't say what I really wanted to say. I continued to seek and find happiness in my life with God, Lisa, Mikey and

Ellena. With all due respect, that's all that mattered to me. Those were my priorities, and I was doing my best to keep them in order. If it meant losing a few friends in the process, then so be it.

All of this isn't to suggest that I did not understand some people's confusion over my life choices and the path that I was taking. I absolutely understood it. I was the one living it. At times I was confused right along with them, but I never once doubted that God had a plan and if I would just continue to seek Him, He would guide me to what was best for my life. And thankfully, and almost miraculously, that path and plan led me to Lisa.

Lisa is godsend to me in so many ways. Daily I am blessed by her ability to give of herself so selflessly. She has become a wonderful friend to my children, and they have accepted her into their lives and love her very much. I will never be able to express fully into words the love and joy I feel each day for Lisa, and I don't know where I'd be without her by my side. I love you, Pooh!

FORTY

The 2009 Stryper tour was a bit of a financial hardship. Our attendance numbers were starting to decrease somewhat and the sales from the album, although respectable, weren't where we felt they should be. Overall exposure of the band didn't seem to be climbing at a rate that we felt it should have been.

In 2010 we toured overseas in Europe, South America, and Australia. Some tension was starting to mount again within the band over what we perceived to be a lack of progress. All of us wanted things to be better for the band — we just had minor, and sometimes major, differences as to how to go about making that happen. Financially, our bank accounts weren't growing and neither was our popularity. Upon returning from South America, we encountered some financial setbacks with promoters not paying what they had originally agreed to pay. To make matters worse, our booking agent had decided to declare bankruptcy and refused to pay us money owed after a show was performed. In the world of booking, it works like this: A promoter sends a deposit to the band's agent. The agent holds that deposit until the date plays and then he remits the balance, minus his commission, to the band within a few days of the performance.

Well, our agent was in such financially bad shape that he was illegally using these deposits for his own personal use without us knowing about it. He was basically "floating" our deposits. He would wait until he received the deposit from the next gig, and then he would send us the balance from the previous one.

Again, all this was happening without us knowing about it. We were extremely unhappy with our agent due to bad commitments and lack of follow-through, so we decided to let him go. Artists and agents part ways every day in this business and it's usually a fairly uneventful passing of the torch, but in this case the agent now had no future shows to collect deposits on from promoters. He had no deposits coming in to "float," and that's when we discovered we would not be getting a rather large portion of the money that he had collected on our behalf.

Although it was a difficult decision, we sued him. We won, but we still never saw a dime of that money. He declared bankruptcy and despite us getting a judgment against him, we never got paid. We probably never will. Things seemed to be going from bad to worse, professionally.

Dave Rose had remained our manager since 2003. The band felt a change in management was the next possible solution to our problems. Dave's not really a "big time" manager in the world of management companies—by most accounts his company Deep South Entertainment would be considered a mid-level management company at best. He's a hard worker and someone we trusted, but he seemed to lack the kind of power we felt we needed to push us through the industry system and get us opening slots with bigger bands, more publicity, and generally more exposure all the way around.

Oz became close friends with a guy named John Greenberg at Union Entertainment. I knew John as well from way back and had spoken to him many times, but Oz and John had developed a much closer friendship prior to our working together. Union managed some fairly large acts like Nickelback, Daniel Powter, and Cinderella. John started presenting the band with some big ideas for taking us to the next level. I had my doubts, but I wanted to see the band go further, and John led us to believe that we would if he was managing the band.

John and I had spoken a few years prior about possibly working together. He and I had several conversations and we even met for lunch in Santa Ana with Oz. We had been speaking to John about a Stryper/Union merge for quite some time. What made me feel disconnected with John was an incident that was nothing short of dishonest. John had agreed to work with us and again had all the right words to make the sale, but last minute we were passed on to a B-level manager at the company and John would not have been directly involved. I politely said that this arrangement would not work for us and that didn't go over too well with the guys in the band. Fast- forward to Oz endorsing John again and obviously I was reluctant, and rightfully so.

I think the band always felt like Dave Rose was "my guy" and not necessarily the band's guy, and because of this it was time for a change. I won't say I begrudgingly went along with it only to keep the peace. I too felt we needed a new energy in the band. I felt Dave had taken us as far as he could and we as a band had to try something new. Whatever we were doing didn't seem to be working, so new management seemed like the best option at the time. We decided to go with Union and give John Greenberg another chance.

I made the phone call to break the news to Dave. This was a guy who had given a toast at Lisa's and my wedding. He had been to Kyle's funeral. He had believed in my music without any hopes of Stryper ever reuniting. So, when I called to say, *"Dave, we're going to let you go and take on new management,"* it wasn't an easy call to make. Dave had become my friend over the years, and firing a friend is never easy. To show my loyalty and belief in him, I asked if he would remain on as my personal manager. He agreed to do so.

Meanwhile, we as a band moved over to new management with all the hopes and promise of a bright future. In February of '11 we released *The Covering*, an album comprising 12 cover songs by artists that had inspired us from our early days and one new original, "God." I'm really proud of that album's production and musicality, and it gave me the opportunity to show what I can do as a producer. Charles Foley, my longtime keyboard player and vocalist for solo projects, and Stryper's touring keyboardist and vocalist, really helped in giving authenticity to the songs that required piano and keyboard parts. He also sang all the background vocals with Oz and me. Everyone really stepped things up on this album, and it was met with great critical acclaim. It sold well by today's standards but failed to meet our expectations.

We toured in support of that album and did our best to spread the word and self-promote the band. Sadly, the tours were losing money and I personally, as the bandleader, was not getting along with John Greenberg very well. Our communication methods were entirely different. In less than nine months with John, we were making less money as a band than ever before and our fan base was not growing either. The carrots that were dangled to convince us to go with Union seemed to continually remain just outside our grasp. Frustrations continued to mount.

Once again, it was time to regroup. We parted ways with John and Union just a little over a year after we started working together, and for us that couldn't have come a day sooner. It was not a healthy relationship and things were getting really bad. Tour numbers were down. Sales were down. Finances were all but nonexistent.

Fortunately, Lisa is an incredibly bright businesswoman and excels at finances and budgets. She helped us orchestrate a plan to bring Stryper management in-house, saving tens of thousands of dollars a year in commissions. She helped in delegating the duties a manager would normally handle to within the current Stryper business team. We brought Dave Rose back in to oversee finances. Lisa brought in an assistant, Marilyn Becrelis, to help with travel and administrative duties. Our tour manager took on a few extra responsibilities as well. We also hired a new booking agent named Sullivan Bigg, owner of Bigg Time Entertainment. As far as management goes, I have basically managed the band since 2003, only now we're not throwing 15-20 percent into the fire by hiring a manager to do what I've done for more than 10 years. If we ever find the right manager, maybe we'll reconsider.

Thankfully as 2012 began, we started to see a turnaround in the right direction. Our finances are growing again. We signed a major, multi-record deal with Frontiers Records, which enabled us to release three records and a DVD within two years. I signed a new multi-album and book deal with Big3 Records and so much is happening now. Our touring entity has become a more refined operation and things are only going up from here. Truthfully, prior to this regrouping and reorganization, I was beginning to think it was the end of the road for Stryper. Thanks to Lisa and her business skills, she managed to help get us back on the right path. We're heading in the right direction now, and for that we are grateful.

I don't deserve all that God has blessed me with over the years. From all of my musical success with Stryper, solo and with Boston to the incredible blessings in my personal life, I am thankful God has remained faithful to me despite my occasional straying from Him.

If I've learned anything in my adventures through life it has been to not predict what God has in store for me. I have learned to accept what He brings into my life and to do my best to remain faithful when He takes something or someone away. More so than I think ever before, I wake up each day thankful for all that He has done. I may not always agree with it, but ultimately I find that God knows best. What He has in mind for my tomorrow, I will never know. Nobody can predict the future. What I do know is that I want to follow His leading and direction, and if I can stay strong on that course then, the sky is the limit.

Conclusion

The three greatest moments in my life as they relate to Stryper are as such:

1. 1983 — Forming Stryper
2. 1992 — Departing Stryper
3. 2003 — Reuniting Stryper

That's simplifying things a bit, but here's the bottom line: I've always had a love/hate relationship with my feelings about being in Stryper. I never, even in my worst moments, deny what God has done through this band, and I am forever grateful for the opportunity to serve Him through music. That said, I can't help but wish from time to time that I could do the same service without Stryper.

I'm so different personality-wise than my band mates. I regularly feel like I'm struggling to further the band, only to take two steps backward because of an opinion or statement made by one of my band mates. It's a huge burden to carry the torch known as Stryper, yet seemingly no one fully understands how difficult it can be. The songs don't just write themselves. The business team that surrounds us doesn't just show up at our doorstep. The career-making decisions have a profound effect on our livelihood. Often when I try to move us forward, it's as though I can feel a force within the band pulling us backward.

We all have a full understanding and appreciation for Stryper and what it has accomplished over the years. I just don't think that we necessarily like each other at times. We love each other. We just don't always like each other.

"So why not just quit?" you may ask. "You've done it before. What's stopping you?"

You'd make a great point if you were to ask me that question, and I'm afraid I'd fall short in coming up with a reasonable answer that would be easily understood by the masses. It's hard for *me* to understand completely, so I certainly don't expect anyone else to comprehend it.

It's not as if I don't want to make music or serve God with all my heart. I do. I just wish at times that I could do it without having to rely exclusively on Stryper.

I love writing songs. I love producing records. The studio excites me and truthfully, I love performing.

What I don't like is the proverbial monkey that sits on my back because I'm the bandleader. The logical question might be "Why not let one of the other guys lead the band?" And again, that is a fair question. Truth is, I don't completely trust anyone else to lead the band. It's not that I think they're dishonest or malicious because they're not at all. It's just that I don't trust their production and or business decisions to be in the best interest of the band. So I'd rather carry the weight and make most of the decisions myself.

In a professional band there are seemingly countless decisions that need to be made on a daily basis. Interview requests. Show opportunities. Licensing and recording decisions. Accounting and travel details. And yes, we have a team to work with us on all of these points, but ultimately the decisions come down to the band — and since there are so many of them to be made on a daily basis, one person has to be the leader, the visionary, the decision maker. And that person is me.

Playing in Boston was incredible for two reasons. First, it was Boston — the influential rock band of my youth. Second, and probably more the reason why I enjoyed it: I didn't make any of the decisions. I showed up and played music to the best of my ability. As long as I showed up on time, well rehearsed and did my job, life was good. That's a feeling I have never really felt before, and I liked it.

Yet in Stryper, I often feel such a burdensome responsibility. I feel responsible for so many things—keeping the band active and progressing forward, keeping the band's professionalism intact, maintaining the financial state of each band member, taking God's message to as many people as possible, and pleasing the fans who have supported us all these years and not disappointing them by leaving or discontinuing the band.

As I touched on earlier, I stick around partially because it's my livelihood. This is my chosen profession. It's not as if I can go back to law school and become an attorney. Bottom line, I'm a musician. So to support my family in a responsible manner, I rely on music. Right now, Stryper affords me the best opportunity to do that. I'm definitely not getting rich playing in Stryper. I make a living. It's not a great living, but it's a modest living.

I'm responsible for bringing home a portion of the bacon (Lisa brings home a lot of bacon, too) and without Stryper, there'd be less bacon.

That's probably part of the problem. I feel trapped at times. I can't really leave Stryper because it allows me the ability to put food on my family's table.

So I feel somewhat caged at times with no way out.

And then, just when I least expect it, I wake up the next day with a fire, fervor, and love for my band unlike anything in my life. I wake up proud of Stryper, and I want to give it my all. And for a while I do. Then something happens—an argument with Oz, a complaint from Tim, a pity party for Robert, or some skeleton from my past rears its ugly head and decides to haunt me, often in regard to bad business dealings we made back in the '80s. And I'm trapped again.

It's a never-ending cycle, and the cycle itself wears me out. Some days I think *"I'm too old for this. Isn't the point of life to just be happy? I should quit if I'm not happy."* Other days I'm on fire for Stryper, wanting to pull the team together again and conquer the world.

And then I look at my life and realize that if I want to be responsible for my family, I need to learn to let go of the things that bother me. So I do, for a while. That is, until those same things are knocking on my door again.

I love Stryper and everything we have accomplished. I love my band mates. I love Stryper fans. Honestly, I'm so blessed to be able to do what I love for a living, and here's hoping and praying I'll have the opportunity to keep making music and touching lives moving forward.

ENDORSEMENTS:

"Sometimes you see someone or something and you think you've got it all figured out, just to find you were pretty far off base. That's a sucky feeling. I learned a long time ago not to judge a book by its cover, and as much as I used to think that I am nothing like Michael Sweet, I have come to realize that we both have had a lot of hardships in common; the same trials and tribulations, the same band problems, and some of the same relationship issues. Fortunately for us, we both believe in the same Jesus, and serve the same amazing, loving creator, so it's no wonder that we would both be standing on the same victorious side of life, once all the smoke clears at the end of the fight. I hope you will enjoy his memoirs and come to a new understanding and a new appreciation of Michael Sweet."
~Dave Mustaine, Megadeth founding guitarist/vocalist

"I've always felt Stryper was one of the more talented bands to come out of the '80s hard rock scene. I'll never forget being blown away by the band the first time I saw them, and I was equally amazed at what great players and singers they still are, when I saw them recently. Michael Sweet remains one of the most powerful vocalists in rock!"
~Eddie Trunk, radio personality and music historian

"Michael Sweet is a pioneer, a virtuoso, a musical genius, a rebel, a hero, an inspiration, a peer and a friend. He's a man who stood up for what he believed in and was idolized by some, but persecuted by many others as a result. His story is amazing, interesting, unforgettable and completely unique."
~Chris Jericho, professional wrestler and musician

"The first time I saw Stryper was on the Soldiers Under Command Tour. They opened with "Battle Hymn of the Republic" as a crucifix in lights lowered behind the band. A stranger gave me my first shot of whiskey and I got hit in the head with a Bible. Needless to say, I was hooked! I went home and put their poster up on my wall right next to Iron Maiden's "Number of the Beast." They were the band that made me realize how much more powerful the Message of God is than the force of the devil. All and all, their music has always made me feel warm inside. Like a yellow-and-black teddy bear."
~Jeordie White (aka Twiggy Ramirez), Marilyn Manson bassist

"I've been a Michael Sweet fan and fanatic of Stryper ever since I popped the album Yellow and Black attack in my tape player and cranked the song 'C'mon Rock' sitting in the parking lot of Baptist University of America in Ga. Not only did they sound amazing but the words Michael sang were powerfully true. A great underrated American metal band that in my humble opinion rocked just as good as Maiden. If you never heard Stryper then you're a communist! I hope y'all buy this book Mike wrote because I'm gonna take 15 percent of it for all the free press I've givin' him throughout the years! In this world of entertainment you need good solid Christian friends to look up to and admire, and I'm proud to say Mike is that for me. Git-r-done and long live Stryper!"
~Dan "Larry The Cable Guy" Whitney

Michael Sweet - *I'm Not Your Suicide* (2014)

Thank you for spending some time reading my story. I wrote a song called "How to Live" for my wife Lisa, and I sang it at our wedding. I wanted to make it available as a gift to you — a thank you — for reading my book. God bless you ~M

Download for free, "How to Live"
from the Michael Sweet album *I'm Not Your Suicide.*

www.DSEMusicGroup.com/howtolive